Prologι

There are significant periods during a life, when we are tested either physically, mentally, emotionally, or spiritually. There are times when we have to let go of people, dreams, careers, our security and our beliefs. It is in these points of time, through experiencing adversity, that we have the greatest opportunity for personal growth. After enduring our life trials, the time afterwards, to reflect and integrate all that we have learnt through our experiences, is imperative.

In 2020 circumstances beyond my control took me on a journey that would test me to my absolute limits and lead me to question who I was and shake my perception of reality. On this journey I would be opened up to a whole new incredible world and witness things I didn't believe possible. This story is about what happens when you truly let go and allow yourself to be taken by the flow of the universe. To live one day to the next without the need to know what is following. This is a story about ancient wisdom, healing, manifestation, energy, synchronicities and allowing the universe to flow through you.

Between 2020 and 2021 I lost my businesses, my physical health, my relationship with my life partner, my home, my income, and my community. Trusting my intuition, and without a clear plan, I set out as a nomad and travelled across Britain. In that time, I created enough space to bring in healing, adventure, new learning, and new relationships. Whilst piecing my life back together I was led along a spiritual path, where I would need to find my courage, grit and sheer determination to overcome a series of challenges that would repeatedly test my faith to the limit. I was shown the true power of manifestation; of how to set an intention and bring it into my reality effortlessly. But first I would need to go on the *'shaman's journey'* and experience the *'shaman's sickness'*. I would need to surrender to a debilitating illness and succumb to my spiritual calling. I would need to go through a period of intense learning in order to heal myself and learn ancient ways of manipulating energy and accessing wisdom.

I embarked on a lonely journey, one that would lead me to the edge of my sanity. I would peer through the veil between reality and the spirit realms, and allow myself to be taught and guided by the spirit world. Through their direction I gained incredible new insights about what we are truly capable of, and the true meaning of my life, that would transform me. I was about to enter a world where incredible synchronicities were a daily occurrence and a thirst for understanding them kept driving me forward.

I have written this as a semi-autobiographical novel. Parts of my story have been fictionalised in order to protect the identities of people in my life that played their part in my story, and to help with the flow of the narrative. I believe that stories find people who will tell them, and this is a story that wants to be shared and I am the one it chose to share it. I aim to inspire you to follow your own spiritual path, and to show you what can happen when YOU answer the call to the universe and embark on your own hero's journey. When you are in the flow of life and fully present to the messages that life reveals to you, incredible experiences will start to emerge through you. This book will take you on an exhilarating and intense journey and reveal aspects of reality that will challenge the conventional thinker.

Chapter 1

Getting Sick

I parked my little white car into a tiny space and squeezed the door open, being careful not to knock the expensive car alongside of mine. I walked over the cobbled stones and entered the beautiful old pub in Abingdon, in the south of Oxfordshire. It was a bitterly cold evening and I'd wrapped myself up in my long woollen grey coat and warm scarf. There was a little ice underfoot, so I walked carefully. As I entered the pub, I immediately felt the warmth from within. Partly from the cosy fire and partly from the people who were gathered together chatting enthusiastically. These people were my tribe, we'd been together a while and were happy in each other's company. I grabbed myself a beer from the bar and headed over to join my friends. I was a little apprehensive of the mood of the group with the world full of ongoing news reports about the virus spreading in the country and across Europe.

I found Tom and Michael as they chatted in an upbeat way. Tom always brought the conversation back to work and Michael listened and nodded, he seemed to be enjoying the optimistic way that Tom spoke. They smiled and opened up a space for me to join them.

'How's your week been?' Tom asked me casually.

He was a broad man, in his mid-forties with rosy cheeks and a patchy red beard.

'This virus has got my attention. I can't seem to pull myself away from the news,' I replied.

'It's all a lot of media hype if you ask me. It's no worse than the flu, that's my take on it,' said Tom.

And Michael nodded in agreement.

'Well, I hope you're right, but my intuition is telling me there's trouble on its way,' I said, not wanting to be gloomy.

Michael pulled a contorted face suggesting he thought I was over-reacting and being pulled into the needless hysteria. Michael was a short man, with a typical English face.

We were a group of business owners who came together twice a month to share our successes, challenges, goals and find solutions and inspiration whilst supporting each other. We had been meeting here for over 2 years, we ate good pizza, had a drink together and had become (at a surface level) friends, colleagues, and mentors. This would be the last time we would meet, but we didn't know that yet. I left Tom and Michael chatting and went and spoke with Nicky about her dress-making business, before we headed away from the bar and into a separate room where the proper meeting would begin, and the food would arrive. The room was a converted old barn, with high ceilings and a long wooden oak table with benches where we all sat communally together.

I stood silently at the head of the table and greeted everyone as they entered the room with a smile. I waited for their chatting to quieten down before getting started. They each had a glass of something in front of them and were in their usual good spirits.

'Tough week, hey? We were going to talk about Steve's business today, but we'll knock that into next week as Steve isn't quite ready yet. He's working on his new website and wants to finish that before the focus turns to him.' Steve nodded and smiled at the group. He was a big man from Newcastle with a booming voice.

'Give me a couple of weeks,' he said, almost apologetically.

'I have some good news to share,' I said with a proud expression on my face. 'I have finished writing my novel. There is still plenty of editing to do, but at least the first draft is complete.' There was a round of applause from everyone.

'Well done, have you got a name for it?' Asked Siobhan.

She was one of my favourite members of the group. She was young, and as lively as a lamb in a spring field.

'The working title is A Networking Tale,' I said.

It was the third novel I'd written and this one was in a different genre to the previous two. It was a business book about everything I'd learnt about building a small business and utilising a business network to help achieve your goals.

'We need to celebrate,' said Tom.

He was always up for a celebration. Tom was known for his barbeques and the late nights that followed.

'Sounds good to me, Tom,' I said.

'Count me in,' added Siobhan.

I had also written two Time-travel novels for young adults, which both featured teenage siblings, protagonists: Emily and Arthur Archer. Both of the books had involved extensive research into the English Civil War and the Roman occupation of Britain. My new book however was all about using my own knowledge and experience. My protagonist this time had been a professional photographer just like me.

'So, tonight we're going to talk about this virus spreading from China that's all over the news,' I said somewhat apprehensively.

There were murmurs in the room as I shared my unease. Despite the bravado, there was clearly a nervous tension within the room, people just didn't know what to think. Like my earlier conversation with Michael and Tom, the consensus was that the media was hyping up hysteria. I listened to the light-hearted joking on the subject. I didn't feel the same. I could feel trouble was coming deep within in my bones.

We had an open discussion. We looked at the facts, we looked at the consequences of what would happen if the virus spread throughout Oxfordshire. How we could protect ourselves, our businesses, and our community. It was a useful discussion and left me knowing in my heart what I needed to do. I would shut down the project for the time being. It was frightening as I didn't have another source of income. I had worked for myself since I was a young man and quite frankly considered myself too long in the tooth to work for someone else now. By the end of the conversation, most of us agreed the government was acting too slowly.

When I got home the house was quiet, Gabriella was already in bed. I took off my shoes and placed my coat in the cupboard under the stairs. I squeezed the leftover boxed pizza into the fridge for us to eat the following day and switched on the news. There was blanket coverage on the virus, it was hard not to get sucked into the pending pandemic. After a while I crept up stairs, opened the bedroom door as my partner, Gabriella turned away from the light and sighed. She hated being disturbed once she had gone to bed. Quietly and unobtrusively, I got myself ready and climbed into the warm bed beside her. I snuggled up to her and placed my arm around her waist gently. She removed it and huffed. I turned my back to her and tried to sleep, my mind was full, I was worried. I needed comfort, I needed reassurance, but I knew from my experience it wasn't going to come from Gabriella. She believed men should be tough and not show their weaknesses. My world was about to tumble in around me and I could sense it coming, fuck... What was I going to do?

The alarm woke us both at 6 am. I rolled over to hug her, and she embraced me. That's more like it, I thought. She kissed me.

'I'm off to London today,' she reminded me.

Gabriella got up and spoke about the importance of her networking event. There were going to be lots of investors there and her start-up company was in real need of an injection of cash. She said she wouldn't be home until late. We lived in Witney in west Oxfordshire; it was at least three hours travelling for her to get to her destination. She had a look of determination on her face. She meant business, but we had been here before. She was a real talent and worked with a small team she had assembled herself. They had developed a piece of software that monitored the movement of fish and birds which with the right investment could make a real impact in the conservation of certain endangered species.

'Will you walk Nester for me? She'll be very grateful,' she asked.

'Of course, I will,' I replied.

Nester was a golden Labrador, a beautiful sweet natured dog who Gabriella had recently brought to our household. She had been a friend's dog, but her circumstances had changed and Gabriella had offered to give Nester a new home.

I had told Gabriella of my concerns about her going before she'd booked the tickets. It was a risk; she would be travelling on the train and the underground and would come in contact with lots of people. The virus was out there, and I didn't want it coming home with her. At the event she was going to there would be over one hundred people, so she was taking a huge risk, not just for her but for both of us. She'd told me that I was overreacting and that she wasn't going to let fear get in her way. I knew I couldn't talk her out of it, so I had to let it go.

I started the day with Nester, she gobbled up her food and then waited patiently for me to finish my tea before we headed out for a walk. It was raining, but she always enjoyed a walk regardless of the weather. Nester was growing on me, I wasn't usually a dog person, but she was so easy, well trained and content to fit in around our lives. I had never had a dog in my life until Gabriella had taken on Nester. Initially I didn't like the idea but despite my objections, Gabriella had got her way as she often did. In the end it was Nester that had won me over.

I continued to think about what to do about the network, but as the news of the pandemic unfolded that day, I knew I had no choice. I would shut the network down, suspend the memberships and cancel all the outstanding events across the county. Typically, I was putting on an event each day and cancelling this would stop the money coming in immediately, with no idea how far into the future it would be before I could resume the events. I had considered that perhaps it would be terminal for the network I'd created and nurtured, there was a strong chance it would never recover. I'd worry about my income later, for now it was about protecting the community and keeping us all safe.

I had run the business network for 10 years. It was my business and passion, or at least it had been. I had been on a journey with it, with lots of highs and lows. Over 800 events later it seemed it was coming to an end. It was enforced, but it also felt like the energy had been leaving the project slowly over the previous two years, so perhaps this was a way out. A clean break, one that would allow me to leave my community and finish at a natural time. The lockdown was coming, it was just a matter of when.

Gabriella said a rushed goodbye and headed off to the capital. I couldn't help feeling annoyed that she hadn't listened to me and had dismissed my concerns about the dangers of the trip. My intuition wasn't often wrong and right now it was screaming at me, saying trouble was looming. Of late Gabriella was taking a new direction. She was following her inner compass which seemed to be taking her away from me. I felt a distance growing between us; her hunger for success at all costs was impacting our relationship and there was a mismatch in our values around money. I liked to tread lightly on the earth, and she wasn't always prepared to make that sacrifice.

I followed through with my decision and posted on social media. All the events across both Mahwe and The Oxfordshire Project were cancelled. I updated the website and sent out an email campaign to all of the members. It was painful work; I didn't know the future, but I knew there was a chance that I had hosted my last event. I felt desperate, worried, and uncertain. I had run the network for a decade, sometimes at great cost to myself financially. Yet I had gained immensely in different ways. I had sat through around 900 business and personal development talks, and you can't do that without learning a thing or two. My reputation had grown from being a professional photographer to a key figure in the small business community locally. I had been inspired and found mentors who had helped me to grow through my limitations and made some close friends along the way too.

Late that evening Gabriella came home from London exhausted. I thought how stunning she looked despite the long day. She was tall and elegant looking with a curvy figure. She dressed in stylish branded clothing and always took her appearance seriously. She slipped off her coat, hung it on the back of the door and kicked off her shoes.

'Put some music on Ben, let's dance,' she said seductively.

'I'm on it, what do you fancy?' I replied.

'Surprise me, something sexy!' she said.

I put on some Gypsy Kings, and we danced. Dancing sensuously with a woman was one of the true pleasures of life for me, and I loved dancing with Gabriella.

After a couple of songs, she kissed me. She still had her red lipstick on, and I thought that she must have put it on specifically for me. She made me feel special that evening, after five years together she could still excite me. She needed to feel desired that night, she was feeling sexy, and she wanted to be wanted…

I'd prepared us a meal, a dish with olives and aubergines and fresh herbs but she didn't want it. She wanted me instead. I could live with that. I wanted her too, but in the back of my mind I couldn't quite shake off the thought of her day, and all of those people she had been in contact with, but I wanted her, and if she had the virus, I'd probably catch it from her regardless. I let fate take its course.

I grabbed her hand firmly and led her to our bedroom. We made love and fell asleep in each other's arms. It felt like we'd connected, but little did I know then that it was the last night it would ever be like that for us. Our world was about to change, and the memory of that night would stay long in my memory.

We woke to the news that U.K government was telling the country that everything was shutting down. I was glued to the news; the whole country was. Everything was up in the air, the world we knew was changing and nothing was certain. It was something that scientists had been predicting for years, they had been saying it was a likely scenario and now it was reaching our reality. Despite all the predictions, the governments across the world were not prepared for the impact of the pandemic, and in the U.K in particular they seemed to be slow to react. The indecision changed many people's lives and with it, my life forever. Had the government locked us down a few days before, as they had been advised to by other European leaders, my life would be so very different, and with it, my understanding of who I am and what lies behind the veil of our reality.

The following day Gabriella told me that she thought she had the virus. She felt funny, it was unlike anything she'd experienced before. She had a fever, a headache and was exhausted. I knew that if Gabriella had the virus, then so did I. She took the day off and told me to keep my distance. Nester sat on the end of the bed and Gabriella asked me to bring her a cup of coffee. I spent the day organising my business admin, tidying up and mothballing my companies. I had to cancel the upcoming events, let the venues know and all the members. I had put so much work into these businesses, I didn't want to think about the consequences of what I was doing. Sometimes in life you just have to roll with the punches. I tried not to feel the pain that was rising in me. Had I just given up on unfulfilled dreams?

I had a restless, sleepless night. I didn't feel well, I was burning up and then really cold. I had shivers and tingles through my body. Everything I had seen was materialising before my eyes and at such a pace. It felt different than anything I'd had before. I was glad to get out of bed and hoped a shower would help refresh me. It did a little and some of my grogginess left me. My symptoms the next day were relatively mild, and I carried on with my work. We both put ourselves into isolation and wondered how we would be impacted in the days that followed.

As the day came to an end, I was unable to sleep again. I tossed and turned but couldn't find a way to drop off. I took myself out of bed and went downstairs to watch movies and eventually fell asleep on the sofa just before dawn. I don't cope well with a lack of sleep, so I took the next day easy. The next night followed a similar pattern. I would try to catch up during the day, but simply couldn't fall asleep.

My breathing had started to become laboured and then the chronic fatigue began to emerge. My normal routine became difficult, simple tasks became hard to complete. I would have to sit down when preparing food and I couldn't think clearly. I took to my bed for longer periods feeling like I needed to rest in between anything that required energy.

Gabriella on the other hand was already back to normal, for her the virus had come and gone and she was frustrated to be in isolation. She wanted to get back to work, she had a business to save, and this inconvenience was frustrating for her. Having to look after me was just adding to her annoyance and it showed. I was made to feel guilty for being ill, not for the first time, yet I fought against those feelings knowing after all how I had become sick.

My difficulties with concentrating got worse, my mind was fuzzy, and I started to find conversations very tiring. I got in touch with my ex-wife, Maria.

'Hi, it's me can you talk?' I asked.

'Yes, what is it?'

'I'm sick, I can't have the kids this weekend, I've got the virus.'

She sighed deeply, 'How do you know you've got it? I'm sure it's something else.'

'I have no energy. I can't sleep and I'm struggling to breathe,' I said.

'Pff! I suppose I have no choice then,' she said unsympathetically.

It would take her months before she'd acknowledge my illness, a story echoed by many suffering with long covid, where people close to them didn't believe in their illness.

She was disappointed, she needed a break but agreed. The kids were now at home full time because of the lockdown, and she was desperate to break the routine. I wanted to see them too; I missed them, but I didn't want them to catch anything from me and I had no energy to spend quality time with them.

I tried to work and sat at my office desk working on photographs I had taken, in order to sell them through a picture library. I was able to do an hour or two and then would find my way back to bed to try and sleep. The days went by fast as a new pace of life set in. I was frustrated, a little scared and impatient to recover.

It was hard to think clearly but I made a plan. I would work as a professional photographer, taking photographs of things I had easy reach to, and I'd sell them through different picture libraries. I searched the internet and expanded the stock libraries I worked with, from one to five. It was slow work as I was limited in what I could do with the energy I had.

I had three children; Sara was my eldest, she was 15, Leo was 13 and Beatrice was 9. They were great kids and got on really well with Gabriella. I would see them often and take Beatrice to school each morning. Gabriella and I lived around the corner from them, so it worked well for all of us. I had a great relationship with my kids, Leo and I would love to see football matches at Oxford United and bond over the drama of a last-minute winner as the ball hit the back of the net. Beatrice loved being at home; I called her my little house cat. Her favourite thing we did together was baking cakes, cookies, and cheesecakes. Beatrice could spend hours joyfully licking wooden spoons, whisks, and bowls of cake batter. What I love about her most is her ability to always find the fun in everything she does. Sara, loves to work on school projects with me, it's then she takes the opportunity to share her thoughts and feelings about her life. When I get to help her revise for exams, we talk about the real things on her mind in between. They were growing up fast and they made me ever so proud of them all.

A couple of weeks passed by. I started seeing my children again but the chronic fatigue, insomnia and breathing difficulties remained and perhaps the most frustrating of all, so did my brain fog. I took photographs what I could find in the kitchen, staring with grains, pulses, spices, and cheese. I then moved on to dishes and an idea popped into my mind. In order to contribute and feed my creativity, I decided I would claim the kitchen and take over the menu and all of the cooking. I would create dishes from all over the world. After the dishes were made, I photographed them for the picture libraries and challenged the kids' taste buds. The idea was exciting, I needed some fun, I needed something interesting, and this was it. I wanted to indulge my senses, I wanted to enjoy myself through food. I started with Tunisia and decided I'd cook 3 meals from each country and then take a route around the world, going from one country to a neighbouring one, I took a cooking pilgrimage across the world and I loved it and so did the family.

I was trying hard to stay positive, but just under the surface I was aware that I may not recover from my illness and return to the life I was used to. My inner world was in chaos and what was going on inside me was matched in the outside world. As the world leaders stumbled for clarity and the best path forward, in my world I was doing the best I could, with the little I had to offer.

It was shaping up to be a hot summer, the hottest on record. Gabriella was working hard looking for investors and I was struggling, trying to get my head around the fact that my businesses would not live up to the expectations I'd always had for them. Had I failed? Would I be left like this, unable to work more than a couple of hours a day? Unable to walk further than 50 metres without needing a long rest? I tried hard to put negative thoughts out of my head. I imagined myself fit and healthy and I had a vision of myself running on a beach, with the blue sky above me on a pleasant day which I repeated over and over again. I knew well about the power of visualisation and how to work with it to manifest into your life what you desired.

My mother, my rock in my life was also sick, really sick. She was in a lot of pain, unable to walk and the doctors were trying hard to diagnose the issue. Now in her early seventies, she was a lady who had been very active and a keen walker. It was the first time in her life that she was unable to do the things her mind wanted her to do. It was all so much to bear at one time. We were in lockdown, the sun was shining and offering its gift to us and I did my best to keep my chin up despite the turbulence all around me. Thoughts about my mother were never far from my mind, but they were troubling and made me feel worse. She was lucky to have Graham, my stepfather. He was a good man, loving and supportive. She was in good hands.

We had a sweet garden. It was secluded with beautiful flowers and it was a sun trap. The bees and butterflies were busy throughout the day as Nester dozed underneath a young silver birch tree. It was idyllic, and I was able to strip off and let the sun energise me whilst I attempted to switch off from my problems.

The insomnia was relentless, I just couldn't get a proper night's sleep, no matter how hard I tried. In the end I turned to sleeping tablets, but even they couldn't get me through the night. I would fall asleep in the early hours and wake just a short while later. Gabriella was a light sleeper so I would find myself heading down to the sofa and doing my best not to disturb her. As my insomnia took hold my condition worsened and so did my outlook. Each day was a constant battle with my inner demons. I was trying to stay positive as I knew a negative outlook would only make things that much harder.

My cooking pilgrimage reached Greece. I planned a romantic evening with Gabriella, the kids were at their mother's and we had the weekend to ourselves. I spent time choosing interesting dishes and settled on chicken with olives and lemon in a white wine sauce. I picked up some wine and found some Greek music. For a starter I picked some of the vine leaves from the grape vine I'd planted the previous year. I went about preparing stuffed vine leaves as a starter. It was an ambitious meal for me, and I just about pulled it off. I had dedicated my whole day to it.

I moved our beautiful oak table outside into the garden, laid the table and put the wine to chill in the fridge. There was a blue sky and the swallows had just returned and were dancing through the sky. Gabriella emerged, she had been soaking in the bath and was delighted to see all of the effort I'd made. She was wearing a beautiful green flowing dress which showed off her long legs. Her long straight black hair was tied up elegantly

15

on top of head. She had been catching the sun and her skin was beginning to tan. I thought how lucky I was to have her in my life. I hoped the distance I had been feeling between us was just in my imagination. I served the stuffed vine leaves, apprehensively. I had no idea what they would be like. Gabriella looked at them unconvinced. She put in her fork and slowly raised it to her mouth and then popped the food inside. She smiled, 'Not too bad,' she said. I felt a little deflated. I guess I had been hoping for more.

The next day the news came through that my mother had broken her back. She had osteoporosis, osteo rheumatica and polymyalgia rheumatica. It was a tough blow for all of us to take. The journey back to health would be long and hard for her and I was unable to help in anyway. Graham was a man who loved the details and was reading up on everything he could regarding the conditions and sharing this with me and my brother. I felt devasted by the news, it just seemed so much for her to have to face.

My world was being turned upside and it had a long way left to go. What I didn't realise then was that this period would be the easiest of my journey. Despite the insomnia and lack of energy, this was a time of rest where little was expected of me. I was safe and secure. All that would soon change and it would take time to appreciate what I'd had in that long hot summer.

The days that followed took a familiar pattern. My children would come every other weekend but sometimes it wouldn't be possible, it would depend on how well I felt. I would work on my photography, I would cook, and I would rest. Gabriella was under immense pressure, the investment in her business she'd hoped to receive was proving elusive. She was facing the possibility of having to lay off members of her team. So, she decided to put the business into furlough.

Gabriella and I had met in Italy, many years before. I had been on a trip to photograph different cities on a whistle stop tour. She had been working as a waitress and we had flirted in a little café and I'd asked her out, one thing led to another and we started to date. Her English was good, but she spoke with a strong Italian accent which I found very attractive. She was driven, focused, and determined. She also had a certain charm that she could switch on and off that was hard to resist.

She had moved to England to explore how our relationship could work. She enjoyed the country and how relaxed business rules were compared to Italy. Her career had flourished, and the start of our relationship had been a whirlwind romance, full of passion and excitement. Now, five years on and in post Brexit Britain, with a struggling start up, an imposed lockdown and a sick boyfriend, I could see behind her smile that she wasn't content. She wanted freedom, she wanted success, and she wanted a man that matched where she wanted to be in life. Initially she thought I was that man, but I had been bogged down in running a community that took a lot of my time and didn't deliver the financial reward for my efforts. I could see her longing for more.

As the days passed through the summer months of 2020, I began to try and start going on a short walk every afternoon. Leo came with me and each day I'd try and get a little further, walking for five minutes and then taking a short break. I was so grateful to have him with me. It was slow work and disheartening. After a walk I would be exhausted but I kept up the practice and after a month I was able to be out an about for up to thirty minutes. I began to believe that I would make some sort of recovery, perhaps not back to who I was before, but maybe enough to work fulltime and be independent, that was encouraging, and my spirits began to lift.

The lockdown began to ease and as it did, I excitedly jumped in my little car with my camera and headed to the nearby town of Burford. There was a blue sky, and I took my camera and photographed the pretty Cotswold town. It felt so good to be out of the house and working with my camera away from the kitchen table. I only had limited energy so Burford was perfect as it was small. It felt so good popping into a grocery store and picking up some fresh vegetables, seeing the colourful arrangements in the quaint shop. I spoke with the shop worker; he'd lost his business and was working there temporarily to keep the money coming in. Lockdown had changed us, the simple pleasure of exploring a little shop was suddenly a sensual delight!

The following day I had managed to get the photographs up on sale on the picture libraries and I was taking advantage of the blue skies to head to Abingdon in South Oxfordshire. I found myself walking even further, along the banks of the River Thames. I was over 3 months into getting sick and I felt at last I was on the mend. I still had to work out how to make a living, but it felt like I was through the worst of it. I was enjoying being out of the house and I allowed myself to hope that I'd restore myself to full health once more.

Photography trips to Cheltenham, Stratford upon Avon, Banbury, and Bicester followed. I was able to walk further and further. Gabriella started jogging around Witney; she had gained weight over lockdown and now at last had the time to get fit. I'd watched her increase her exercise routine daily and felt inspired to join in. She had a thirty-minute run mapped out and I asked if I could join her. She told me to be careful and reminded me that I was prone to overdo it, but she'd be glad of the company.

It felt good, exciting even, to put on my running gear. I did some light stretches and we set out together with Nester. We ran down a steep hill and into the town centre. As we reached the bridge, I told her to go on ahead with the dog. It had been just five minutes and I was out of breath. I walked for a little and then tried again. I passed some shops and again after just a few minutes had to stop. This time I turned and headed back. This would be my starting point, I would only improve from here, I thought positively.

The following day I headed off to Southampton to photograph the city. I was excited to be on the road, to be going further and further. Once I'd parked up, I wandered to the seafront and photographed the docks. I soaked up the atmosphere and watched the large gulls on the rocks. I wandered the old city walls and enjoyed the views and imagined how the city once looked in mediaeval times. I spent hours meandering around with my camera, taking in the sites.

The next day I felt different, I was overcome with tiredness. I'd over done it. The culmination of the jog and the day out exploring Southampton had taken its toll on me. The following day was the start of the summer holidays. I had my kids, and I was heading to Dorset to spend some time with my mother. My stepfather Graham was overseas working, so it would be a little longer before we could all catch up. I found the drive hard and when I arrived, I headed straight for the bed. Gabriella had come down with us in a separate car, she would stay for a few days before flying off to Italy to spend the summer with her friends and family. I began to seriously worry about my health. I had put so much hope into my recovery and I was feeling it all slip away and there was nothing I could do to halt the decline.

Within two days my health had deteriorated so much that I actually thought I was going to die. Gabriella was extremely concerned. She was trying to be strong and trying to be upbeat. She was far from a natural carer and seeing me lying in bed struggling to breathe was quite shocking for her. There was a smell of sickness in my room, I wondered if she felt responsible, guilty perhaps, although I never mentioned it. I sensed she wanted out; she hadn't signed up for this. Her business was down on its knees, and she longed for her culture, Italian food, Italian cuisine and above all Italian coffee. Did she long for the excitement of a new romance too? Unhelpful thoughts filled my mind.

Every breath I took was laboured and it felt to me that if I stopped trying to breathe my body would simply give up. I didn't have any energy at all. I told Gabriella that I believed that I couldn't get any worse, there was nowhere left to go, worse was death. Perhaps that wasn't the case, but right then that's where my thoughts were leading me and that's how I felt.

I decided it was time to be completely honest with her. I sat myself up and with a laboured and breathless voice and said,

'I'm struggling. I don't know if I am going to pull through this.' I paused to catch my breath and then very slowly continued. 'I think I might die. I feel like I am at the edge of my life and that almost all of my life force energy has been taken from me. I have been regressing, like I'm walking backwards and there is a cliff behind me. If I take a few steps more backwards I'll be gone, over the edge!'

She stared at me and was completely lost for words.

'I'm sure it's not as bad as all of that,' she said sympathetically.

She kissed me on the forehead and left me to rest. I will never forget the look of dread on her face as she left me. She had always been an open book, hopelessly unable to hide her feelings. I knew she didn't know how to respond; she didn't want to think about the situation. She called the doctor and was told that I was in the best place and for her to keep an eye on me. It wasn't very reassuring, but they were run off their feet with sicker people than me. I didn't want to go to hospital, but I packed a bag just in case.

I lay in bed staring at the bag packed up beside the door. I was scared, this wasn't the end I had expected for myself. I thought of my children and if I died, how I would watch over them from the other side of the veil. I would stay close and keep them safe. When I thought of their reaction to my death, my eyes filled with tears, and it was the trigger for me to feel the pain that was welling up inside of me. I let out a cry of emotions and then sobbed loudly with tears streaming down my cheeks. After a little while of letting out the raw emotions, I managed to pull myself together again. Feeling sorry for myself had felt helpful, good even, but also a little indulgent. It was time to act. And so, doing the only thing left available to me, I decided it was time to call out to God and ask for help.

And so, alone in a room at my parents' house I prayed. I sat myself up and cleared my mind and mentally prepared myself.

'Dear God, It's me. It's been a long time since I've prayed to you. I'm sick, I have nothing left to give. Please don't leave me like this, with no energy, living some kind of half-life experience. I want to live. I want my life back; I want to be strong again. I have so much to offer. I want adventure. I want to be the best version of myself, I've always wanted that, but I haven't got there yet. Help me heal, help me be strong again and I will do whatever you want me to do. I will serve you. You know that I've always done all that you've asked of me. Please, I beg of you, help me recover. Show me how.'

It was done, I felt enormous relief. I felt like I had been heard and then I remembered times in the past when my prayers had been answered. I had faith, I'd be okay. I smiled to myself and tried to sleep.

My prayer was heard. I felt God had been waiting to hear from me. The stars were aligned, I had reached a predestined point in my life, it had all been unavoidable, this was my path. I was exactly where I was supposed to be. As much as I wished to have control over my life, there were times the mere idea was ludicrous.

Gabriella left for Italy, with a kiss. My mother and I would look after the kids between us. We weren't in great shape, but we could just about feed the kids and they were so pleased to get away from their home and have a change of scenery. My eldest two already knew their way around the kitchen. They were always really helpful and contributed whenever asked. My mother had a large comfortable house, the weather was great, and the kids were happy. I got to spend some good time with them, even though my energy was very limited, and I was back to walking fifty metres or so. It was now four months since I'd first got the virus.

I decided to change my approach to getting well. I would no longer try and slowly build up my fitness and keep busy by working on my photography business; it was time for a completely new approach. After all, I had made no progress, and I was back at square one. I made the decision that, I would stop trying to work and fully focus on getting well. I would research and learn all I could, and I would also turn to my spiritual side in order to heal myself. That decision would lead me down the rabbit hole and send me on the adventure of my life.

At this stage on my journey, I was struggling to think clearly. I had the real fear that I'd never fully recover, I'd be an observer who was no longer able to play a fully active role in life. My relationship with Gabriella was unravelling and I was too scared to think of the future and the implications of all of this on my life.

I decided to post on social media a blog about my journey with long covid. I shared a warning to anyone going through long covid about the chance of a relapse if they over did it and I told those that didn't believe their partner or colleague who was experiencing the illness, to trust and support them. My post resulted in two really helpful conversations with thoughtful people. Abigayle was first, she had once been a customer of mine and we'd stayed connected on social media. She was making a very slow recovery from Lymes Disease. We had a long conversation about nutrition and which vitamins she was taking in order to make her recovery. She was still struggling and had some good days and bad days. Following her advice, I got busy ordering vitamin tablets. One of the problems with brain fog, a symptom of long covid is that thinking is really difficult and, conversations can be exhausting. So, the obvious things, like taking vitamins was something I hadn't done until then. I got some magnesium tablets, which would help me sleep and vitamin C, vitamin B and fish oil tablets.

I then had a conversation with Jessie. We had once worked together when I was a teenager and she had spent the past twenty-five years with M.E. which had left her with chronic fatigue, like Abigayle. Jessie told me that it sounded like my symptoms matched hers. She told me that people with M.E. were usually very active people and catch a virus that attacks their immune system. She gave me a stark warning, every relapse I had was likely to leave me with less chance of making a full recovery. Although a terrifying thought, it was just what I needed to hear. She told me about pacing myself, how I'd need to take a break between everything I did. She also pointed me towards the M.E. website where I'd be able to read all about practical things that I could do, in order to help myself. It was eye opening. I felt that, if I had been given this advice from the doctor at the beginning, I could have saved myself months of recovery. However, I was one of the first to get this new illness, so I knew it was pointless holding any blame towards the medical profession, or anyone else for that matter. This was my journey and I needed to own it.

The next positive step was joining an online group with over one hundred thousand people who were also suffering with long covid. Each day people would share their stories, there were messages from people who had recovered and people in despair. I shared what I'd learnt from Abigayle and Jessie and checked the threads each day. The group became a real positive anchor in my life.

I started walking again. I took my son Leo with me and we walked to the end of the drive, past the petrol station and to a bridge crossing the road. I took the pace slowly. What used to take me two minutes to walk was now taking ten. I had to rest and then head back. It was frustrating, but a necessary step towards my recovery. Leo was patient, he must have been worried to see me able to do so little, but he never showed it.

I followed advice from my friend and started pacing myself. I would rest in between each activity. Resting consisted of lying down doing nothing at all. I was taking my recovery deadly seriously. I was determined not have another relapse, each improvement in my health would be built upon, step by step I would get back to full health again.

Chapter 2

Surrender

A couple of years before the pandemic started, I had been doing shamanic journeys with recorded drumming music. To explain further, I'd learnt how to do an inner journey whilst in a meditated state in order to communicate with my soul guides. It was a technique that I had found really beneficial. I would communicate with guides who always seemed to be able to answer my questions with profound wisdom. If you were to ask me who were those guides, I spoke with, I wouldn't be able to give you a concise answer. Perhaps they are a part of me, or they are spirits who have lived many lives, perhaps it is the universal energy or from a religious perspective you may simply call it God. They knew my life inside out and offered me support, showing me the path ahead and a different perspective that I so desperately needed.

So, I decided to reach out to the spirit world for advice and support once again. I put my earphones in and listened to the drums as I focused on my breathing: four seconds in, hold, four seconds out, hold and so on. It's a technique known as box breathing. I imagined a beautiful large oak tree in a lush field on an idyllic hill. The sun was shining, and I could feel a warm breeze on my face. There was a large wooden arched door with a black handle leading inside. I opened the door and saw the familiar black and white chequered flooring. On the left was another door which led down to the Lower World. On the right a spiral staircase led up to my spirit guides and the Upper World. There was a beautiful window flooding the inside of the room with a golden ambient light. I walked up the staircase which then led me through the centre of the tree. At the top of the stairs, I walked out on to a thick branch and waited for my lift to the Upper World.

A giant eagle swept down and invited me to hold on to his talons. We had made this trip together before. As he took off upwards, I grabbed on and watched below as the trees became smaller and smaller and I flew through the clouds. After a short and exhilarating ride, the huge bird gently placed me on some sturdy clouds and took off the way he had arrived. I was met by one of my guides, it was a journey I had made many times. My guide had taken the form of a graceful female in a white robe with a hood. She looked ethereal and smiled benevolently, showing me into a room which opened up to a beautiful garden. We sat down on two ornate wooden chairs, and she asked how I was coping. I shared a little of how I was feeling, just a little as I was sure she knew exactly, and I was here to listen and not to talk.

'How can I heal myself?' I asked.

Her answer was short and simple.

'Surrender to your spiritual path, only when you fully surrender will you start to become whole once more. You are in transformation right now. You have been a caterpillar and right now you are in a cocoon, transforming into a butterfly. It will take time, but if you accept your path, you will become that butterfly Ben, and you will fly,' she said.

After this profound message I found my way back to the tree and opened my eyes. I was left in no doubt. I had surrendered to my spiritual path once before and it had led me to huge growth and opportunities. I trusted my guides and I wanted so desperately to be well again. I prayed to the highest power imaginable and surrendered and asked it to show me my way back to health. I would await instructions and see where it would lead me.

Although I was excited, I found it hard to take on the enormity of the impact this would have on my life. It wasn't as if I was being pointed towards a new career as an artist or graphic designer, which were occupations my peers would be able to relate to. This was out of the ordinary, from a source I had found deep within my inner world. The idea of the cocoon seemed to fit well. I was going to transform and become a new version of myself. I felt uplifted and also privileged. It was all part of the plan the universe had in place for me. I would find purpose in my life again, but first I needed to get well and that was going to be one of the biggest challenges I had ever faced.

My days were spent painting, playing with the children, reading, cooking and resting. I tried to increase the amount of walking I did each day. My children were happy, relaxing by the pool and playing computer games. I was reading Charlotte's Web to Beatrice, and she was loving the story, like so many children before her. In the classic novel a wise spider talks to her friend the pig and weaves words in a cobweb to make him appear more special than he was. I thought how many times in my life that I had been like the pig in the story. I had been able to achieve things through my work, whilst weaving my personal web of dreams and taken the credit for it, but I felt that it was always the spirit world working through me. The spider was a great metaphor for the spirit world. No one could see it hidden away on the ceiling of the barn, yet it was forever patient with the pig as the spirit world was with me. It offered advice, pointed me in the right direction and allowed me to take the full credit.

My first significant dream since becoming ill came as a complete surprise. I knew very well the difference between a normal dream and a dream in which the spirit world delivers a powerful message. These dreams are the ones you wake from bright-eyed and remember every detail. A knowing sensation inside tells you that was important, and you must pay attention and remember as much as you can. In my dream, I was visited by a spirit guide in the form of a serious man with a black cape with the hood lowered. His message was short and stark,

'You are to become a Shaman. You will be taught by the spirit world. Watch out, for the lessons are all around you. Your training has already begun!'

It was a clear instruction; my path had been revealed to me.

But what did this all mean. Would I have to go to South America and study with indigenous tribes. Visions of tribal dancing filled my mind, huge open fires against a backdrop of clear night skies studded with stars; drumming, chanting and psychedelic adventures through the veil of reality. I pictured wise, tattooed men with beards wearing animal skins, handing me pipes of plant medicine and encouraging me to smoke!

It was thrilling, uncomfortable and challenging all at once. The adventure seeker within me punched the air in delight and the old crone gave me a knowing smile. That day I kept receiving the same message through my intuition. I needed to make my own set of cards for divination. Inspiration formed in my mind, to gather wisdom from around the world, from all of the great minds past and present and make a set of cards that I could use to channel from the divine. I'd tap into the wisdom of geniuses to help me find my path. I had a message in my head, be led by the wise. I had spent many years living in Witney in Oxfordshire and the name was an Anglo-Saxon name, from the word Witan, meaning a group of wise people who would advise the king. I would gather my Witan and put their wisdom into a set of cards.

I had started a new audio book, a novel by one of my favourite fantasy authors. I'd really enjoyed reading his previous books and quite coincidentally, he had written a portal to an alternative reality outside the house I grew up in North Oxford. As always, books I'm meant to read find me, and this was no exception. My father had bought the first book in the series a few years earlier and it had been sitting unread gathering dust until now. I needed to read it at this precise moment. I purchased the audio book and listened to the first volume in just a couple of days and then bought the second in the series. It was set where I grew up, around Oxford and Wolvercote in particular. The river I swam in as a child played a major role in the books and I felt like the author was almost talking about my childhood, but in an imaginary world. There was something special about that stretch of the river, which could also boast links to Alice and Wonderland.

I took out a pan and poured in some water to boil, whilst engrossed in my new audio book. I was thinking about making these new cards and how it could help. Just then the story I was listening to mentioned a set of cards that could discover hidden knowledge. I had been thinking of these cards and immediately it played out in the book I was listening to. It was a clear sign, confirmation from a book I am linked to geographically.

I was also a fantasy novelist, although of very modest success. I had a keen love for the idea of time travel, historical novels, and fantasy worlds.

I began making my first set of cards. I took sheets of A4 paper and cut them up into rectangles and started writing words and sentences on them. I wrote intuitively with whatever came into my head. Things like overcoming an obstacle in your path, facing your fear head on, it's time to act on an idea you've been holding on to. I just allowed my mind to open up and overflow with instructions the spirit world could guide me with. By the end of the day, I had over two hundred of these cards and I decided to try them out.

I shuffled the cards and laid them out face down. I didn't know if it would work or not. I had been reading the Tarot for many years and had come to an understanding with them. They always seemed to match what was in my head, my fears, and aspirations and they gave me good guidance.

Would these homemade cards be able to carry a similar energy and foretell the future or give me guidance? I had been led here so I expected them to work. I asked my spirit guides to talk to me through the cards and tell me the most helpful things I needed to know right then. Through this initial set of cards, I was told to heal myself, to work with energy and develop a greater knowledge on the subject. I was encouraged to let go of my need to earn money. To free myself mentally from the pressure and surrender to the sickness within my body. It was a time of transformation for me and an important part of my life path.

Over the next few days, I increased my cards and continued with the readings. It was an inspirational and enjoyable process. I was confident they would work, I just needed to source the wisdom I could use. The next step was to improve the look of the cards and so I got to work on a simple design for the cover.

The summer holidays continued. My children were incredibly supportive, and it was so good to spend quality time with them. I continued cooking around the world and they were delighted one morning when I told them I was cooking Brazilian churros for breakfast. Their Spanish culture was rich, and they loved the Spanish food and churros was a favourite for them. My mother got involved with the cooking and we all laughed heartily at the strange shapes they were emerging into. We made far too many and added a rich chocolate sauce and sugar to dip them in. It was a happy moment from a difficult period, and we all ate too much.

By the end of the month, I had read my first book since getting sick. It had been about reversing chronic fatigue by working on your inner world. I had chosen the book intuitively and it would be the first of a long line of books that would teach me exactly what I needed to know at exactly the right time. My guides were leading me through the wisdom contained within books. They were choosing my mentors and the order would take me on a profound journey of healing and spiritual growth.

I was able to walk for fifteen minutes without stopping, which was up from five minutes before I'd arrived in Dorset. I would progress from that point, and I was grateful for every little gain. I continued to work on my visualisations of running on the beach. I was using a beach in Tasmania I had been to in my early twenties. In my mind I would connect energetically to the rising sun and have the whole beach to myself.

I arrived back in Oxfordshire in much higher spirits than when I had left. Gabriella had enjoyed the break and showed no signs of missing me, in fact she never did. When I was away, she seemed at her happiest, in her element, working on herself, her career. I questioned our relationship and knew I needed to talk through some of our issues of with her.

I was beginning to feel confident in my improvement in health. As long as I was careful, I felt I could pick up my camera again and begin to start photographing small towns around Oxfordshire. I went to towns within an hour's drive. I took it slow and easy. I paced myself every step of the way. I would treat myself to a coffee in an independent quirky café which was the highlight for me of these photography trips. Money wasn't finding its way to me. I had just a little each month coming in via the picture libraries and was mainly living off my savings. I was trying hard not to get stressed about the situation. Stress was a big factor in relapses with long covid, the more stress you were under the more likely you would be to fall backward again with your recovery.

There was something I had been considering for some time and I couldn't find a clear answer as my judgement was clouded with so much emotion, so I asked for help. I decided to ask my guides if I should restart my business networking community. I laid out the ever-increasing cards at my disposal and asked the question. The answer I received back was insightful. I was told that it was an endeavour that didn't serve me and that had little financial reward. That sounded true. After years of toiling away, there was the business summed up in a nutshell. Now was the time to let it go, but it would be hard to do. It had given me so much more than money but perhaps I had learnt enough from the project. I would miss the community aspect of my businesses most of all. One of our basic needs as a human is to play our role in a community and feel part of something bigger than ourselves that we believe in. By being a leader of a community, I had filled an important role in my needs. I had gained respect and been able to contribute to something that impacted many lives in such a positive way.

I noticed on my bookshelf a book on Egyptian Shamanism. It was calling me. I felt I needed to read it again. I had read it once before but hadn't finished it. Simply its time had now come. I devoured the book in three days. I knew a lot of the techniques in the book but there was information in there I hadn't learnt, and I was able to deepen my knowledge of certain practices. The ancient Egyptian Shaman was connected to the leopard, and according to the book, the leopard spirit animal would work with the shaman on his shamanic journey. The leopard would come to me too, but not yet. As summer began to draw to an end I escaped into the astral plain and began to meet my spirit animals in the underworld.

I got comfy in my bed, I put on the shamanic drumming music. I concentrated on my breathing until I was deeply relaxed and found myself outside the large oak tree. Inside the door I stood on the familiar chequered floor and this time took the door leading down into the ground, into the Lower World. I walked down the wooden steps, spiralling deep into the earth, all the while hearing the rhythmic drumming in my ears. I opened the door at the bottom of the dark staircase. In front of me was a rich terrain with a red sun casting a golden light across the landscape. To my left was a cliff leading to a valley, with a jungle aside a blue lagoon. To my right lay a dark dense thick forest and straight ahead was a clearing which I walked towards. I reached a fallen tree and sat and waited for my spirit animals to approach.

A white owl landed upon my right shoulder. He didn't speak, but I knew he brought with him certain strengths: intuition, listening and of course wisdom. A stag made its way through the trees until it stood before me. It appeared to be so beautiful and graceful. He gently bowed his head and invited me to dance with him. I felt like I was in a children's movie. The owl flew up into the air whilst I stood watching and the stag started to dance in time to the drums playing through the music in my head. My inner child took over and I danced too. Together we made quite the sight. The owl above us hovering in the air, seemingly joining in his own way. I felt free, I felt liberated, and it all felt rather magical.

After the dance I thanked the deer and asked him if he had a message for me. He said he brought stamina, grace, and spiritual enlightenment, that was his gift to me. He told me to come back, and he'd perform a healing on me. The following day I returned to find a small fire lit and I was told to sit beside it. The stag danced and chanted around me with the owl working some sort of magic with its flapping wings. It felt awe-inspiring to connect to these friendly helpful magical spirits. I was building a new support network which I would need for the journey ahead. These were the spirit animals that had been with me all my life. It was brilliant to finally meet them and share an unforgettable experience with them.

I would later read that dancing with your spirit animals was a common experience for shamans. As my journey unfolded, I would be joined by more animal spirits that would bring exceptional gifts with them.

I was drawn to go to the library and pick out some books with wisdom that I could use for my cards. I found books on trees and animals containing spiritual meanings. I was learning another language, similar to that of the Tarot. Each tree, plant and animal contained a spiritual meaning. I made cards for all of these and added them to my collection. It seemed an endless list. I also looked at dreams and their meanings. I searched for books with well-known quotes and made cards for these as well. I was inspired through the process. As the volume of cards increased my readings became more accurate and helpful and were able to tackle a wider range of problems and subjects.

I had been spending a fair bit of money on paper and ink and with little money coming in I asked the universe for some help, for some money to arrive. It came with a clear signal that I was doing exactly what the spirit world wanted me to do. When my next five packs of paper and ink came through, there was a delay beyond the three weeks that had been promised, as a result, I got it all for free. It came through the day after the allotted time. It had been lost in the warehouse and then found. I said a big thank you to my guides and knew the support was there, they had my back. It was the reassurance I needed.

My friend Tony called around for a coffee to see how I was. He caught me unaware as I was knee deep in writing cards with books piled high all around me. I brewed him a coffee whilst he flicked through the books.

'What are you doing?' He asked curiously.

'Well, I'm gathering wisdom and creating a tool to translate from my spirit guides in order for them to teach me and guide me along my spiritual path,' I said rather sheepishly.

I felt like I needed to justify my actions. I was expecting him to raise his eyebrows or question me. However, he acted in the opposite way. He was fascinated and asked if he could flick through the cards. The cards seemed to inspire him, and they were a great conversation starter. He asked me to let him know how I got on with them. It was comforting to realise that someone I respected deeply had not judged my thought process in making them and allowing them to guide me.

To my surprise I started picking up messages through the cards that Gabriella wasn't the right partner for me. That it would be better for both of us if I was to leave her and find a new path, one that would lead to me rapid spiritual growth and help her grow too. I was told that in time I would find someone else who would gladly offer me the level of support I needed. I was brought to tears. They'd revealed an unwanted truth that I'd been fearing deep down but had been ignoring. I didn't share this with Gabriella, but I started to reflect upon our relationship. It was a hard thing to consider. We had been really happy in the first few years of our relationship. Since Brexit she had changed her opinion of Britain, and the British and I could see that she longed to be back in Italy. I felt more and more rejected and couldn't remember the last time she had made me feel special or valued as a partner.

Most of the instructions from my spirit guides led to further studies, but it wasn't just ancient wisdom and shamanism they wanted me to learn. They told me to write about environmentalism and politics. I spent days researching biodiversity, the plight of the oceans, the issues with the party-political system in the U.K, plastic pollution, the pollution of our rivers, the historical impact of the British Empire and the impact of modern farming on the environment and our health. I truly felt like I was back at school, it was fascinating but the more I learnt the more frustrated I became about the world and our leaders.

The shaman is a human connected to the spiritual world and the natural world. They wanted me to increase my knowledge on the natural world too. It was fascinating, I was learning so much and I was publishing my blogs and getting great feedback. I was delighted when a retired professor of ecology at a world-famous university got in touch to say how well written and accurate my blog was.

Something else was happening within me. I felt closer to nature and more agitated with human behaviour. I was becoming hyper-sensitive to capitalist greed, the political elite, the destruction of our planet and general thoughtlessness regarding the path humanity was heading towards. I could see our collective behaviour from a new perspective, and I didn't like what I was seeing one bit.

I was now able to start walking my daughter Beatrice to school again. It was a pleasant thirty-minute walk there and back along a country trail, beside a little picturesque stream. It felt so good to get to that stage of my recovery. I decided we could contribute towards our community, and in particular to the natural world on the way to school. I suggested to Beatrice that we pick up litter on our walk and do our bit for nature. Thankfully she needed no persuasion. I was so proud of her attitude. We took an empty carrier bag each and a pair of gloves and every day as we walked to school, we would pick up a bag of rubbish each. I had hoped the school would get involved and start a campaign to get the other kids helping too. Beatrice would take her bag of rubbish into school to show the teacher what she'd collected. She was given the star of the day and that led to extra determination on her part. We continued each day and soon people started to notice what we were doing whilst we were in action.

I was joined by the local priest Daniel. He would get off his bike when he saw me and walk with us. Over the next few weeks, we got to know each other quite well. We had fascinating conversations about spirituality, our community and the impact that lockdown was having on the local people. I told him about my personal journey with sickness and losing my businesses and how I had been led to shamanism. I told him how I had allowed my spiritual side to be my guiding light. He was intrigued and asked me all manner of questions on my practices and the communication I had with the divine. He told me he'd been praying for me, and I was deeply touched. I would look out for him in the mornings and hope we'd get a chance to talk, we were becoming friends. He shared with me that the biggest issues his community were facing were loneliness and isolation. The world hadn't fully opened up again and many people were too afraid to leave their homes. It was a strange time, the walk to school was eerily quiet as most other children were being home schooled.

During one of my reading, I was told I needed to learn something new that would help me to heal. Apparently, I didn't have a card for it, so I picked up the dictionary and opened the page randomly with my eyes closed and when I looked down, I was pointing to the word Qabalah. The Qabalah links back to early Judaism and is a set of esoteric teachings.

I did a little research and picked up a book on the Qabalah. I had never heard of it before, but it was ancient and spiritual, so I was intrigued. As I saw it, it was a series of inner journeys which were similar to shamanic journeys. There was clearly a lot more to it than that, like astrology, one could spend a lifetime studying the Qabalah, but that wasn't to be my focus. I was told to do a crash course.

Through the Qabalah I would come face to face with myself, the elementals, my karma and much more. This was the beginning of some much-needed inner work. I would heal myself from within. I needed to let go of the load I was carrying and make peace with my life. On starting, I knew nothing about the Qabalah or Judaism, but I embraced the book and its teachings. Some say its origins go back to ancient Egypt and the time of the Egyptian Shaman. I had to create a series of rituals and do a visualisation to an inner world, much as I was used to. The rituals involved using a sacred space, incense, gemstones, herbs, offerings, and plants. I was very much within my comfort zone and looking forward to seeing what was revealed to me. I was also told to pick up an Egyptian ankh for good measure and wear it around my neck. It was an ancient symbol that had a powerful impact upon the energy of the wearer.

In my first journey I had to look to balance the elements within me. I was to journey to the Temple of Malkuth and meet the four elements face to face: fire, water, air and earth and it would be revealed to me, what I was depleted in. I set up my altar as instructed and did breathing exercises and followed the path to the temple in my mind. There I faced them, they were imposing figures, they looked like gods and through their density I could see how strong each one was within me. I felt nervous to be in their presence as I focused on the vision. The elements of water and air appeared strong, however, the fire within me was faint, as was earth. I thanked them for revealing this truth. I needed to connect with nature, I needed to get out in the country to feel the wind blow through me and touch the earth with my hands. I needed to rekindle the fire within me. I vowed to get myself out in nature and connect to the forest. From that point on, hardly a week has past by that I haven't spent time in a dense rich forest, no matter where I have been.

Increasingly I was led by my intuition. I would leave the house not knowing where I was going until I got there. On a cold Tuesday morning I told Gabriella not to worry about me, I was going out for a walk. I followed a path that led me across a muddy farm and through a narrow wood. It was a blustery day, and the wind was getting stronger and stronger. I was guided by my instincts to the middle of a large open field. I felt something important was about to happen. My hairs stood on end, and I felt a tingle over my shoulders. I stood there with my arms outstretched, and as I did so, the gale whipped up around the field and thrust against me. It felt amazing, I was at the centre of a storm. In that moment I connected with the element of air, and it made me feel alive, full of energy and vigour. I laughed and shouted to the wind. 'Thank you, I feel you, I hear you.' When I'd left the house there had been a fair wind, but it seemed right here in the centre of the open field it was circling me, going through me, dancing with me. I was in the moment, and I was connected with the natural world. Every day I was becoming more the shaman.

The weather was now becoming autumnal and to be within the forest filled my heart with joy. I couldn't walk the whole distance of the circular walk without taking a long break in the middle but if I took my time, I could make it round. I found it healing for me to be alone with the forest and I was beginning to connect with nature at a higher level, a connection that hadn't seemed open to me before. I was soon doing the same walk almost every day. I was connecting to earth, and it was helping me, and I fell in love with the forest. It became a filter for my thoughts, emotions, and my energy field. I would arrive in one state and always leave in a better one, calmer and with new insight. I connected to the trees, and they aided in my healing.

The Qabalah isn't to be undertaken all in one go. You take each journey at your own pace, reflect upon it and integrate it into your life. The first journey had proved very beneficial, and I felt ready to take on the second, to the temple of Yesod. There I would meet my subconscious mind. The Yesod is where I would come face to face with my past and all the things that I had done. On this journey it was revealed to me that I was holding a lot of pain in me regarding my business, The Oxfordshire Project. I had given so much of myself and hadn't fully understood all that I had gained from the experience. I was invited to reflect on the lessons and to accept that was the nature of business networks and how people treated them. I needed to understand that it wasn't personal, and it was harmful to hold on to the pain. I needed to let go of those feelings and as a result I would travel lighter. It was part of my healing process. It was about moving on and appreciating all I had gained from the venture and letting go of the negative experiences and my expectations of people and their behaviours.

I sat in the garden with my shirt off soaking up the sun and spent the afternoon reflecting on all the positives I had gained from putting on several hundred networking events over ten years. I thought of all the wonderful people I had met. I pictured my mentors and what they had all taught me. I remembered the opportunity I'd had to appear in a dancing competition and dance on stage at the theatre. I had been a regular guest on local radio and television and through that exposure, I'd met some really interesting people. I'd developed new skills in communication and been thrilled by the impact we'd had in helping various charities. Taking what I'd learnt from the Qabalah, I would travel light; I'd only carry the positives forward and leave the regrets and pain points behind. I would rewrite the past. It was a huge moment for me and one that would lead to another step along the path towards my full recovery.

Each journey of the Qabalah was equally profound and helped me to change my perspective towards my illness, my past and my life. It seemed that with every journey I was given some insight that would lead me to be able to heal an old, deep inner wound. On one such journey I was led to a desolate path where I was heckled by my children for my failings as a parent. I was told to ask them for forgiveness. Afterwards I sat down with them individually and went through my mistakes, as I saw them, and I asked them if they could forgive me. They did so effortlessly, and then in turn they asked me to forgive them for what they had done. It was a cleansing process; it was deep, and it was a very emotional, positive experience.

I wasn't the only one making progress, my mother was also on the mend and was reducing her medication each month. She was growing stronger and able to do an ever-increasing number of things. It was such a wonderful relief for the whole family and helped to lift our spirits.

I was beginning to lean further into my intuition, and it led me to study energy and how I could generate more of it. I was drawn to understand more about ancient practices that worked with energy, and these included sexual practices and techniques from the East including Tantric Sex and aspects of Taoism. I still had chronic fatigue so the idea of creating new energy to use, store and to help me heal seemed like a wonderful idea. I started with some of the individual exercises I had read about. I told Gabriella what I was doing, and she listened intently and was open to getting involved and trying it out. She had been withdrawing from our intimate relationship slowly over time and we both thought that this could help bring us closer together.

Working with energy at a higher level, by giving it intention, to easily move and store throughout your body was important shamanic work, and my next module of my spiritual university course. I was moving quickly through my intensive training, and I was using the new knowledge to heal myself. I read numerous books on working with sexual energy and all the benefits attached to it. Before long I was putting the techniques into practice and gaining tangible results. I had more energy; I was healing at a quicker rate and my connection to the divine seemed to open up to a greater extent than ever before. It all felt right, my energy was increasing, and I was learning how to use it in a different way. Gabriella and I enjoyed the new techniques and because I was used to working with our chakras and healing with energy, none of it seemed alien to me.

Chapter 3

Letting Go

It was during a Qabalah journey that I spoke with a spirit who took the form of an angel. As we sat beside a clear pool in a Japanese garden, I asked how I could receive more financial support. The sun shone in between the trees creating dappled warm light all around, and the angel told me to turn my hand to a little magic. I should try and create a money spell. It wasn't the answer I was expecting. I was suddenly really curious, and my mind was full of questions.

I started researching money magic on the internet and found several articles with clear, step by step instructions. There were also loads of books I could buy that were packed full of spells, as well as blogs. So, I found a simple money spell and got started. I needed: fresh basil, bay leaves, green gemstones, green candles, incense, and to write the actual spell. I also needed a knife, to open and close the magic circle. I remembered that a couple of friends had given me a whole load of stuff from their kitchen when they moved to South Africa. So, I rummaged through the garage and found the boxes they'd given me, and of course, inside was exactly what I needed. Not only was there a beautiful brand new knife, but as I took it out, I noticed it had the words 'Magic Knife' written along the side. Wow, that was incredible. Just like the cards and ink coming to me for free, the knife was here and clearly marked for its purpose. The spirit world was encouraging me to add the use of magic to my toolbox for my training as a shaman. It made sense and I marvelled at my spirit guide's methods. I remember finding my first pack of tarot cards in my wardrobe and having no idea how they got there!

For my first spell I chose to work with Ra, the Sun God of ancient Egypt. As instructed, I created an energetic safe space with the knife and asked my guides to aid me. I channelled with my guides and asked if I'd forgotten anything. The answer was yes, I still needed to make an offering. Of course, I'd forgotten that bit. I went into the garden and picked some flowers, and I took some fruit from the kitchen and laid it out on the altar.

I raised the energy in the room. I used drums, music, and chanting, and then read out my spell in a strong, commanding, and dramatic voice. I had done my best to write my words into a poem, which is a more powerful way of expressing words. The curtains were drawn, and I allowed myself to lose my apprehension and not question whether it would work. After I read out the spell I thanked the spirits, the elements and Ra for their help, and closed the magic circle with my knife. I didn't know what to expect, I was certainly hopeful I'd been heard.

The next morning with a cup of tea in hand, I did what I usually did, I checked to see how many photographs I had sold on my various picture libraries. Usually, it would be between five and ten. To my utter amazement I had sold eighty-five images overnight, more than ever before by a considerable distance. One particular library had sold its very first image for me. I'd been with them for six months. I was speechless. Magic seemingly worked, magic was real, and what's more, I could do it. Now didn't that make life a lot more interesting! My mind buzzed with possibilities. I felt like Aladdin with his magic lamp, except I had endless wishes instead of just three.

I ordered books on magic; some worked with the sun, while others worked with the moon. I ordered ancient books, and second-hand books out of print. I went right back to the earliest of sources, to Solomon himself. It wasn't easy reading, but it was the next module of my training, and it was transforming how I saw the world. I set about creating spells for healing, and spells to tap into my intuition and spiritual connection on a higher level.

I invested in the craft. I bought trinkets representing the elements. I bought a range of different gemstones, candles, incense, and clothes of natural fibres to wear only when I was working with magic. I started to feel confident in the process and realised the similarities between magic, rituals, and prayer. I also saw it all like cooking; once I decided on the spell, I needed the ingredients to make it come to life, things like the gemstones, plants, candles, incense etc. Then I needed to raise the energy in order for the spell to 'cook', much like turning on the oven. But instead of lighting an oven, I raised the energy of magic with chanting, drumming, or dancing. And finally, there was the casting of the spell itself, which was like the cooking of the dish. Closing the magic circle was the turning off of the oven and the clearing up!

I had immersed myself well and truly into my studies. I was learning the craft of magic, tantric sex and I was still making my way through the Qabalah. The spirit world was pushing me to learn the ancient forgotten ways, and I was learning fast. As this new world continued to open up to me, I so desperately wanted to talk to like-minded people about my experiences. Gabriella was pushing me further away with each new development. When I told her the story about selling extra photographs because of the money spell I cast, she got cross with me and dismissed it as mere coincidence. I was excited by what I was learning, but she just wanted the old version of me back. My vibration was changing more and more, and we were becoming less and less compatible. It came to a head one Sunday afternoon when we chatted over lunch. She was upset with me, because she felt like we could no longer have a 'normal' conversation without spirituality being involved. I disagreed, and said she was exaggerating. I felt hurt and misunderstood. She felt she couldn't relate to what I was experiencing. She started to question my mindset and accused me of living in a fantasy world.

I took time to truly reflect on my experiences. Was she right? Every time I questioned myself, I came back to the same answer: everything I was learning was working. All the advice I'd taken from the spirit world had benefited me and enriched my life. I was recovering and was gaining wisdom that would unlock new opportunities for me. I wasn't hurting anyone, and I was enjoying the learning of each new modality. So, I continued, choosing to stay true to myself. And next I was told to learn about the world of dreams.

Lucid dreaming had fascinated me ever since I first discovered the concept in the early nineties. To lucid dream is to be become aware that you're dreaming when you are inside the dream. For most people it's hard to induce a lucid dream, although a few do find it easy. To stay in a lucid dream whilst remaining aware, is like ice skating for the first time and trying to keep your balance, it's a tricky business. As children we often lucid dream without even realising it, but sadly we lose the ability as we grow. One of my repeating dreams as a child was flying down the stairs. I told my daughter Sara about this reoccurring childhood dream, and she said she had experienced a similar. She described her dreams about stairs and flying, and the similarities were uncanny. It must have been a genetic imprint that had passed between us.

I then read five books on the subject of dreams in quick succession. The world of dreams gives us incredible insight into what is actually possible in our waking state. To study lucid dreams is to study what we are truly capable of, without limiting beliefs and societal conditioning holding us back. Following the guidance of the books, I started recording all of my dreams by keeping a dream diary beside my bed. As soon as I woke up, I would try and remember what I'd been dreaming about. When I first started this practise, I could barely remember the dream I'd literally just woke from. But things began to shift, and I was learning how to work backwards in the dream to gain more insight and information. It was like catching a thread of wisdom that lived in the dream world and pulling it into present moment reality. Within a month I was recording seven dreams a night. As I started to pay attention to the dreams, they became more and more relevant. I found the spirit world would visit me in my dreams and teach me there. I was taught about energy, healing and I was taught magic, lots of magic. I was shown bits of my future life too. I had opened a channel for the universe to teach me without the constraints of the waking world.

I chose an object to stare at before sleep, whilst setting the intention that when I saw the image in my sleeping state I would awaken inside the dream, becoming lucid. I chose a tree of life trinket, that was covered in tiny, chakra coloured gemstones. Before long I saw the trinket in a dream state and took the opportunity to become lucid. In my dream I was in bed with Gabriella, it was dark, and we were in a small unfamiliar bedroom. I got out of bed and walked around the room looking for the light switch, but I couldn't find one. I saw a plant pot in the corner of the room, and inside the pot were five small plants, and they were all moving. They had orange eyes, and sharp threatening teeth; they looked like they were hungry new-borns, and they were vicious. I continued moving around the room and found a large green gemstone. I tried to identify what the gemstone was but I woke up. I'd spent too long looking at it. It was frustrating to awaken back to reality so quickly, but I had succeeded, it was a good start.

My next lucid dream was a month later. I was standing in the street outside my house and realised I wasn't actually standing in the street outside my house, but I was dreaming. I wanted to try some of the cool stuff you can do when you're lucid dreaming, so of course, I took to the air like Superman. I was flying above the houses feeling the wind on my face.

I was so excited, but sadly I woke up soon after.

I discovered that you could speak to the characters in your dream. You can ask them for an explanation about the dream you're in. Why are you there? What is there to learn? You can even speak with the maker of the dream and ask them questions too. You can transform and recreate the scenery in your dream. You can bring anyone into your dream that you want there. It's like working with the law of attraction; without the constraints of the awakened world, and without your limiting beliefs getting in your way. A new miraculous world awaits exploration, you just need the willingness and openness to believe in the possibility of lucid dreaming.

It became obvious to me that human beings were only just touching the surface of what we are truly capable of, the Western world had lost connection to our spiritual ways and followed science as the only path of truth we could rely upon. We were relying on scientists to solve all our problems; we had forgotten how to look within and find the answers there. I was experiencing something so rich: ancient wisdom taken from different cultures all over the world, going back thousands of years, which was stretching my open mind ever further.

Whilst tapping into this rich source of wisdom, through my dreams, I started getting profound and powerful messages. In one such dream, I was in my kitchen standing still as the front door flew open, and into the hallway blew autumn leaves. I was sucked out along the corridor and out to the front of the house. I stood there looking at the building, and then looking down I discovered my old wedding ring to Maria (my ex-wife) which I'd previously lost, and next to it was the ring Gabriella had bought me a few months prior. I was told I was gaining powers and would have to be very careful not to undo the past, it was possible that my actions could change the past, and my time with Maria and Gabriella could be undone.

In another dream I was watching a tidal wave sweep across the land; I couldn't save the people, only observe them being lost to the water. My family were stood beside me, and I felt a deep intense pain for all those people who had perished.

I didn't just visit my spirit guides in the Upper World, I would also visit my spirit animals in the Lower World. And it was during this time when the spirit of the bear began to accompany me on my path. He had first showed himself to me in the shamanic journey, but I soon felt his presence with me in the waking world too. His presence was powerful and reassuring. I decided to honour the spirit of the bear with a necklace; I found one online, it had a leather chord with a wooden disk with a bear paw print on it. Intuitively I bought a second necklace, very similar, only it had a leopard paw print on it. I wore the bear necklace, and put the leopard paw necklace in my bedside draw, not knowing why I had bought it.

Around the same time, I decided to step up my fitness, I 'd become stronger and was now comfortable walking for up to forty-five minutes at a gentle pace. So, I invested in a personal trainer. Her name was Nikki, and she was a tough cookie. Her gym was outside on farmland; there were tractor tyres, ropes, weights, axes, exercise bikes, resistance bands and a whole lot of other interesting devices to build muscles. It felt like bootcamp, and I loved it.

I told Nikki about my journey, and how I'd gradually got myself back to being able to walk, but besides walking I'd done no exercise in quite some time. Over a period of a few months, she pushed me to the edge of my limits. We started with core strength. I'd gained weight through lack of exercise, and my cooking around the world pilgrimage hadn't helped. It was time to get fit. It was during these training sessions that I began to connect with the spirit animals to give me additional strength and stamina. I would pull long heavy ropes with a tractor tyre attached to the ends, through the mud. I'd jump up and down on tyres that would get higher with each new set. It was hardcore.

I learnt to love these work-out sessions; they were the highlight of my week. I did squats and push ups and worked on my tummy. Every time I was spent, I would evoke the strength of the bear or the leopard, whose presence I was beginning to feel and use more and more, to find the strength to finish the circuit. I was able to harness energy that I'd never had before. I would picture the animal beside me and then see it merging within me. It worked every time. I was able to gain as much as 50% more strength. Nikki was fascinated by my process, and it wasn't long before I was teaching her various new spiritual techniques I'd been picking up. I was getting stronger, and at last I knew I would make a full recovery. By working one to one with Nikki, I was learning important techniques I'd be able to take with me on my solo journey ahead.

I continued making the cards and could now boast over two thousand. To my surprise my spirit guides told me to start reading my cards for other people, and to charge for the service. I was to become a shamanic life coach and work with my clients' spirit guides in order to help them as I had helped myself.

I contacted Clara, she was a friend of mine, a Greek lady I knew through my business network. She found it remarkable that I'd contacted her as she'd just been thinking about me earlier that day. I asked her if she would like a free reading to see what we could uncover, and she was delighted to give it a go. She told me she loved anything involving divination. I laid out the cards and asked her to ask her guides to communicate with me through the cards. The reading was insightful and full of wisdom for her; she needed support and guidance to find more balance in her life and help her to move towards her life's purpose. It obviously resonated with her, because after the first session she signed up with me as a paying client. I would work with Clara weekly over the next twelve months and in that time, she completely transformed her life, saved her marriage, and gained the strength to be able to maintain the good habits that had been eluding her up until now.

The next potential client was one of my closest friends, Mark. He was a little older than me and a single guy who was happy to remain that way. He was a successful architect and entrepreneur. He was open to his spiritual side, and he too jumped at the chance of a free reading, and soon followed Clara in becoming my second paying client. By reading for my friends, it gave me a safe space to explore my abilities in tuning in to the teachings of the spirit world. I also discovered that the readings not only had a meaning for the client, but also for myself; there was always something in a reading for me to gain insight too.

In a short period of time, I had picked up almost a dozen clients, and was learning so much from the sessions. The guidance always seemed to follow a similar path; in a nutshell it was about helping people back to wholeness. They were encouraged to let go of what no longer served them, and be guided towards finding more balance, meaning and harmony in their lives. The sessions were about raising their vibration, forgiveness of others and themselves, as well as asking for forgiveness from others. We were moving them towards a purposeful life and helping them to find harmony within their close relationships. They would be guided through the difficult obstacles along their path and made aware of the repeating cycles that no longer served them. We would guide them towards ancient spiritual practices in order to help them gain a better understanding of themselves and the world around them. I was in awe of the guidance and incredible insight that was being revealed.

Every time I would contact someone as a potential new client, they would marvel at the coincidence that they'd been thinking of me at some stage in the previous twenty-four hours. I would pop up in their mind and then soon after, I would message them out of the blue. I considered this to be their spirit guides giving them a positive sign, or perhaps my energy was becoming stronger and when I decided to contact someone, they would pick up on my energy beforehand. Perhaps both were true.

I was gaining confidence in my shamanic abilities, and I allowed myself to consider the possibility I would be okay financially after all. I'd always trusted that the universe would give me all the resources I needed if I worked in service of a higher cause. This belief stemmed from an incredible moment I had experienced earlier in my life; I had been sat in my office working, I opened a drawer to take out my cheque book, which was inside a canvas money bag. I took my cheque book out of the money bag and opened it up to discover a thin long-legged spider squashed on the signature strip. Incredibly it was squashed exactly into the shape of my signature! I know it sounds bizarre, but the dead spider was squashed identically into my signature, and it felt like a miracle. I called my wife at the time, Maria, who came and witnessed it and she was as blown away as me. It was that moment in time when I knew that the spirit world existed, and that they were communicating with me. I understood the message, there was a blank cheque and it had been signed by the spirit world. It meant I would have all I needed, that the spirit world would work with me and I shouldn't be fearful of having a lack of money. Just like the free paper and ink, and the magic knife. And now in the form of my new clients who I could guide and learn from all at once and possibly make a living whilst doing it.

My awareness was on the rise; I was seeing things more clearly and I was seeing signs from the spiritual world all around me. I went for a walk into Witney and followed the setting sun. I didn't know where I was going, just for a walk, as it was such a beautiful day. And as I walked past my old house, I recalled the old car I used to have at the time, and suddenly I got a bizarre new insight from that period in my life. Back then my car had been vandalised whilst I was overseas on holiday with my family. We'd clearly been targeted and I was very concerned. I reported it to the police and suspected it had been the man who'd originally sold me the car. I'd been pressing him to honour the warranty, which he had refused to do, so I left a negative review on his website. But for some reason this version of events didn't match the new insight I was being given as I was standing there at the historical scene of the crime. The truth was being revealed to me as I returned to where it all happened. It was not the man who sold me the car as I suspected, but one of my neighbours who was disgruntled with me. I was speechless. I was receiving information about the past that was completely unknown to me before. I had a vision of my old neighbour walking into my garden in the dead of the night, and saw him scratch the word 'fuck' on the bonnet of my car.

What should I do with this new insight? Initially I was angry. I wanted to go over and knock on his door and confront him with the insight I'd been given. I wanted to see his face when the accusation was delivered and see how he'd deny it. Instead, I reflected on the vision, and realised it had been revealed to me now because I was ready to accept and forgive him. I could choose to release the negative energy that was still tangled up inside me; so, in my mind, I knocked on his door and gave him a piece of my mind. But in reality, I forgave him because I knew he was just playing out his role of the pantomime villain in the story of my life, giving me an opportunity to learn and grow.

The new insights were coming thick and fast, and I was picking up all sorts of information. It was like I was tuning into a new powerful radio frequency, and each new level of awareness was like a turn of the knob. I was transforming rapidly. I felt called to put salt in each of the rooms of the house to absorb negative energy, I even started to feel that there was energy in the words of books and record albums in the house, so I took certain books and records out of the house and stored them in the garage. I changed my diet, cutting out all processed foods, and I started blessing my food before I ate it, in order to change its vibration before it entered my body. I connected to the food and expressed my gratitude to it; my appreciation and love.

I was finding it harder and harder to lead a conventional life. By allowing myself to connect to the spiritual world, I had opened myself to transformation and no longer fitted in with 'normal' conventional society. I was feeling a deeper connection to a much simpler and more natural way of life, I was reconnecting to the roots of why we're actually here. Within the collection of my artwork that I had drawn some ancient cave paintings, and a couple of these were framed and hanging in our bedroom. One night, lit by a handful of candles, a solitary flame danced underneath one of those cave drawings, and as it did, I was transported in my mind back in time, and sat in the cave with a tribe of neolithic humans. A fire lit up the walls to reveal the original cave art. I studied their faces, whilst they also stared in awe at me. In some way I was reconnecting to my ancestors and an ancient part of my soul. A man sitting beside the fire, who I believed to be an ancient shaman, offered me a vessel with liquid in it and as I reached to receive it, I came back to the present moment in my bedroom. I was overwhelmed, it was the stuff of movies. It was an intensely powerful vision, and I felt that these ancestors were now with me on my journey going forward.

There were so many things I was drawn to do, like drawing animals, creating cave painting art and holding on to trinkets for many years without knowing why. Now all those actions were starting to make sense and have meaning. Unbeknown to me, I'd been preparing for this adventure for a lifetime, and now it was all unfolding in the most unexpected ways.

On my next shamanic journey visiting the Lower World, I was met by the spirit of a brown black bear. He led me through a forest to the water's edge, and as we arrived, I saw another six bears seemingly awaiting our arrival. I was told to trust them, that they had something important to do for me. The original bear then suddenly struck me down, and I fell to the ground where I was attacked by the six other bears. Fear rose in me, I wanted to return to reality, but I'd read about such uncomfortable journeys before and chose to trust in the process. I would face my fear head on. I lay there as the bears gnawed their way through my flesh. I felt nothing, no pain. I was simply a spectator, watching the bears clean my bones until they were spotless. The whole ritual took just a few moments. I knew the symbology of what was happening, I was being cleansed, I was being reborn. My journey as a shaman had reached the next level, I was leaving the past behind.

During that time period I was being repeatedly told by the spirit world that I needed to leave Gabriella, and go off into the unknown alone, to continue my training. I needed to trust this guidance; this was about my life purpose. I knew this was why I'd been incarnated into this body, at this time. I had no choice; I could leave willingly or I could be forced. Of course, the idea scared me, I loved Gabriella despite our widening gap. We had a better relationship than most couples we knew; It wasn't perfect, there were areas we needed to work on, but we were doing okay. I was conflicted. I was told I needed to be free to follow my path, but I wasn't sure about walking away from Gabriella. And then the spirit of the horse joined me on my journey, it came to me during a meditation. It was a chestnut-coloured horse, I was standing in a field alone and the horse walked towards me and lowered its head. It then turned away and rode quickly and powerfully into the distance. It was beautiful, and I accepted my fate. I would work towards leaving Gabriella.

A friend got in touch out of the blue, Lucia, she lived in Belgium, and I'd known her ever since she and I were teenage friends. We didn't speak very often, but when we did it was always as if there had been no break in our communication. It felt good speaking to her again after so long, and she told me she was now a keen astrologer and offered to read my birth chart. I accepted gracefully, and in return I offered to do a reading with my cards for her. We arranged a time one evening and set up a video link. I went first, and as I pulled the cards I could see her marriage was in trouble and that her partner had been less than honest about the goings on in his life. He had been with other women, and it was clear that pain and heartache lay ahead for her. She did have a choice: a new start or more of the same. It was time for her to consider ending the relationship. It was hard to reveal such stark news to her, she stared hard into the screen at me and then revealed her husband had indeed had many affairs. She wasn't ready to leave him yet though, she was trying to work through the issues as she was very much still in love and wanted to keep this man in her life. A few months later she would tell me she had left him, and they were getting a divorce.

A week after I read her cards, Lucia did an astrology reading, as promised, for my year ahead. She told me I would go off on a journey on my own, I would leave Gabriella and go on a spiritual quest; the hero's journey of self-discovery. I would get all the support I needed along the way, and it would come from many different avenues. I would meet new people, and plenty of them. It would be a difficult year which would test me and take me to the edge of my comfort zone and well beyond. She said everything would be in the right place at the right time waiting for me, and she told me that within six months all of my strength would return. I asked her when I would leave on this hero's journey, but she couldn't say for sure.

It was a significant moment, my solo journey into the unknown was there in my astrological chart. My guides were right, I had no choice, it was preordained. My head was spinning, what should I do? I had offered myself up to my spiritual path when I lay there on my sick bed all those months before. I was receiving the training, the healing, and now I was being asked to make a huge sacrifice. To give up my woman, my children, my home, my security and go off into the unknown. Gabriella and I were living in rental accommodation, and the lease would be up soon.

But I still wasn't ready to broach the subject with Gabriella, I needed to be further down the path of recovery. As I battled with the Gabriella dilemma, my coaching work continued. I picked up a new client in Mike, he was a psychotherapist I knew, and he jumped at the idea of having conversations with his spirit guides. During one session his guides asked him to read the 'Book of Exodus', which was quite a surprise to me, but it had a significance to Mike. At our next session Mike shared what happened to him when he followed the spirit guides instructions and went to buy the book.

As requested, Mike had gone to a second handbook shop and picked up a copy of the religious book. He opened the book and a piece of paper dropped out, and that piece of paper was a shopping list he himself had written several years beforehand. Someone must have picked up his old shopping list and started using it as a bookmark, in the very book that he had just picked up in the second-hand bookshop. It was an almost impossible coincidence which certainly got his attention. He took the book home, and as he read it, he noticed the word for God was written as Yahwe, the Hebrew meaning for the God of the Israelites. When he retraced the same passage later it then read God, and there was no mention of the word Yahwe. The word had changed its spelling, the letters had incredibly changed to reveal some kind of a message. As he recounted the story, its significance was not lost on me, I'd never heard the word Yahwe before, but I had created a business about spiritual and personal development that I called Mahwe.

I had created Mahwe a couple of years before, I'd come up with the name intuitively; when I was first creating the community, I had sensed the name I was looking for was in a piece of music by the composer Karl Jenkins. I listened to all his lyrics on a particular album, but none of them had any meaning, they were just letters put together because of their harmonious sound. However, there was one word that I kept hearing, which sounded like ma-way, and for some reason I wrote it as Mahwe, and used that as the name for the new spiritual community. Everything, all the information crossing my path, it all seemed to connect to my life somehow.

I was starting to see significance in everything; in things that I would come into contact with, people I would talk to, certain numbers that popped up everywhere, the names of places. The house I was born in was on Divinity Road in Oxford, and then I grew up on Sunderland Avenue. Divinity, Sun... could this be connected to the Egyptian Sun God RA? I discovered that my name, Benjamin, had the Hebrew meaning - The Right Hand of God. Was it possible that all this, all of my life, was leading me here to this hero's journey? It seemed to all be pointing the way to my being a servant of God; a messenger of sorts. It felt like a role I had committed to before I was born. What exactly I was supposed to do was still unknown to me, but I was okay with that, I trusted all the guidance I needed was coming in divine timing. When travelling on a spiritual path you have to surrender and watch and marvel as everything unfolds before your eyes.

I continued picking up more clients, most notably my latest clients were coaches who had once coached me. I was in awe of the role reversal, I found it fascinating to be on the other side of the table. I so enjoyed working with people who had spent time and effort working on themselves; their minds and hearts were open, they were hungry to learn, to grow and continue their journey of self-discovery.

During a reading with one of my clients, Ness, her guides asked her to consider having a soul retrieval. A soul retrieval is a shamanic term for when the healer helps a person to reintegrate lost parts of themselves in order to heal. The guides revealed to her, through me, that a piece of her soul had been cast away as unacceptable in one of her past lives, thousands of years ago, and if she wanted to experience wholeness, then she would have to reintegrate the piece of her soul that was missing. I would have to travel back through time and space, find this missing piece lost in a past life, and ask it to return to join with the rest of her soul in the here and now. It was a challenging assignment that I'd never done before. I had read about in shamanic books but had no experience in it whatsoever. So I consulted with my guides who said they would help me, that I just had to allow the process to unfold in a shamanic journey.

Ness insisted that we needed to proceed with the soul retrieval, she was excited because she had always felt there was something missing within her. We lay side by side on the floor, under blankets, whilst drumming music played in the background. I relaxed myself through deep breathing and travelled to my sacred garden within my mind. Once I was there, I met with my usual spirit animals and a black wolf that was there on behalf of Ness. I was then pulled back through time, and as I travelled through what seemed to be a black hole, my breathing changed and became stronger, faster, and more powerful. It felt like the spirit world had taken over my breathing. I arrived at a beach with a leopard, a bear, an owl, and Ness' same black wolf. The leopard was there for me, it told me it had come to be one of my spirit guides. I thanked the leopard and welcomed him; it was a special moment; I could immediately sense the powerful bond between me and my new guardian animal.

I looked out from the beach at the vast expanse of the sea, with the spirit animals standing by me. I cast out a huge fishing net, as far as I could throw, and after a short while we heaved the net back into to the land. There were two women caught inside the net. I immediately released them and they stood before me; one was a maiden and another a high priestess. I approached the maiden, a young woman in her early teens, and told her that I was a shaman and I'd come to reunite her with the rest of her soul. I told her that she was needed, missed and she would be welcomed back by a beautiful open heart. I also told her that her soul was sorry that she had be cast out. She looked so young, so anxious and so innocent. She agreed to join me on the journey back. The wolf approached her, smelt her and looked directly into my eyes and nodded his approval. This was a piece of Ness that I had to bring back to her.

I then approached the high priestess. She seemed to know why I was there but wasn't trusting of me. I explained who I was and my intention for being there, but she needed some convincing. She was protective of the maiden and didn't want to let her go. I gave her space to share her fear, and eventually she gave me permission. She was hurt and angry and I sensed her immense power. The wolf went over and sniffed her too, this time more suspiciously, but he eventually nodded his acceptance. I returned to the sacred garden and then I slowly came back to the present moment, laying there next to Ness. When I opened my eyes, I was freezing cold and trembling with exhaustion. However, I instinctively sat up, placed my hand on Ness' heart space and blew into my hands, and returned to her the part of her soul that had been missing.

It took me a few hours to recover, and regain my energy, but afterwards I spoke with Ness, and she told me she had felt the two women's newfound presence within her. Over our next few sessions, she revealed how integrating these two lost parts of herself had changed her dramatically, she was feeling a wholeness that she had never experienced before. She had learnt and grown so much from the experience, and I had too. It opened my eyes to the importance of accepting and integrating all parts of ourselves, even the shadow side. People shut parts of themselves away that aren't deemed acceptable by society, culture, religion, family etc, whether we do it in this life or did it in a previous incarnation.

From there I was guided to learn about the ancient historical King Solomon. I had known the name but nothing else. But after starting to read about him, I wondered if Solomon had been a shaman too? He had been visited by an angel who gave him great wisdom, and he had also been taught magic. I couldn't help but think it sounded familiar to what I was going through. Maybe it was a common experience throughout history, but hard to explain and make sense of, so maybe these 'shamans' or spiritual people throughout history, were simply explained and rationalised in different ways depending on the lens and time it was looked through. Some might see it as a spiritual awakening; being touched and guided by the divine. Whilst in our modern-day Western society, the general consensus perhaps, would be that such a person was experiencing a mental illness that should be treated accordingly.

Christmas 2020 came and went. Gabriella and I had a quiet Christmas without my children. We were both exhausted after such a challenging year, we simply rested and as we did, I wrestled with the continuous nagging feeling that the spirit world wanted me to leave Gabriella and embrace my freedom. I decided to be brave and broach the subject. I told her I had something difficult to share with her. I told her that the spirit world had told me that I must undertake a spiritual journey that required my freedom. It was an extremely uncomfortable and difficult thing to tell her, even though I wasn't telling her I was leaving, just that I had being advised to go; that every message and sign I received from the universe pointed me along this path.

She looked at me long and hard with a stern face.

'You are insane, you have really gone and lost the plot this time.' She shouted and stormed out of the room, slamming the door behind her which made our dog Nester yelp nervously.

I felt guilty. Perhaps I had lost the plot? But I knew deep down in the core of my being that things were no longer right between us, and that perhaps a fresh start was better for the both of us. We just didn't fit anymore, I could see that she missed Italy, and that I was the only reason she was here. I couldn't see her business ever getting off the ground the way things were, she was out of her depth, and she knew it.

My friend Jay invited me to spend the day with him and our mutual pal Quinn in the countryside. They were both interesting characters who thought outside the box and lived unconventional lives. I enjoyed spending time with such characters, and I had a feeling this excursion would be powerful and significant in some way. All I knew was that we were going on a walk in the countryside, they hadn't told me anything more than that except that I needed to bring some lunch, a flask and be at Quinn's house in South Oxfordshire for 10 am. I arrived on time, with the addition of my homemade divination cards. As we huddled together in the utility room putting on our walking boots, I asked,

'Would you like me to do a reading for you Quinn, before we go?'

He immediately stopped putting on his boots and agreed and went to make the three of us a cup of tea.

The cards that I drew for him were: water, radical change, and ancient civilisation. I wasn't sure of the meaning, but Quinn knew exactly what they meant for him. We then took a long drive to the base of the White

Horse Hill in Uffingdon, Wiltshire. It was in the heart of the countryside, with steep green rolling hills dotted with picturesque grazing sheep. We parked and started walking until we reached a stream with a natural spring running into it, and Jay filled a tin cup with the fresh cold spring water, drinking it with clear appreciation and gratitude. He then asked me to take my shoes off, roll up my jeans and walk into the centre of the stream. He joined me in the water and handed me the now empty tin cup and asked me to drink from the stream. I did as he said, it tasted pure, fresh and cold. He then poured some of the stream water over my head and did a cleansing ritual. I had no idea he was going to do it, but I enjoyed the ceremony. Afterwards, as I dried myself with the towel he gave me, Quinn became the modern-day bard and retold the story of two ancient Britons, who were brothers and kings. One had become a king of France, and the story brought the brothers to the brink of war with each other, only for them to discover that they'd been tricked. Quinn, a tall gangly guy with a long face, spoke in a dramatic voice, booming loudly above the running water of the babbling stream. I was enjoying myself; it was definitely a day out of the ordinary.

We continued on our adventure, walking across fields chatting merrily, until we found ourselves standing on Dragon Hill, an ancient site with powerful spiritual significance. I climbed to the top as Jay instructed, whilst they both walked the circumference in a clockwise direction three times, representing the past, the present and the future. Whilst they did so, I meditated on the top of the hill about those three aspects of time. Jay and Quinn joined me at the summit. Jay had a long wooden staff and he stood beside me, whilst Quinn perched on a rock with his hands in his large sheep skin coat's pockets keeping warm. Jay banged the hand carved staff hard into the centre of a barely visible pentagon that he'd traced into the earth with the stick. He summoned the energy from the earth, calling upon the ancient druids and ancestors of times gone by to share their power and wisdom with us. I sat in the centre of the invisible pentagon as he instructed, and he told me to imagine myself inside the hill, being one with the earth. He then told me to imagine I was flying and to connect to the spirit of the air.

Afterwards we continued walking on to the top of White Horse Hill. I was tiring and needed a break, all of the walking and spiritual work was taking its toll on me and I was still sensitive to the possibility of triggering another health relapse; although excited by the day I was still acutely aware of my limitations.

Quinn continued his story about the brother kings, how they had poisoned their enemy and slayed the giant who'd been stealing their food. We walked up the Dragon's tail to the eye which is known as the White Horse; It was a neolithic chalk drawing, a historical site of great significance. It was a steep climb, and I was soon out of breath. We were sat on a major ley-line and Jay said we should all make a wish, I asked that I could deliver on my life's purpose, whatever that may be.

We continued our walk to the centre of the hilltop fort, where we stood between the feminine and masculine energy lines that ran through the hill. Quinn took time to explain about the ley-lines and how they mapped their way across the country. We ate our lunch, we laughed and spoke of politics and history, we shared our food with each other and the moment was sacred. Finally, we took the long walk along the Ridgeway to the Wayland Smithy, an ancient neolithic burial tomb. Once there, Jay told me to walk in a clockwise direction around the tomb three times, again representing the past, present, and future. He then performed a ritual at the front of the tomb and told me to enter the darkness of the burial chamber and wait inside there for five minutes. I was surprisingly accepting of all that was unfolding and thought 'Here goes,' as I headed inside. It was pitch black, cold and damp inside, I had to squat down on the earth to fit in the little space. I didn't question Jay, or myself for allowing these strange events to unfold, or ask my guides why I was there, I just knew this day was significant on my hero's journey, that it was all part of the story unfolding. I made an offering to the tomb; a beautiful feather I found on our walk and I sat in the dark and silence. I imagined the people who'd built the tomb and the spirits that watched over it. I pictured the people over the years who had an experience similar to the one I was having sitting there in the darkness. I wasn't afraid, just accepting.

After the five minutes was up I stepped back out into the light of the day, I had to squint at the brightness. I was glad to be out of there. Jay came to my side and poured more of the spring water over my head and to my complete surprise, he baptised me as a druid. He recounted a poem he had written, or perhaps he had found somewhere in a book, and then he told me to choose a new name, my druidic name. And the name came to me straight away, it was Bear, after my spirit animal and the name I had chosen for myself when my daughter Beatrice had once asked me to give her another name she could call me by.

Away from the tomb and back on the path, Quinn finished with his third story of the day, as we slowly made the long walk back to the car. It had been one of the most bizarre and unforgettable days of my life and it had been fun. On the drive home a large white owl flew beside the car for some time and I remembered what I had been told in the stars, that everything I needed would be provided for me at the right time and the right place. I hadn't even thought about whether I wanted to be baptised as a druid or not, the thought had never entered my mind. I'd always seen a druid as an ancient shaman, the British shaman, so for me this was a ritual about the acceptance of my path; the path of the shaman.

As my journey of self-discovery progressed, I continued my daily spiritual practice of walking through the ancient wood near my home. I was encouraged by my guides to touch the trees and connect to them, to offer them a gift and ask for an energy exchange of sorts. So, I'd sit at the base of a tree, put my hands against its trunk and connect with the flow of energy going through it. It was transformative, it was healing, and it was invigorating. It was like recharging the battery of my soul, I would become almost light-headed and giddy after the connection.

I was learning to love the forest, to feel deeply for it. I would take a carrier bag with me each day and pick up any litter I found on my walks; I wanted to play my role in protecting the planet and keeping it sacred. When the wild garlic came up, I picked it and ate it. It was delicious; I was taking a part of the forest into my body as nourishment. It felt important to consume a part of the forest, so the forest could in some way become part of me.

I was getting stronger and continued with my personal trainer, she pushed me harder with each session and we were getting to know each other well. In the spring we even began running together, I couldn't remember the last time I'd been able to run and I loved it, although I found it hard.

When I returned from that challenging first run, I discovered Gabriella cooking us a special meal. Despite her Italian roots, her favourite cuisine was Thai, and she was preparing a beautiful dish with sweet potatoes, prawns, and a sweet chilli sauce.

'I'm ready to talk about us.' She told me, as I sat down at the table after my shower.

I could already see the sadness in her heart.

'I've given our relationship a great deal of thought.' She continued, as I tucked into her tasty food.

'This journey you're on is obviously important to you, and I can see that it's actually more important to you than I am.'

I tried to interject, but she stopped me.

'Please, let me finish.' She took a sip of her wine.

'I'm ready to let you go Ben, because I feel like you're holding me back too. We're both stopping each other from making a success of our lives somehow. Don't ask me to explain more than that, it's too hard and painful. I'm giving you what you want, a way out without it playing on your conscious. I'll be fine, I'll be better off back in Italy. To be honest, since Brexit, I've been liking this country less and less. I know you hated the idea of Brexit too, so I don't blame you. I don't blame you for all this weird stuff you've been learning and going through either. I might not understand it, but I can see that it's not all a figment of your imagination.' She made a small smile, relieved of speaking her truth and rested her hand on mine.

'I love you. I always will,' she finished.

Gabriella closed down her business, and organised to stay with her parents in Milan for a while; to think about what her next step would be. We hugged, we were both sad and we both cried. There was no more talk from either of us about trying to fix things or work through any part of our relationship. We had been happy for a while, but we both knew it was time to explore the next chapter of our lives. When our rental contract was up on the house, we would both go our separate ways. Until then, I was on the sofa, as the intimate part of our relationship was now over, she no longer needed to pretend that she was interested in me in that way anymore.

I received a message from my guides through the dictionary, about birds singing and calling to me. I couldn't understand what the message meant but considered that maybe I was being told to go for a walk to find inspiration. It sounded like a good idea. I needed a break from all the biodiversity research I was doing for the blog on my website. I found writing blogs challenging and needed frequent breaks in order to get the best content out of me.

As I walked out my house, a tune popped into my head, it was familiar, an old song from the eighties. I couldn't remember the name of the song, but I knew it was important. I left the estate where I lived and reached the main road as a white van screeched up onto the curb, and stopped at an angle on the grass verge with a sudden thud. The van, and its exact position, were identical to a photo I had just sold on the picture library that morning. I knew the moment was significant, but what did it mean? I had to solve the mystery. Behind the van was a muddy path onto private land, so I crossed the road and followed it for a short distance until it led me to a magnificent large oak tree. I was being drawn to the tree. I walked up to it and put my hand upon its bark and connected to its energy. This tree reminded me of the oak tree in my mind's eye that I used to travel to the Lower and Upper Worlds, and I immediately felt called to do a shamanic journey and see if anything interesting would be revealed. I sat on the earth, leaning against the beautiful large oak tree, and closed my eyes, focusing on my breathing. In my mind I walked around the tree three times, representing the past, present and the future. I entered through the ground at the base of the tree where a hole had appeared and as I did, I immediately remerged in the exact same spot, but my picture of the world had changed slightly. Everything felt different, yet still the same. I spoke with the tree and offered it a blessing. I was unsure what to do next, so I brought myself back to the present moment mystified as to what it all meant. Had I missed something important? I was confused. There were too many strange things happening that I couldn't piece together.

The next day I spent more time trying to remember what the eighties song was that had popped into my head during my walk. I sang the tune over and over until I finally remembered; it was a Nick Kershaw song called 'The Riddle'. I immediately googled the lyrics and it certainly was a riddle, and I was trying desperately to connect all the pieces together. The words to the song were more significant to me than I could have imagined; they matched my vision; they matched the shaman's journey to the Lower World. Nick Kershaw sang about a tree, and about a wise man going around the tree and even mentioned the hole in the ground that I would enter into. He sang that the wise man was a beacon in the veil of the night. What did that mean? As I continued to read the lyrics, I got goose bumps from head to toe. Was I the wise man going around and around? Had I passed through the veil in the night? Without fully understanding it, so much more had just happened. I had just officially started on the journey of a lifetime, the hero's journey. The guidance was coming true.

It would be months before the full significance of this moment was revealed to me. I had just undertaken the exact same journey through time as the protagonists in the novel I had written, twelve years prior. I was living in a reality what I'd written in fantasy many years before. The book was called 'Arthur Archer and the Time Traveller's Chronicles', and in the book the characters had been led to a time portal in a tree by birds calling to them. The characters in my novel had been led to the tree of time, whilst trying to solve a riddle of two missing people. And here I had received the same message through the dictionary, that birds were calling to me and a song called, 'The Riddle,' had magically appeared in my head. The synchronicities were uncanny.

I couldn't get my head around it all. How could my mind conjure up a song that I hadn't heard for decades and that I didn't know the words to, but that lyrically matched the moment I was now experiencing? I was in awe, like I'd been when I found the dead spider signature in my cheque book all those years before. The universe is capable of delivering the most remarkable divine guidance, if we are open enough to follow its signs, believe in the possibilities, and take the time to try and understand the meanings.

The following day, during a simple mediation, a strong vision took over my mind. I saw a wolf walking alone across a desert-like barren landscape. It was so clear and detailed, like I was watching a movie on a high-definition television. It was the clearest vision I'd ever had in my life, and it had appeared during a light meditation. I searched for its meaning on the internet, and I discovered it was a sign for me to leave 'the pack'; to go off on my own without knowing exactly where I was going. The time had come, I was being pushed out of the nest.

My life purpose was calling me, and I could no longer ignore it. I told Gabriella of my vision, and she suggested I take a break from my spiritual side, from connecting to the guides and channelling. She suggested that maybe I needed a new perspective. She made sense, but I ignored her advice. I knew I had no choice; I was too deeply in this now, there was no turning back. I had prayed to be saved all that time ago lying in my sick bed; I had asked for adventure and had offered myself up to do the work of God. It was time to go forth and live the life I'd prayed for, the life I had always been destined to live.

But before my journey could properly begin there was still something I intuitively felt that I needed to do; I needed to ask for forgiveness from those I had wronged, to clear all blocks in my energy field. First my guides suggested I complete a ritual where I asked God for forgiveness. I prepared as if I was performing a spell, and I apologised for anything I had done in my life that needed to be forgiven. It was a powerful experience and I felt an almost immediate healing.

I was then told to reach out to my first girlfriend, and my brother. There were unresolved issues with both from my teenage years, that I needed to ask for forgiveness for. I did as was asked and had a couple of unusual, but real and honest, conversations. It felt good to let go of these past stories and move forward, lighter than I was before.

The final person I was asked to clear the karma with was Gabriella. We got a bottle of red wine and some nibbles and chatted long into the night. We both agreed to lay to rest anything between us that was unresolved. Like a writer finishing a novel by tidying up all the loose ends, we spoke about how we felt, what had been good and what we hadn't worked through. It was refreshing and liberating and brought up tears. We both forgave each other and freed each other from the binds of our relationship. The path ahead was now clear.

I travelled down to my Mum's to break the news in person. She had made an impressive recovery since I'd seen her last. We both had a mug of tea in hand as I began.

'I've got something to share with you Mum. I've left Gabriella!'

Her jaw dropped; she hadn't seen it coming. I decided it was better not to share the spiritual reasons for my decision. I told her that we were growing apart, that we both wanted different things and that our relationship had lost its connection. I told her I needed to leave and find my purpose in order to be happy and as always, she was wonderful, understanding, and supportive.

When the kids broke up for the school holidays it was time for me to leave, we had just a couple of weeks left on our rental property and I had taken most of my stuff already to my mother and stepfather's house in Dorset. Gabriella and Nester saw me off, we hugged one last time and I thanked her for our journey together. I told her that I still loved her and would always think fondly of her. She wiped the tears from her eyes and stood and watched as I drove off. My heart sank, It was so sad and heart wrenching. I was in pain, but I was creating space in my life for something new. I drove the short distance across town and picked up the kids, we filled up the rest of the car with their things and they hugged their mother goodbye. She waved us off and we put 'our' cd into the car stereo, as we always did at the beginning of a road trip. Queen's greatest hits, it had to be done, it was our driving soundtrack.

It took a couple of days before I told them that I'd left Gabriella, and it hit them hard. They wanted to know what I was going to do, so I told them I was going to become a nomad and travel for a little while until I'd decided what I wanted to do next. The truth is, I didn't know what to tell them, because I didn't know what I was going to do next. I had taken a leap of faith into the unknown and was trusting the universe, my spirit guides, my intuition, and my life path. I was trusting the fact that I had something important to do, and I would somehow find it on the path ahead. I'd seen too many signs, visions, and messages to ignore the guidance.

I was able to take my children out for day trips, unlike the previous summer. We went to the beach, we went on country walks and we explored local towns. We often purchased our clothes second hand from charity shops as a way of treading lightly on the earth. In one such shop, Leo found a book about politics and told me the book was meant for me. He had been guided to the book and it would later fill in the blanks I needed for my writing. My children were very intuitive, and often pointed out signs for me to see and learn from, and I always trusted and listened to what they had to say.

I had been invited to stay in Oxford at the end of the summer to look after my friend Tony's house whilst he went on holiday to France, where he had a summer house. He needed someone to look after his cat, Cindy. I could have the run of the place and my kids would be welcome to come and stay. It was a lovely house and not far from where my children lived. The universe had supplied the first place I would stay on my nomadic journey. But I had no clue where else I would be going. I was waiting for a sign; I was waiting for direction and then it came.

I got a call out of the blue from someone who used to attend my business network. He was a website designer named David. He'd never called me before and I hadn't spoken with him for five years or so. He had randomly called me to see how I was, which was strange as he'd never done so before. I knew there must be a reason for the call beyond him checking in on me. I explained that I had broken up with Gabriella and I was drawn to becoming a nomad, that I was going to look after Tony's house and after that I didn't know what followed. And he had an answer for me. He told me his wife Rebecca looked after people's pets at their homes through an official website. The website worked on trust, once you had joined and paid your yearly fee you could apply to pet sit for people, and they could choose from the applicants available. You got a review after each pet sit and once you built up a few reviews it would become easier to find more other house sits. It was the answer I'd been looking for and it had found me through a completely unexpected source. I was to become a pet sitter and travel Britain, allowing the universe to take me wherever it wanted to take me. I would go with the flow; I would put my trust in the hands of the universe.

I joined the website, and straight away applied for house sits from September through to December. I trusted that the universe had a plan, and I would only be accepted to the houses which I was meant to go to. I would only sit for cats at first because I wanted to focus on my work, and felt I would have longer to do that without the need to walk dogs a couple of times a day.

Before long I received my first response, it was for a young couple who had a modern comfortable house in Nottingham. They had two kittens and were going away for two weeks. I had a video interview with them, and they hired me. It was their first time using the company, and they were happy that I didn't have any experience with the website either. We were all new to this and that worked in my favour. I would finish up the summer with my children and work my way up to Nottingham. However, there was still a few days to fill between then, so I decided I would check in with my good friend, Maggie in Bath. She said she'd be delighted to have me for a few days, so it was agreed.

I could no longer see my personal trainer Nikki, now that I was constantly moving around, so I started running and doing home workouts using what I'd learnt from her. I was disciplined and kept it up. The previous summer I'd been able to walk for ten minutes and now I was running for twenty, I still had a way to go, but it was a huge improvement and I was pleased with my effort and determination. Both Beatrice and Leo came out running with me, and Sara would come on longs walks. I was filling myself up with quality time with my children before leaving them for a while. I was going to miss them all very much whilst I was away.

I delivered my children safely back to their mother, and the following day went and said goodbye to my mum, before setting off to live the nomad's life.

Chapter 4

In the Flow

When I was twenty-four, I travelled to the south of Australia with my then girlfriend Rihanna. We stayed with friends, and at distant relatives' homes and I'd had the time of my life. Now at forty-eight, at exactly twice the age I was then, I found myself repeating that cycle of adventure. My car was packed up, I said goodbye to my mother and headed north from Dorset, with my first stop Glastonbury. I intended to spend the day in Glastonbury soaking up the atmosphere, seeing the sights, whilst photographing the small quaint spiritual town, before heading on to Bath to see Maggie and stay with her for three nights.

The drive was smooth, and as I parked my car, I immediately noticed a tall ancient tower at the top of a big hill. It was standing like a spiritual lighthouse on holy ground. I took out my camera and ventured into the pretty town. I photographed the colourful buildings, the people, and the church. I listened to a busker singing about the Queen of Sheba, and after a little while I stopped for a coffee in a little café and checked my messages. My eldest daughter was checking in to see how I was, it lifted me, I felt her love. I tried hard to resist the delicious cakes and succeeded, but only just.

Once I was satisfied that I'd taken enough photographs, I wandered into some of the little independent spiritual shops. I was drawn to one in particular, it was full of wooden sculptures of animals imported from Africa and Asia and two sculptures in particular caught my attention, a large wooden eagle and two leopards on a tree. I couldn't take my eyes off those leopards. I'd felt the leopard's presence and now I was embarking on a nomadic experience looking after people's cats, it felt like it was relevant.

But I wondered why I was drawn to the sculpture of two leopards, and not just one. I had also recently felt the presence of a spiritual eagle, and Maggie would later confirm she could see an eagle sat on my right shoulder. I couldn't justify buying either, but in the end, I bought the eagle and headed back to my car. I was tired and ready to head on to Bath when a text message came through, it was Maggie, she was going to be home late. There was stocktaking needing to be done at work, and she couldn't avoid it. She asked if I could I arrive after 10 pm instead. I now had plenty of time to kill and the spiritual lighthouse, Glastonbury Tor seemed to be flashing its imaginary bright light towards me saying, 'Come and say hello!'.

But I felt tired and lazy and wanted to rest, so I picked up the dictionary to communicate with my guides. I preferred this way as it often showed me things I'd never thought of before, and I felt it removed my own inner filter from the message.

I said, 'I'm getting a strong pull up to go to the Tor at the top of the hill. Am I supposed to go?'

I closed my eyes, opened the book with my eyes closed and put my finger onto a sentence contained within. The words my finger touched were: 'Follow the path ahead.' I tried again and this time my finger took me to 'A girl guide.' I was intrigued, so I put aside my tiredness, paid for some extra parking, packed away my new wooden eagle sculpture and slowly made the walk to the top of the Tor with my camera. The views were lovely, it was a warm late summer evening and I was feeling excited about the journey that lay ahead of me over the coming weeks.

As I made my way up the Tor, I passed by plenty of others on their way, either in small groups or alone with their dogs. There were a few teenage girls lying on the grass, enjoying each other's company and listening to music. It was a pleasant walk. At the top someone was playing a guitar inside the tower, he was dressed in colourful clothing and wearing a flamboyant hat and his little dog sat next to him with a bandana around its neck. I walked through the tower looking up at the ancient brick work and noticed the pigeons sitting on the ledges high up. I tried to imagine the building in its former glory, and the people who used it back then. It felt strange to be here on my own, I wanted to share the experience with somebody. I saw a dozen or so people meditating around the edge of the hill, looking out towards the green fields of the Somerset countryside. Some people had their dogs seemingly meditating by their sides too. I was warm, tired, and hungry and found a place to sit at the edge of the scene. I stared off into the distance, it was all quite beautiful, it felt as if I was being shown what to do by the people who were already there.

I closed my eyes and took a deep breath in, holding it for four seconds and then slowly breathing out. I imagined a divine light above my head and brought the light in through my crown chakra, and then down through my spine. I connected that light down, through me, into Mother Earth and allowed the powerful energy of the Tor to enter me through my root chakra and complete the circuit to the divine. I sat there for some time, clearing my mind of thoughts as new life filled my soul.

After I'd finished meditating, I stood up, feeling a deep profound calmness within and decided to head back to my car. It was then that I heard my name being called out.

'Ben, is that you?''

I snapped out of my solitary moment and turned around to see a woman with blonde hair and a familiar face smiling at me.

'Hello,'' I said.

I raced through my mind trying to remember who she was.

'Ella?' I guessed, feeling that wasn't quite right.

'Eleanor.'' She corrected me in a friendly manner, not being offended that I'd got her name wrong, just pleased I'd remembered her.

Immediately I knew why I was there at that particular moment, and I marvelled at the universe and its synchronicities. I was a long way from anywhere I called home, so it was a strange moment to bump into a former member of my business community. Eleanor had once attended my network in Oxfordshire, I remembered that day, I remembered at the end of the meeting, Eleanor sat me down and told me she could feel the energy work I was doing within the community. She'd told me I was a light worker, and she'd said this without me talking to her about anything remotely spiritual.

'What are you doing up on the Tor?' She asked.

'I'm not sure to be honest, I just felt drawn to walk up here. But now I expect I'm here to speak to you.' I replied, 'Why don't you come and sit with me, and let's see if we can figure out why we're supposed to meet today,' I said.

'Okay' she replied, sitting on the exact spot I had beckoned her to.

She stared at me, as if she was feeling into my energy again, all these years later. It felt like her eyes were reading an obscure language hidden inside of my aura, that only a handful of people could decipher.

'I see you travelling Britain, far and wide. I see you meeting the people you need to meet. I see energy lines in the earth. You are connecting to people and connecting to the land. You are expanding your territory, like a male lion roaming new lands. You are on a solitary journey of discovery. You are in the flow of the universe. You are building a web of energy,' she said.

Swap the lion for a leopard I thought, and she'd hit the nail on the head. Somehow, I wasn't surprised by how much she knew about me, I trusted her words, and her skills of insight and vision.

She continued, 'I see you opening your mind and letting the wonders of the universe in Ben. You're truly in the flow right now. Let go of your fears, and fully embrace the adventure ahead.'

I thanked her for her insight, and told her about my journey, and what had led me to meet her on the Tor. She then introduced me to her friends that were gathered nearby and offered to show me a few things in the area that she felt I should experience. I agreed, the time delay for Maggie's stocktaking had been created exactly for this. Eleanor said goodbye to her friends, and we headed down the hill a different way from the direction I'd come. On the way down she told me she was a guardian of the Tor and that I had in fact been led to what is known in the spiritual realm, as the heart chakra of the world. Those words carried a deep significance for me, my very first spiritual experience was some 12 years before when I'd also gone to visit Maggie, when she opened my heart chakra through my first ever reiki session with her. And now I was heading back to Maggie again, and on route connecting to the energy of the heart chakra of the world. There were so many repeating cycles to find meanings in.

As I walked down Chalice Hill with Eleanor, we chatted more about her life in Glastonbury. It was an idyllic evening, and it an interesting conversation that covered Avalon and the legend of King Arthur and Guinevere. I was happy, and as she had pointed out, in the flow. I enjoyed her retelling of stories that had endured for centuries.

As we reached the bottom of Chalice Hill, she took me to the two sacred natural springs, the White Spring, and the Red Spring. Their location was hidden from the majority of tourists that travelled through Glastonbury each year. Eleanor shared the story of the springs, and later I would research even more about them; drinking from the springs was a sacred act, an opportunity to receive blessings and healing. I drank from both the springs, poured the water over my crown, and thanked the sacred waters for their gift. It was reminiscent of the moment when Jay and Quinn had taken me to the springs of the White Horse Hill and connected me to the energy of the land and the ancestors a few months before.

I thanked Eleanor for our brief but powerful time together, and we vowed to stay in touch. And as the darkness of night came, I headed off to Bath to meet up with Maggie. I arrived five minutes after her, to a very warm welcome and a fridge full of delicious food, and I was very glad because at that point I was starving. We ate well, drank wine, and chatted long into the night. I shared my story about Eleanor and the Tor, and what had happened with Quinn and Jay at White Horse Hill. And Maggie reminded me of a similar experience I'd had a few years before, when another member of my community had taken me to Avebury in Wiltshire, which was another neolithic site. He'd performed a ritual with me by the huge sacred stones, whilst connecting me to the energy of the land, the ley-lines. He'd also taken me inside a burial tomb and left me inside to connect with the ancestors of the land. Interestingly enough I hadn't connected these two experiences up until that moment and was grateful that Maggie had tied the two very similar experiences together. Sometimes we just need another person's perspective to help us connect the dots.

Maggie had taken a few days off from work to spend some quality time with me. She loved day trips and visiting different cultural heritage sites, so the day after I arrived, after a delicious breakfast, we headed to Wells in Somerset and wandered around the small cathedral city taking in all the beautiful historical sites. I took off my shoes and socks as we sat on the lawn of the cathedral grounds and connected to the energy of the earth. I realised that people were continually taking me to spiritual sites and energy ley-lines, I was continuously connecting to this energy, and it was transforming me, healing me. It felt like I was receiving a powerful spiritual kick-back from timeless prayers and worship over so many years, that remained within those buildings and was now helping me to raise my vibration.

Inside the cathedral stood a huge clock. I was mesmerised by it. It was an astronomical clock dating back to the fourteenth century. My intuition was telling me it was important, and that I somehow had to listen to the message the clock was giving me. The clock was connected to the stars and the planets, and I felt the message was about time, time for me to live out the reason why I was here on this planet at this moment. It was time to be bold, courageous, and let go, it was time to grow, time to act on all I knew, and it was time to embrace my spiritual path. I knew that this was a moment of major significance, and if I didn't follow my path to the letter, I would miss out on my reason for existing at this time. All I had to do was follow my intuition and allow the universe to guide me, although at times that was easier said than done.

After leaving the clock and the cathedral, we strolled around the beautiful ancient city, and I photographed it for my collection. We enjoyed a tasty and rather unhealthy lunch of fish and chips, wrapped in vinegar-stained paper, and headed on to our next destination. We drove through Cheddar Gorge on the way back, another ancient historical site where early humans had lived in beautiful caves. Sadly, it was closed due to the pandemic restrictions, so instead we walked around the area nearby and climbed the side of the Gorge. We meditated together a little way up, and as we did, I noticed two mountain goats perched high up on the rock face. The spiritual significance wasn't lost on either of us, the goats represented spiritual ascension; to have faith in the path ahead. It was the first time I had seen mountain goats in the wild in the U.K and their timing was impeccable.

The day was running away from us, so we headed back to Bath, raided the lovely food in the fridge and took to our beds. That night I was visited by a spiritual creature, I slept restlessly and felt it working on my energy field as I slept. I had the vision of a little creature eating its way through me, but unlike the shamanic journey when the bears had eaten me to bare bones and I hadn't felt a thing, this time I felt its tiny teeth eating through me like maggots placed in an infectious wound in an attempt to clean it out. This little creature wasn't there to do me harm, it was eating through the things that no longer served me. I remained in a light restless sleep throughout, it's the only time I can remember the feeling of pain in a dream state. I woke in the morning feeling quite overwhelmed by the experience, but I let it go, I trusted my guides to keep me safe. It was a rough night, and I didn't feel rested at all.

The following day Maggie did a reiki healing session on me, as she passed the healing energy of the universe through her and into me, I fell into a much needed, deep, and relaxing sleep. My mind went blank, and it was a rare moment of peace in a usually turbulent mind. Maggie on the other hand was receiving plenty of insight through messages from the spirit world and her guides. Over coffee afterwards she shared that a huge eagle was with me, sitting perched on my shoulder. She saw a leopard to the left of me, and a bear to my right, both protecting me and she saw a white owl above me.

The following day Maggie and I said goodbye, I thanked her enormously for her hospitality and I hit the road for Nottingham. I had a night to kill before my first pet sit, so I would stop at a bed and breakfast in the city centre. During the drive I started to reflect on the past year or two, and saw a pattern I hadn't noticed before; my life was starting to resemble the life of the two main characters in the book I'd written twelve years before. When Maggie had first read my book, she'd told me that I was both the main characters, Emily, and Arthur. It had made me laugh at the time, but her observation had never left me. Emily and Arthur had travelled through a time portal inside a tree and gone off on an epic journey through time. Inside the tree they had looked at the pages of a book, and the images inside had come to life and they'd found themselves thrown back in time.

The first book was set during the English Civil War, and it followed a specific year, 1643. I noticed that I'd been following the same route as my characters in the book, with my camera, ever since recovering from covid; I'd been to Oxford, Witney, Burford, and Gloucester - all places that had played a significant role within the book. Emily had got the plague during the story, and I too had suffered at the hands of a virus that had taken the lives of millions across the world. My novel was set against the backdrop of a pandemic just like the one the world was currently enduring. Could I be reading too much into this? I considered the possibility, but kept seeing more coincidences, nonetheless. My characters had been forced to leave their family behind because it had been revealed to them that this was part of their destiny. And the character, Emily, felt like time was against her, and there I had just been, looking at a big clock in Wells cathedral feeling the exact same way, - the clock was ticking. And then, as I drove to Nottingham, I realised in my second book, called 'Arthur Archer and the Warrior Queen', Arthur was summoned by the ancient druids and taught their ways - he had become a druid. And that had happened to me too! I knew I was on to something and my mind started racing, it had been a long time since I'd looked at the two books that I wrote all those years ago, but the similarities were uncanny.

In both books my characters were tested to the edge of their endurance; Emily was accused of witchcraft, sent to prison, and got the plague, she almost drowned, and she was sold into slavery. Arthur was attacked numerous times and captured by a mad man who planned to perform experiments on him, he fought in two wars, was left for dead twice, and became a drummer boy. I was a drummer now too, only mine was the drum of the shaman. In my books the protagonists are led to a time portal by birds, and the time portal is a tree, and there was the day when I was led to the big Oak tree and heard the Nick Kershaw song 'Riddle' in my head, and I'd been led there by birds singing, via channelling in the dictionary. And later I did a shamanic journey into the tree, which could have been me going through a time portal too. The manifestation of that scene was playing out in my present life. The implications of this were huge, this was serious stuff. This was a test that I had to get through.

I arrived at the bed and breakfast, and I was welcomed into a house with angelic figurines scattered everywhere, and little candles illuminating the space. My room was tiny, just big enough to fit a single bed, and the wallpaper was of grey brick. It immediately dawned on me that this room was also a manifestation of one of my novels. Emily spent a night in a prison cell in 17th century Oxford. On the wall in my tiny single cell-like room there was a ridiculously huge clock, another sign, it was time for me to step into my destiny. The landlady showed me the facilities and said goodbye, as she had a late shift at work. I wouldn't see her again; I was to let myself out in the morning and I could help myself to some breakfast.

I brain stormed on all the similarities of my life and the books I had written and ruminated on the meanings of everything. I picked up my dictionary and channelled a conversation with my guides. The message was clear, I was failing in my duty; I was only doing the parts of the job I wanted to do but was ignoring some aspects of what I was being told. The guides told me to remember that I was at university being 'educated', but it wasn't like being a teenager where you could choose which subjects to drop so you could just focus on the ones you liked. The guides stressed that I couldn't do that now, that I had to embrace all of the teachings, and this meant (for now at least) no alcohol, no heavily processed food, no refined sugar, no wheat, no meat, no dairy, no eggs. I needed to raise my vibration.

I spent the whole evening in my cell like room meditating. It was a profound evening, I felt I had been reprimanded. I had given up so much, I had followed the call and here I was failing. I needed to live a purer life, which meant I needed to go forward with a very strict diet. I needed to increase my daily exercise too. I was hurt, I felt I was being asked to do too much and I was feeling the pressure, but regardless, I would try and do as I was instructed.

The following day I was pleased to leave the bed and breakfast. I left a little note of thanks on the kitchen table, and as I was leaving, I observed all the angel figurines, and realised what a spiritual and profound experience I'd had in that strange little house that was surrounded by bars. A few hours later I arrived at my first pet sit and met the young couple as they were packing up their car for their road trip holiday. They were charming and showed me around their comfortable home; how to use the appliances, what the kittens needed and how to set the alarm. I instantly warmed to them both. The house was large and modern, I would be happy here for the next 3 weeks. The kittens were adorable, playful, loving and just a little bit naughty, just how they should be.

My guides told me it was time to change my work focus; taking what I'd learnt from all of the books I had been studying, I was told to begin a new project. I was to write a document, with my guides' help, on how humanity can transition to a new evolved society. It was apparently part of my life purpose and of significant importance - a document on a new way of living that would be in harmony with the planet, the individual, the local community, at a national level, global level and above all, for humanity to live in harmony with the natural world.

It was a rather daunting mission, but I didn't doubt the download I'd received from the spirit world. I knew the help I needed would find its way to me like it always did, should I need it. So I'd give it a go, what an incredible challenge! I was missing my children already; I had these two little kittens I was taking care of and couldn't help but think how much my kids would love to be playing and cuddling with these little fur balls. I picked up the phone and called them. They were back at school; Beatrice was now walking to school without me. A chapter of our lives had closed, and it made me sad.

I started with my new diet, I would follow the instructions I'd received from my guides and see how I did. It was a strict way of eating and I would take it one day at a time. It was a challenge but my previous cooking journey around the world during lockdown had taught me many ways to cook delicious food, so I would eat well, and study hard. I also found time to catch up with my good friend Dawn, we'd stayed in touch for many years after having met through work when we were in our early twenties. Dawn was now a fulltime artist, so I visited her at her craft stall, at a nearby local market. We sat at her stall together all afternoon and chatted about her work and my recent life changes. It was great to see her, she had such an infectious positivity about her. I suggested that perhaps we could share a pop-up gallery one day, with her artwork and mine, and she loved the idea.

It rained a lot during those days. I wanted to get out and about to photograph Nottingham, but the rain just didn't let up. Eventually I decided I just needed to escape the house for a little bit, rain or not, so I went into the city to write. I found a trendy café in the centre of town and ordered a coffee. I sat at a long communal wooden table, set up my laptop and I got to work, I enjoyed the clatter and chatter as people came and went and the strong aroma of coffee

After a little while a tall, attractive blonde woman walked over to where I was sitting,

'Do you mind if I sit next to you and write as well?' She asked politely, her accent sounded local.

'Of course not.' I replied smiling.

She settled down and we focused on our writing. After twenty minutes or so, we both looked up from our screens at the same time to take a breather. She asked if I knew where the toilets were, and I shrugged.

'Will you look after my laptop whilst I go?' She asked.

I smiled and nodded, and she disappeared. When she returned, we struck up a conversation. Her name was Jo, and she was from Lincoln. She was in Nottingham for the day as she'd just met up with a friend for lunch. She said she felt drawn to writing here in the café instead of heading back to her desk at home. Had the universe brought her here to chat with me for some unknown reason? After all, the universe did have a habit of doing that!

So, I chanced-my-arm. I told her I was new in the city and didn't know anyone, that I was a life coach and a photographer, and she smiled. She told me she was a life coach and a photographer too. What were the chances? I felt drawn to her. I asked her if she would like to meet up again over the next few days. She didn't need to think about it, she immediately said yes, and that she thought we'd have a lot to chat about, of which I agreed.

She obviously knew the area better than me, so she chose a restaurant between Nottingham and Lincoln for our meet up together. I got there a little before her and read through the menu, it was simple with pizzas and a few other dishes. I decided I would allow myself to break a few rules, I would treat myself to a veggie pizza, but I would steer clear of alcohol. Jo arrived; she was taller than me with her high heels, she was dressed elegantly and gave me a warm captivating smile.

'You look nice,' she said, looking happy to see me.

'Thank you, and so do you,' I replied, and I meant it.

We both ordered our drinks, a non-alcoholic beer for me, and a non-alcoholic cocktail for her as she was also newly off alcohol. We started by talking about photography, she'd been to Africa and showed me examples of her work; there were giraffes, leopards, elephants and more. She was really talented, and shared with me the stories behind each photo. I showed her some of my drawings on my phone, and then the conversation went to shamanism, and we chatted about our coaching. I told her about my cards, she was intrigued and full of questions.

When I told her about the document I was working on for the spirit world, her eyes widened with interest. She was drawn to the concept and offered to help. I was delighted, she was the first person I had told about it and here she was, offering her services. It was a promising start. I didn't know what she could do to help, but I accepted her help regardless, it had felt like an enormous task so to have a little help made me feel less overwhelmed. I thought of Lucia's message in my astrological birth chart, that help would be there each step of the way.

As we continued to chat, we started finding more and more synchronicities between us, two in particular stood out with bright flashing neon lights. I had been right; this was no chance meeting. It turned out her father had grown up in Oxford, that was a coincidence, but the fact he had lived just a few doors away from the house I'd grown up in was incredible! Especially as Jo was living in Lincoln, and we had met by chance in Nottingham. The other coincidence was that she was drawn to the leopard, like me. As we chatted about the leopard, I told her about the sculpture I had seen in Glastonbury of two leopards climbing a tree: the female protecting the male. Jo's eyes widened again.

'Ben, I have that exact statue on my mantlepiece,' she said startled.

It was an exceptional coincidence.

We represented the two leopards, and she would be my protector as I ploughed ahead on a dangerous spiritual path. The leopard is the spirit animal of the Egyptian shaman, and here I'd found another shaman to go on an adventure with. One chosen for me by fate.

We both decided to meet up again before I headed to my next stop, Oxford. I drove home unsure if I had just been on a date, or was it something else like friends getting to know each other? There were plenty of reasons to think it could be romantic, but something was missing - the chemistry. I arrived back in Nottingham to be greeted by two very excited kittens, a puddle of wee on the floor and a message from Jo. She'd had a wonderful evening but didn't feel a romantic connection between us, but wanted to be friends, she wanted to be clear that I understood that. I wasn't sure how I felt about it, I didn't want to dwell on it so I let it go. I'd found another piece in the jigsaw, and now I didn't feel like I was on this journey alone. And then a thought came to me about my book, was Jo perhaps playing the role of Tom or Rebecca, or both? They were the best friends of each of my characters in the book, Arthur and Emily, and they'd met at the very start of their journeys. It would prove to be a correct assumption.

I started working on the document of how we can change to an evolved society living in harmony with the planet. The working title was, 'The Project' and I began by listing the aims of the document, which was the easy bit, as we can set aims without any restrictions. My aims were utopian; a global society that shared their resources and knowledge freely, that lived peacefully together through collaboration and without competition. The only way to do that was through societies that operated without money, that were joined worldwide under the same values and ideology and governed locally by decent people all pulling together.

Whilst working on the document, I would pick up the dictionary and speak with my guides to ask for their help during the process, and they would usually highlight a new concept or movement for me to look into. It was fascinating and before long I was researching people throughout history who were instrumental in bringing forward new ideas, either through social movements, essays, or novels. I asked for understanding about what was happening to me regarding my novel, and how I was seemingly playing the role of the two main characters. The answer they repeatedly gave me was the word 'prophecy', I interpreted this guidance as meaning that the books, I had previously written all those years ago, were telling me what was going to happen in my life going forward. So, the word prophecy made sense. The guidance also told me that this connection between my books and my life would be of great significance. Well, I had no doubt about that, it certainly was already very significant for me, it was turning my life upside down and inside out!

Every email that reached me, or chance phone call, seemed to contain information I needed. So when my brother sent me a link with an article he'd been reading I was surprised that it didn't connect with me. After watching ten minutes of the video he sent, I switched it off. He later pressed me for my opinion, so I was honest and told him I hadn't finished it, but he was adamant that I needed to watch the whole thing. So I did, and what I found was quite unexpected. At the end of the clip the narrator spoke about the Bible code; I'd heard about the Bible code when I was trying to find links with Judaism and the Qabalah. I'd watched a documentary that showed how there are prophecies and information hidden within the text of the Hebrew Torah, Rabbi's and professors can spend their lifetime looking for the hidden messages revealing the truth about the future or the past.

The video my brother had sent me also had a link at the end that took me to a software program where you could type in keywords to see if they were hidden inside the Hebrew Torah. So I tapped in a few things, one of them being the name of the lead character of the book I had written, Arthur Archer. When I clicked enter, the word prophecy immediately popped up. It could have been anything, but no, it matched the word I'd been given by the spiritual world. This was just too strange, so I asked a good friend Nick to double check for me and he got the same answer. My mind was spinning and I vowed I'd do whatever it took to understand the meaning behind the novels I'd written twelve years before.

Arthur and Emily Archer travel through time, and that had happened to me already. They also changed history and at the end of the second book, through their writing, they'd inspired the world to unite together and share their resources. That was what I was writing in the document the spirit world had assigned to me. This couldn't all be a coincidence. Had I manifested into my life another part of the book, the writing of a document like that of my characters? Perhaps that's what I was doing, fulfilling the story in my book.

I checked if there was any spiritual meaning to the surname of my protagonists, and there was, Archer meant 'to let go'. I had been letting go of everything recently, so that certainly matched my experience, and perhaps that was what the world also needed to do; to let go of the need to own things and for endless growth. Then I looked up the meaning of the name Arthur and found another major discovery, Arthur meant Bear, my druidic name. I had effectively named myself Arthur without knowing it.

I then looked up the meaning for Janus, the name of my publisher I'd worked with all those years before; the only publisher to be interested in my book. And what did I discover? Janus was the god of time travel! How did I not know that? How had nobody ever shared that information with me after 12 years of the book being published? These were remarkable revelations. I had only left on my journey a week before and already I had found adventure; I was uncovering the meanings behind my book and my journey had only just begun.

Eventually the rain stopped, and the sun came out over the River Trent, so I was finally able to take out my camera and wander around the city of Nottingham. It was a beautiful Sunday morning. I took my time soaking up the sights and smells of the exciting Midland's city. I found my way down to the town hall, and watched as the children jumped through the water fountain and the pigeons took flight in their hundreds when the small children chased them. It was a very European scene, and I could have just as easily been in Prague, Milan, or Oslo. I filled my boots with good photos of people, old buildings, trams, and side streets.

As I approached the university, I saw a lady with binoculars and a camera. She walked up to me and told me there was a peregrine falcon nesting on the university roof. I made a mental note to find out the meaning of the falcon and would later discover that the falcon meant freedom and transition. Well, that fitted; I was on the road and I was free, I was following my path and I was in transition. I had escaped the rat race and was heading somewhere else. I just didn't quite know where that was!

I photographed the university buildings and then found myself a quiet café in an atmospheric part of the city on Carlton Street. I sat outside at a little table and people watched with the late summer sun on my face. It was just marvellous, I was in the moment, I was free, and I was alive. I thanked God for that moment, after all I'd been through, here I was making new memories and having wonderful and meaningful experiences. I walked down to the castle and eventually found my way back home. It had been a good day; my feet were tired, and the little kittens were ready for their lunch.

The following day I was ready to start exploring a running route from where I was staying, into the city and back. I was near the Trent Bridge so decided to run along the river, I put on my trainers and set off. I was surprised at how well I could run, and what's more, that I was enjoying it. I passed the football stadium and headed on towards the Wilford Suspension Bridge. I was getting stronger each day and now I was fitter than I had even been before my illness. The extra pounds I'd been carrying on my body were starting to drop off, I had turned another corner but how far could I go?

I ran to West Bridgeford and heard music coming from a street nearby, so I followed the sound and found people singing and playing instruments in the street, neighbours all gathered around, listening, and applauding loudly between songs. I stopped to listen and catch my breath. It was wonderful, a community joining together for a doorstep concert. There were all the generations of the neighbourhood together; small children playing, babies on laps whilst parents chatted with a glass of something, elderly people, everyone was engaged in some way. One of the locals walked over and handed me a timetable, turns out that a dozen or so houses along the street were performing on their doorsteps at different times during the day. It was such a wonderful concept, and the quality of the singing and playing that I heard was excellent. I wondered if there was a reason why I was here, perhaps I was supposed to meet someone? As I had that thought, a man in his sixties started chatting with me and told me about some good nature walks nearby, and some landmarks to photograph. I made notes on my phone to make sure I remembered, and after a very enjoyable break from my run with live music, I thanked him and headed back.

Jo and I met up again. I picked her up from her home in Lincoln and we went for a Thai meal. We ordered from the vegan menu which was plentiful in choice and quite delicious. We chatted about our lives, our former partners, our families, and our work. We were getting to know each other; we were becoming friends and shared our hopes and aspirations. It was a lovely meal and afterwards we went back to her house and carried on chatting, we were trying to work out how she could get involved in my work. I suggested that fate had brought us together, so why didn't we ask the spirit world what the purpose of our work together would be? She agreed.

'Let's ask,' she said handing me a dictionary from her bookshelf.

I showed her how to do it, to go into a trance through breath work and then open the dictionary with her eyes closed and see where her finger pointed. She relaxed and took her time, breathing deeply, and put her finger on a random spot on a random page - 'Hera, The Greek Goddess.' We both had the same raised eyebrow look on our faces, and immediately laughed. The next word was 'blood' and then 'save the warrior'. Was she the warrior or was I? I thought about the two leopards and the female protecting the male. Finally, her finger landed on 'past life regression'!

She looked at me as if to say, 'Are we going to do this?'.

'I can do past life regression through hypnotherapy if you'd like to try it?' I responded to what she said without words.

'Of course I would,' she smiled, 'Let's do it!'

We lit some candles, and she got comfortable on the sofa lying under a blanket. I took her on a guided mediation into a deep state of relaxation. I led her, in her mind, into an old wooden shack and invited her to take a book from the bookshelf, which was up against the back wall, so she walked over to the bookshelf and picked out a book. It was a small book with a red cover, and I asked her to open the book and look at the pages. This was how the time travellers in my novel had travelled through time and the significance was not lost on me. I had taken the idea of time travel through books from the very first past life regression I'd experienced, when I'd travelled back to the life of Jane a Victorian girl who would have many children and live a long life.

'Now look down and describe your feet to me,' I said, as she journeyed deep in the recesses of her mind peering into the pages of the book.

After a long pause she said,

'I have some kind of sandals on, and I'm wearing a long blue dress.'

'What can you see around you? Are you alone or are there other people with you?'

She went on to describe the scene.

'I see a pigsty, horses grazing in a paddock, and children running bare feet with grubby faces and old clothing, very old clothing. There are warriors fighting; they're practicing though, not really fighting each other. There are huts made of straw and mud.'

And then what she said next almost knocked me off my chair.

'My name is Boudica.'

In my second novel 'Arthur Archer and the Warrior Queen', the Warrior Queen happens to be none other than Boudica herself! Boudica was the Queen of the Iceni who led the Britons to rise up against Rome. Out of all the lives Jo could have gone back to in history, she went back to Boudica, the major character and love interest in my second novel.

Jo's awareness returned to the room, I watched her slowly open her eyes and blink herself back to the here and now. She smiled excitedly.

'Oh my god, did that just happen? Was that really me?' She asked, in awe of the experience.

'I don't know, maybe. Or maybe you just tapped into the universal consciousness, or we somehow manifested something from my book. Who knows?' I said, believing all of it could be true or none of it at all. I had been caught completely by surprise. What did this mean, would Jo become my love interest, matching that of the book, after all?

We chatted about the significance of it all, it had been an intense day and needed a lot of reflection. In my second novel, Arthur and Boudica fell in love and changed history; and by doing so set the world on a new path - one of global unity, peace, and prosperity. Would Jo and I eventually fall in love and do the same thing? Was this me manifesting Boudica into my life in a strange way? I couldn't get my head around it all and needed to sleep. I said goodnight to Jo, and headed back to Nottingham, grateful for the bizarre evening and enjoying how my adventure was unfolding. Each day of my life was turning out to be a page turner in a novel, a novel I had actually written twelve years before!

The days in Nottingham passed quickly, and my document on world change was starting to take shape. I was guided to a world without money, and to research all I could on the subject, I was led to a book by William Morris who wrote 'News from Nowhere' in the 1890s about a time traveller who turns up in the future, to a world successfully working without money. I set about reading the book as it too was planting the seeds of doing things a different way.

I was hanging out with the kittens, whilst applying for future house sits when I saw a post for one in Edinburgh, Scotland. It was at a beach house on Portobello, but I wasn't sure it was a good idea as it was such a long drive, and so I asked my guides. I picked up the dictionary and the first words my fingers came to were, 'A profound experience.' Well, there you go; I was meant to go there. I could see on the post that there'd been a lot of people applying for the pet sit but I sent them an email regardless. Promptly I received a reply saying that they had already found someone, so I suggested they should keep my number just in case. I knew I would be going.

My trip to Nottingham came to an end, and it had been a successful trip; I'd connected to a new city, made a new friend and moved further along my path. The kittens had been great fun too and had reminded me of the importance of play. My next stop was Oxford, the place of my birth and my childhood, I was to stay at Tony's whilst he was overseas and look after his cat. I knew the house well as I'd stayed there for a month after my divorce, it was a repeating cycle in my life, one of many I was starting to see.

Chapter 5

Adventure

It was good to be back on familiar ground, I set about unpacking and taking over Tony's spare room. Tony was a good friend and someone I could always rely on; he had a silly sense of humour and a love for the drums which he played loudly. He'd built his home and it was large, stylish, and comfortable. I created a sacred space in his dining room for my spiritual readings and continued with a mixture of photography, study and working on the document. It was stimulating and peaceful, but I was looking forward to the weekend when I would have my children come and stay with me. I couldn't wait to see them.

As I continued on the document, I picked up my dictionary and asked my guides what they wanted included, and the word 'Transcendentalism' came up. I did some research and discovered that transcendentalism was a philosophical movement started in the 1820's in New England in the U.S.A. As I started reading about it, I saw how similar their philosophy was to what the spirit world was teaching me. The word 'Meritocracy' also came up and the guides suggested that what I would write would be the love child of Meritocracy and Transcendentalism, I should take the best bits from both and leave out what didn't feel right. I was amazed at the wisdom I was tapping into and how accurate it was, as I worked on the document each day, I learnt so many new concepts, and opened myself to the potential of all of it.

I discovered that the founder of transcendentalism was a man called Ralph Waldo Emerson, and that the movement believed that the divine is all around us on earth, and they saw the spiritual world and the physical world as interconnected. They believed that large organisations such as political parties, corporations or religions were instrumental in the corruption of the individual. They believed we could tap into knowledge and wisdom intuitively, but we needed a deeper connection with the natural world; spending more time in nature and protecting it. The transcendental movement were anti-capitalist, spiritual and environmentalists, and they were clearly way ahead of their time.

I looked into meritocracy, and discovered it was a movement that believed people should all be given the same chances in life; they believed in equal opportunity for every child. The meritocracy movement believed in taking power away from the global cartels and giving it back to local people; people before profit, and the abolishment of political parties.

I could see how the spirit world believed these two philosophies could be moulded into something new and monumental, and so much of the ideas matched with my views of the world too. None of what I was learning was new to me, they were all ideas that had somehow emerged within me throughout the course of my life; creating a new form of government based on collaboration and not competition, a new society trying to support each other rather than shaming and blaming each other. This was a great project, and I was making good progress, I just hoped I could do it justice.

I was drawn to study books on land ownership and learnt about our very limited right to roam in England; how our main natural resource, our land, was often owned by people living overseas and how we didn't have access to most of it. I discovered that these landowners registered the land overseas to avoid tax on their inheritance, and much of the land had been in families for generations and had been gained through activities such as slave trading. It felt very unfair and served to keep the rich at the top of society.

Jo called me to share some news.

'You are not going to believe this. I saw my friend today, we were having a coffee and he said I looked like someone, but he couldn't quite put his finger on who. But then it came to him and he said I looked like Hera, the Greek Goddess! Isn't that weird? How does he even know what she looked like?' She was speaking fast from her excitement, 'And since I opened that dictionary with you, I've been seeing books and all sorts of things popping up mentioning 'Hera'. It's uncanny!'

At that very moment I noticed a book on the shelf near where I was standing. It was a book about Greek Gods and Goddesses, me too, I thought to myself.

'It's weird and I don't really understand the meaning of it all.' I said, feeling perplexed.

I told her about Janus, the Roman God of time travel, and how his image was on the spine of the novel I had published as my publisher had been named after Janus.

'Hopefully we'll understand more about Hera before long.' I said, whilst adding Tony's book on Greek Gods and goddesses that I spotted on the shelf, to my ever-increasing reading list.

'I asked my guides about you.' Jo told me, 'I asked if I was to work with you. They said I should, but it would be a poison chalice.'

Those words stung me. I knew my path wasn't an easy one, but I was doing my best and didn't want to hurt anyone on this journey of discovery.

Jo followed up with a text message later, asking me not to overthink what she'd said. She clearly picked up on my concern. She clarified that the guidance was about her not choosing the easy path, and it wasn't a reflection on me. Still, the words stayed with me. I knew my thinking was expanding, I was operating in the liminal space between perceived reality and what lies beyond the veil, and my confidence wasn't keeping up with my progress.

The weekend finally came, I went to pick up my children and brought them back to Tony's house. My daughter Beatrice didn't like spiders, but my friend Tony did; he left them well alone to do their thing and catch all the little bugs around the house. So, I got to work on her bedroom first, getting rid of the cobwebs in the corners, and then did the same in the lounge until she was quite satisfied that it was safe. Leo and Sara helped me prepare a meal. It was family life, and boy had I missed it.

Leo chose a movie for the night; it was Troy with Brad Pitt. Out of all the movies he could have chosen, of course we were going back to ancient Greece. I was intrigued and wondered what would come up for me. Being cuddled up on the sofa with my children was a real treat, I had missed them so much and they were grounding me back in reality away from the spirit world, the document, and all the incredible coincidences I was trying to make sense of. I passed around the chocolates as we got settled in.

The following day we went for a walk along the Oxford canal, it was the beginning of autumn, and the sky was blue. I took my camera, and we meandered along the path soaking up the atmosphere of those free minded folk who lived on narrowboats along the water's edge. I shared stories with my children of growing up in Oxford and pointed out where I used to swim in the river as a child. After a nice long walk, we ended up in Jericho, a trendy suburb of Oxford and sat in the garden of a Greek restaurant where I had coffee and they had hot chocolate. It was a happy morning full of smiles, jokes, and good memories. I was loving their company. Afterwards we popped into a charity shop to see if there were any bargains, and I purchased a book that was jumping out at me demanding my attention, it was called 'Plato, the last days of Socrates'. What was is about ancient Greece right now that was calling to me so loudly?

In the afternoon we all settled down at Tony's to do our own thing. I started to read the little book on Plato I'd just bought and managed to read the whole thing in a couple of hours. It turned out that Socrates was executed because he was teaching the young people of Athens about the importance of working on spiritual development, and not just working on the accumulation of wealth and perfect physical form. How interesting that my guides should want me to be learning about this now; in a time when society had lost its way, turning away from spirituality and focusing once again on wealth accumulation and other individualist pursuits. Was it history repeating itself with another repeating cycle?

We put on another movie and this time I got to choose. I wanted to watch The Time Traveller's Wife as I hadn't seen it for a long time, and I thought they might enjoy it. Immediately I noticed that the actor was also in the previous movie from the night before, Eric Bana. We all enjoyed the movie and as I watched the credits role, I noticed Brad Pitt's name came up under the production; there he was in both movies as well. Beatrice called out from the kitchen.

'Dad, come and see this.'

I walked into the kitchen and there was a sculpture of a man's face that looked just like Eric Bana. And the face was half formed and half disappearing, just like in the movie!

'It's the man in the film!' she said and she was right.

This was the start of countless synchronicities I would discover in my house sits.

Over the next few days, I felt very drawn to Tony's books. He had a wonderful collection of esoteric books on ancient spiritual practices and wisdom. I scanned the bookshelves waiting for a book to pull at my attention; it was a technique I used in the same way as I pulled cards during a spiritual reading. I'd ask my guides to show me a book that I would benefit from, then I would relax, and a book would simply beckon me, it would almost become brighter and call out, 'pick me, pick me!'. It was a technique I relied upon and how I found my greatest learnings, and one book would always seem to effortlessly link to the next. There was a set of three books on Tibetan monks, their practices, and the journey we go on after death. They were old books that I guessed had been sat on various bookshelves for decades, passed on to Tony by his grandparents. They spoke to me, so I chose one and sat down on his comfy sofa with a fresh cup of coffee.

I opened the first page and began to read, and to my utter amazement the book started in the exact place the previous book about Socrates had finished, with Socrates' final hours before his execution. How was I supposed to comprehend this? The chances of this happening were unbelievable. What was the message? I put it down as important, I was on a path to wake up others from the spell of a materialistic and superficial world, just as Socrates had done. So, would I also face the wrath of the people, and have to justify myself in the same way that Socrates did at his trial? Or was I just manifesting into my life the wisdom I needed to write my document? Again, there were more questions than answers.

I heard my phone receive a text message it was Emma from Edinburgh, she asked if I was still available to come and look after Mikey, her cat, in their beach house in Portobello. I had been waiting for this message, I knew it was coming. The person who was originally booked in for the pet sit had pulled out for some reason. I immediately confirmed I was available, so we planned a video call to talk the details through, and I started to wonder what my profound experience up in Scotland would be.

I was in the flow, allowing myself to go where I needed to go and learn what I needed to learn. I felt like I was growing faster than I had at any other time in my life. I called my children for a chat and spoke with Beatrice, we chatted about her friends and what she had learned that day. She told me she was studying the Greek Gods, and told me how Hera was the Goddess of life and Zeus was the God of everything else, apart from what the other Gods were in charge of. Of course she was learning about Hera and Zeus! Here it was again, but what was the connection? I was sure it would come to me at some stage.

My time in Oxford was coming to an end, and Jo had kindly invited me to stay with her in Lincoln for the few days I had between Oxford and Edinburgh. But my first nights would be at an Airbnb in Lincoln as Jo had a prior engagement. I was sad to leave Tony's because I knew I was leaving my children again. I cleaned up the house, said goodbye to the cat and headed out onto the A34 towards the Midlands. I arrived at the Airbnb, which was on a housing estate, in the evening. The host greeted me with a warm welcome, the room was small and had a fridge. I squeezed as much food as I could get into the little fridge and lay down on the bed. I took an early night, but became increasing frustrated by the loud buzz from the little fridge as I struggled to sleep.

The following day I searched for things to do in the area and saw that the Magna Carter was also here in Lincoln. Magna Carta, meaning 'The Great Charter', is one of the most famous documents in the world, originally issued by King John of England. I had seen part of it in Salisbury earlier in the year, and whilst at my mother's house she'd asked me to watch a movie with her about Robin Hood and the Magna Carter. I had the feeling it was significant, I had something to learn from it. Then it dawned on me, I was writing a document that signified a huge change in how we do things, that would challenge the ruling elite and give more power to the individual. Was it connected? I expected it was at some level. I came to the realisation that I needed to finish the document in the next few days whilst I was in Lincoln, because I needed to be free to start a new project when I got to Edinburgh the following week. I didn't know what the next project was, just that the document needed to be finished in Lincoln. I realised that

I didn't need to have the answers to all my questions, I just needed to act on the guidance I received from the spirit world and my intuition.

So, I found a café that I could work from in Lincoln; I needed good coffee, and I couldn't get that in my room at the Bed and breakfast. I set about putting in a good few hours' work on the document and by the time I headed to Jo's house, I had finally finished writing, 'How to move to an evolved society in harmony with the planet.' It was vague, as I was no expert, but the principles were all there; it would be a moneyless society that ran alongside the normal capitalist model. I didn't see people with money giving it up without a fight, well not very many of them anyway. Those that were thriving were often the decision makers, they'd reached the top in the current system so of course they'd be opposed to the changes I was suggesting. My idea was a transition to a new way of doing things; two systems that would give people a choice: a) they could remain as they were or b) move to a vocational way of living, where there was no need for money, and everyone contributed. There would also be continued learning throughout a person's life, as each person would be assigned a personal mentor. There would be a local approach to governance, and education would be created specifically to the individual's needs, no longer a one way fits all approach to learning, and a move away from exam-based teaching. The document mentioned local communities sharing resources and knowledge, locally, nationally, and globally, a form of global localism. It was a radical approach to just about everything and offered a huge potential for change, but all within the model of democracy. I'd found ideas from several different sources and put them all together in a new way. Some of the ideas were my own, or at least I hadn't seen them before, for instance the way the transition could come about, two systems running side by side giving everyone a choice, and how we could bring about an end to party politics as well as handing some of the land back to the people.

I was proud to have finished it, but I didn't know what I was supposed to do with it; I just felt I had to allow the wisdom to emerge through me, just like all those years ago writing my first two novels and my business networking community. Both had gone further than I could have ever imagined. For now, I would just tuck the document away until the right time came to be.

It was lovely to see Jo again, I turned up with a car full of bags of clothes, photography equipment, spiritual stuff, and food. She gave me a warm welcome and told me she'd ordered us take away pizzas. As we chatted over some tasty comfort food, I told her that I'd finally finished the document on Global Localism, and she asked if she could read it. We chatted about Edinburgh and my novel, and how I'd seen various scenes from my books playing out in my life.

I was manifesting the stories from my books, and I knew what may be coming next, but I didn't want to face it. I decided to rewrite my first novel to see if I could prevent the drama that seemingly awaited me in the near future. I was aware that it would take me a little while to rewrite, but it would give me an opportunity to improve the book; add more detail and bring my characters a little more happiness and less trauma in the journey they encountered. By now I was convinced that Jo was playing the role of the close friends of Emily and Arthur in the book, and one of those friends, Tom, was going to be murdered. That bit needed to be rewritten as quickly as possible. Over the years many people had asked me why Tom had been killed, so now I would retell Tom's story and give him an easier time of it, and I'd also make Arthur and Emily's time considerably less challenging. It then dawned on me, the café I'd been to in Lincoln that day had a strange name, it was called Tom 2.

It was time to teach Jo some real magic, how to raise energy and give it intention. We set about preparing for the spell; we cleansed the space, washed ourselves and set up the altar. I had a copy of each of my books which we placed at the centre of the altar and added trinkets, gemstones, and offerings of fresh fruit and we lit candles. We chanted sounds, we danced elaborately in circles around the altar, we played our drums, and we asked the elements and the moon for support. In the book Arthur and Tom became drummer boys in the Parliamentarian army and go off into battle together, but for Jo and I, our battle would be the battle within ourselves, although we didn't know that then. As we danced around the altar, Jo looked over my shoulder and said,

'I see her Ben. It's Hera, she's standing behind you.' I turned but couldn't see anyone.

'She's with us, protecting us,' she continued, 'She wanted us to know, and Zeus is here too, although I can't see him. I can just feel his presence.'

As the spell ended, we thanked the gods and everything that had helped and guided us, packed everything away and sat together on her sofa. I wished I could have seen what she saw. We channelled into the dictionary, and were told that the spell had been successful; we had managed to add a layer of protection to ourselves from the magic contained within the book. Not just for us but for our families too. It had been a strange night and so we said goodnight and took to our separate rooms.

The following day I made us scrambled eggs for breakfast and afterwards Jo had a bit of work to do; she had a couple of client calls to make so I left the house and went for a walk around Lincoln with my camera. I walked to the old castle quarter, up the steep hill and took my time photographing the attractive old town. The light was tricky to capture good images, with too many long dark shadows. Jo joined me after her calls and said we should go inside the Cathedral, so we did. She insisted on paying for my ticket to go inside; she said she'd channelled that morning with the dictionary and it had been quite adamant that she should pay for me, I accepted gratefully and we wandered around inside the beautiful historic building.

I soaked up the atmosphere and we visited the Magna Carter, the world-famous ancient piece of writing that was the world's first human bill of rights. The cathedral was splendid and had a lovely sacred energy to it. There was a sermon going on while we were there and Jo listened intently whilst I kept to the shadows looking around reading the signs to see if there was something I should be picking up on; a hidden message on a plaque or something similar. Jo told me the sermon was really relevant for her, and timely, the words were just what she needed at that moment - it was about having faith in her spirituality.

The following day Jo and I said our farewells, and I headed out on the long drive to Edinburgh. I had good music playing and the wind behind my back, it felt like my adventure was moving on to the next chapter. I arrived around the time I'd planned to, the traffic had been kind and the drive enjoyable. I let myself in and immediately noticed the hallway wallpaper was covered in little birds of all different colours. It matched what I wrote in my book, where the tree of time was covered in birds of all different species. My senses were immediately alerted, and I started paying attention to every detail.

The room I was staying in was full of symbology, and everything matched my current life, just like Jo having the exact sculpture of two leopards that I'd seen in Glastonbury, here in my room were figurines of a bear, and a leopard. There was also a blanket with a tree covered in owls, much like the tree where I travelled through time. I had a deep sense that I was exactly where I was meant to be to rewrite my novel; it felt right, the room felt like an outer expression of my book. As I started unpacking, I accidently knocked a curtain that was hiding a bookshelf and something fell off the shelf and landed on the floor. It was the most unusual item, a decorative medieval face mask that doctors would have worn when treating people with the plague or an infectious disease. The only reason I knew what it was, was because I had written one of them into my novel; Emily was treated by a doctor wearing such a mask. There was no doubt in my mind that this was a sign to confirm I was in the perfect house to begin writing my story all over again.

I met Mikey the cat, he was strong and beautiful with silver fur. He had a wonderful life; he had a cat flap to come and go as he pleased, and I was to leave food all around the house for him in little bowls so he could eat whenever he wanted and wherever he wanted. If I was a cat, I'd definitely want to be Mikey.

On my first day in Portobello, I decided I'd first reread my novel from cover to cover as I hadn't read the book since reading it to my son Leo about 5 years before. I wanted to immerse myself in the story before I began formulating a new narrative.

The lounge was comfy and quirky, with interesting posters framed on the walls. There was a theme of music that pervaded throughout the house, and it was clear that music from the 60's and 70's was Mikey's parents' preference. I got comfy and set about reading the whole book in a day, I took notes as I read, and it wasn't long before I started seeing things I hadn't noticed before. The most incredible thing I noticed was that when I wrote the book, I chose to have the characters living by a secondary school in Witney, and five years later I ended living on the very same street as my characters in the book!

The novel was just riddled with significance for me; Emily's friendship with the priest matched the conversations I'd had with the priest when I'd been picking up the litter. By the time I'd reached the end, I knew I'd need to rewrite a safer passage for the characters in the book, because it was far too intense and dangerous if I was going to live through it myself, which seemed highly probable.

Reading the book again brought back many memories for me, most of all how much I had enjoyed reading the books to my children; they had loved cuddling up in bed with me, whilst I would read the stories that I had created, to them.

I didn't have much food with me, so I needed to find a supermarket and stock up for the week but I was too tired after the long drive, so I cooked a simple pasta dish and took an early night. I awoke at 5 am, everything was quiet, when the neighbourhood was fast asleep like this, it was the perfect time to speak with my guides, I got out of bed and said hello to Mikey. I made myself some tea, went back to bed, took out a notepad and a pen, and asked my guides for a message through the dictionary. The message I received was that I needed to get into the sea, apparently it was part of my journey here, to cleanse myself in the salt water, as part of my healing, and offer myself to Neptune, the Roman god of the sea.

Let's just say I am averse to cold water; on a hot day I'm the person that doesn't get into the pool because it's just too damn cold. I closed the dictionary, thanked my guides, and decided I really didn't like what they were suggesting. It was October, it was cold, and I was in Scotland, and now they were telling me they'd brought me up here to swim? Couldn't they have asked me to do that during the summer months instead?

I eventually got myself up, showered and began rewriting the book and as I did, I looked up to see 'The Great Wave of Kanagawa,' a famous Japanese painting by Hokusai, on the wall.

'Okay, okay I'll think about it.' I said to my spirit guides out loud, 'But I'm not happy about it at all!'

I made a good start on my book. I didn't have the original electronic document anymore, so I started a new one and dictated to myself from the paperback version, making changes as I went. It felt good to be writing fiction again, I'd missed it. This was creative, this involved diving into my imagination and I was connecting to a part of my history; I was finding meaning in the story of my life.

That night, whilst I was dreaming, I was visited by one of my guides and introduced to a new spirit animal that was now with me in the form of a salmon. The salmon represents cycles, determination, and adaptability, and it also happens that salmon live in cold water, of course! My guide told me that this new spirit animal, the salmon, would help me face my issues regarding getting into cold water, to help me get into the North Sea. I awoke from the dream knowing I had no choice, I needed to do this.

I decided to have a hearty breakfast to warm myself up for what lay ahead, and then I walked to the beach with a towel and a bag. I didn't have any swimming shorts with me, so I used the shorts I'd brought for running. The beach was long and quiet, I chose a spot far away from anyone else; from the cafes, restaurants, and little shops nearby. The only people I passed were the occasional dog walker. I found a big rock on the beach near the water's edge and stripped down to my running shorts. I put all my belongings into my bag and stood facing the formidable sea. I was already cold. Despite the deceiving blue sky, there was an ice-cold wind blowing off the water straight on to my bare skin. Was it safe? I didn't know. There was certainly no one nearby if I got into any difficulty, but I trusted my guides and I trusted my path. So, I slowly walked into the water and invoked the salmon to help me navigate the cold.

I went in at a slow and steady pace, and soon enough the cold water had passed my nether regions, I tried to ignore the discomfort as each wave went higher. My body was numb to the cold water now, I felt very little at all. Something took over me, like the shamanic journey when I completed the soul retrieval, and I suddenly knew why I was here. I was here to connect to the element of water, like the day I had stood in the middle of a field and met the wind, and I was here to connect to Neptune, the god of the sea. Perhaps they were the same thing, I didn't know. I called out to the god of the sea and asked him for a cleansing and offered myself to him; I said I would do all I could to help protect the oceans from man and pollution. And then I plunged myself under the water, and held myself there, letting the ocean hold me in its grip. I was perfectly in the present moment, I felt so alive and knew I was connecting to the water. It was surreal, and then I re-emerged from beneath the water and screamed an undiscernible noise. It was a release; I felt cleansed and revived, and also really, really cold! As I made my way back to the sandy beach, I thanked the sea for the cleansing. It had been another extreme moment that I would hold with me until the end of my days.

I wrapped myself up in a towel, dried myself off and headed along the beach to grab a hot cup of coffee. I deserved it! I sat on the terrace, wrapped up warm, looking out at the sea with the hot drink in my hands, still shivering slightly. I marvelled at the beauty of the water and its power, and contemplated who I was becoming. This new version of me, in the flow, being 100% my authentic self, was so far removed from the businessman I used to be, who'd organised all those events, or the photographer who had taken all those family portraits. I was reconnecting to a deeper part of myself, reconnecting to my roots; I was connecting to the elements, connecting to the gods, and connecting to Mother Nature herself. I had become a modern-day British shaman, and realised how far that took me away from Western culture and conventional society.

When I got back to the house my guides told me not to wash but to leave the salt water on my skin for as long as possible as it was part of the cleansing process. The hot shower I had been looking forward to would have to wait!

The sun came out later in the week and I took the opportunity to photograph Portobello; I wandered down the beachfront and took photos of the coastline, people walking their dogs and couples walking hand in hand along the promenade. I took photos of the houses and the high street, and when I passed a small church that I was drawn to it. Standing on the street directly opposite to the church, I grabbed the dictionary from my camera bag and connected in my usual manner. I asked if I should visit the church, and the answer I got was, 'You think you are more important than you actually are. You have no right to be here.' Something had hijacked my reading, and I instinctively knew I wasn't in a safe place. I'd attracted the attention of a spirit that had attached himself to the area, so I quickly put the book back in my camera bag and walked away, not wanting the attention the spirit was giving me. I popped into a little gift shop further up the road, and thought I'd managed to give the curious spirit the slip. I found some time travel books which I asked the man at the till about; he told me the author lived down the street and she'd just dropped the books in that day. I purchased the books for my daughter for Christmas and carried on my way.

Something was niggling at me, so I picked up my dictionary again and asked my guides, 'Is there something I need to see here, a sign perhaps to understand?' The answer was yet again weird and unexpected.

'I see you're a shaman. You think that everything happens for a reason, don't you? You think there are signs everywhere and you have to understand them all!'

It was the spirit again, he was following me, but I didn't want to talk with him. I closed the book and walked further away along the street to make some distance between me and the church. As I increased my pace I looked back around and saw a cyclist seemingly being pulled to the ground by an invisible force almost to the spot where the spirit had been. Oh my! I went to see if he was okay, but before I got to him, he'd dusted himself off and cycled away. I felt responsible, I suspected the spirit was trying to show off, or perhaps I'd annoyed him by ignoring him and walking off. It seemed that not a day would go past without me having an adventure of some type!

When I had been sick with long covid and had chronic fatigue, I'd pictured myself running on a beach and being healthy as a way of manifesting myself back to good health. I decided that this was a pretty good place to play out that vision, so I put on my running trainers and shorts and took to the beach. I'd done a little running in Nottingham, but hadn't in Oxford, so I wasn't at my best, and the sand under my feet made the jogging that much harder. Nevertheless, there I was, running on a beach, and not worried at all about my health. I'd done it; I was living out my visualisation from all those months ago, and was feeling perfectly fit and healthy. In that moment, with the cleansing of the sea from the day before, and the run on the beach, I knew I had closed the chapter of sickness in my life. My long covid recovery was complete.

Jo had said I could come back to her house in Lincoln and see her on the way back down south and stay with her for a few more days. I was pleased, I'd already secured my next pet sit in Potters Bar on the outskirts of London, but I needed somewhere for the days in between. Things were continuing to fall into place. That afternoon I did a reading, and the word 'entrails' came up, it made no sense to me and I assumed I had misread it, until the following morning when I was packing and found the entrails of a mouse on the floor next to my suitcase that Mikey had left me as a thank you and farewell gift. Nice! I didn't attempt to look into them and read them as the ancient shaman's would have done. I had really enjoyed the house and my time there. I'd pushed myself way out of my comfort zone and grown as a consequence, and perhaps I'd even connected to the God of the Sea, Neptune himself.

I arrived back in Lincoln, and Jo took me for a walk in the local woods, she'd just finished reading my first novel and wanted to share some of her insights. She told me that the book was full of meanings for us to decipher, and that it was beneficial that she was seeing it from a different perspective than me. I asked if she wanted to get involved with the rewrite of my novel and she jumped at the chance. I was certain she was somehow playing out the roles of the two best friends of the protagonists in my book, so it only seemed right that she could work on Tom's, story. He was going to meet with a grizzly end, and we had to get that bit changed as soon as possible as I didn't want to tempt fate. I gave her a test section of the book to work on first and she was excited, vowing to start the very next day.

That evening we went into the old quarter by the cathedral and had a meal out; the restaurant was small and quiet, so we tried to keep our voices down. I told her what had happened with the spirit in Edinburgh that had pulled the man off his bike, and she told me that when she asked her guides about my novel, the word 'prophecy' had kept coming up. She also said she'd been told the changes I was making on the book would be of great significance.

The food arrived along with a couple of drinks. We were both off meat, so it was easy to share the food between us which all looked delicious. As I kept talking, I noticed Jo's facial expression had changed, as if something had visibly spooked her.

'Did you hear that?' she asked, putting her hand on mine to stop me from talking.

'No, what was it?' I replied.

'The table over there, the man just said something really odd.'

'What did he say?' I asked.

She leaned in to whisper.

'He said the Devil is with us tonight, and that he was referring to us.'

I turned around to look at the table of people she was referring to, but all I saw was a normal family enjoying a meal and chatting together.

'It was those people,' she said, still clearly freaked out, 'spirit was talking through them for me to hear!'

Now I was spooked too, what she said sent a shiver down my spine, and we vowed not to talk about such things in public again; this was the second time in a week that the spirit world had eavesdropped on my conversation, and I didn't like it one bit. I needed to be more careful when I was out of my protected spaces. We were near the old castle and the cathedral, and I suspected many old spirits lurked in this part of the old town.

We ate up quickly and left the restaurant, we needed to get back to the house where we could talk safely. On the way back to the car I felt something attack my energy field, something I couldn't see and as we got in the car I felt an immediate restriction across my chest, and a darkness attach itself to me. It was the most horrible feeling. I explained what I was feeling to Jo, and she told me she felt the same; whatever was happening to me was happening to her as well.

'Just get us back quickly and when we're at your house we can deal with it, we'll banish it,' I said, more confidently than I felt.

It was uncomfortable, but I had read enough about these spiritual attacks to know that we should be able to clear it.

Once we were back at Jo's place, I asked my guides what we needed to do; first of all, we needed to raise our vibration, so we channelled divine energy and radiated it out of our heart chakras, filling the room with love. Then Jo spoke with the negative presence we were both feeling, and told it to leave; she spoke with a strong and powerful voice demanding it to leave us alone and not to return. She picked up the dictionary and talked to it through the pages, but it refused to go, it was angry and demanded to know what we were up to. She gave it no choice and with a burst of energy and some strong words she wrestled with it. I asked my guides to help her and after a few moments we finally felt the presence leave us. We cleansed ourselves with incense and renewed the protection on the house. It was a powerful lesson to learn from; from now on we would be discreet and keep our business away from eyes and ears we couldn't see. Thankfully we were fine, Jo had risen to the occasion, her bravado had matched that of Tom's character in the book. I noticed the two leopards on the mantlepiece, the exact one I'd seen in Glastonbury, with the female protecting the male. And that story had just now played out. I was rattled, as I knew what was ahead in the book and it got far worse than this.

I realised that we'd reached the part in my novel where Arthur and Tom had been attacked by Royalist snippers on the road to Gloucester, the book was further ahead of me on my rewrite, and I knew I needed to catch up in order to stop what was going to play out in our lives. Suddenly it felt like we were against the clock, and it turned out it would stay like that for some time.

The following day, we went for a cross country run together. It was the first time I had been for a run with anyone else in a long time. We ran through muddy farmer's fields and forests, and as we passed an old church the bells rang, and we could hear people sing from inside. It was a special moment and we were forming a great friendship, just like the characters in my book. In the story, Emily had been taken into the service of the queen in Oxford and had befriended Rebecca a queen's maid; whilst Tom and Arthur had joined the army and were heading to Gloucester to be trained as drummers in the Parliamentarian army.

I arrived in Potters Bar where I met Steph and Nick, a personable Australian couple with a beautiful house. They had no children, but they did have two very beloved cats. Molly was poorly, she had an issue with her eye and had just had an operation on it, so she would need to have eye drops and eye cream on the eye twelve times a day. Steph had got in touch with me just before, to say that I could pull out of the house sit if I wanted to as it wasn't what I'd signed up for, but the cat breeder had agreed to call in for a few days and administer the medicine, I just needed to deal with it for the first day and the last couple of days before they returned back from their cruise. I had a hunch this was where I was supposed to be next, so I was happy to be Molly's nurse for the next few days.

The following morning after Steph and Nick had left, I found myself a nice little spot in the house to write and I was spoilt for choice as the house was vast. I placed myself at the end of their large dining room table and studied the art on the walls that surrounded me. Each picture had a common theme of a tree in the centre, some of the pictures had birds, and three pictures had a proud stag stood beside a tree. The trees were so reminiscent of my books and the time portal, and I decided to write the stag into the rewrite of the book. The stag had come to me on my shamanic journey and been the first spirit animal to dance with me, so including the stag in the rewrite felt like my way of thanking the stag and confirming our connection in words. I would take inspiration from my inner journey and the art on the walls and write a new scene in the book, then I looked down and saw in the corner of the room a picture leaning on the wall that hadn't been hung up yet, and surprise, surprise, It was a stag by a tree full of birds and I knew, I was on the right track.

After a steady morning writing I found the poorly cat, wrapped her up in a blanket and applied the eye drops. She didn't like it and she didn't like me, she hissed, and I felt terrible for her. It wasn't surprising, she'd only just met me and here I was causing her distress. Afterwards I sat with her for a while and tried to comfort her, my heart went out to little Molly, she had a big plastic vase shaped collar on and seemed very upset about it.

The following day the cat breeder arrived; she was a quirky lady who certainly wasn't a people's person. She clearly didn't want to chat, so I left her to the cats and headed out to Saint Albans to take some photos of the town. I'd never been to Saint Alban's before, it certainly felt like I was close to London; the accents had changed, the atmosphere had changed, and people seemed to avoid eye contact. I wandered through the old town trying to find some good angles to take photos and I visited the cathedral.

When I got back to the house the peace of the cathedral was immediately replaced by drama, as I came back to find the cat breeder struggling to breathe.

'Can I take you to the hospital?' I asked concerned, but she shook her head.

'I don't want your help,' she managed to say.

I ignored her reply. She looked like she was having an asthma attack!

'Shall I go to the chemist for you then?' I asked.

She stood up, grabbed her keys and walked out of the house without saying goodbye.

I didn't know how much medicine she'd given to the poor cat and didn't want to give Molly more than she needed. I had the breeder's number so I called her but she didn't pick up, I messaged her but she didn't reply. I was stressed. Was the breeder okay? And what should I do about the cat? I didn't know if the breeder would come back. She'd left me worried, and unable to work on the book.

That was the last I ever saw of the cat breeder; she never phoned back or messaged me. Steph told me the next day that she had just got in her car and drove all the way back up north to her home and that was that. So, I got to be the main carer of a sick cat, but I didn't mind; it was an opportunity to be kind to Molly, Steph, and Nick, so I made sure the poorly cat had all she needed. Molly began to relax around me a little, and even looked for my company in between the eye drops.

On my last day there I cleaned the place from top to bottom; I was learning that the bigger the house, the more work it was to hand over. The couple turned up before I'd finished the clean and were pleased to see the animals well cared for, especially Molly. I said goodbye and I headed off to Dorset to spend a few days with my mum. My next pet sit would be back near Jo and Lincoln, I'd picked up a house sit in Worksop in the Midlands; another place I'd never been to.

Steph kindly wrote an exceptional review for me on the pet sit website which opened the door to many more house sits. So, had it not been for the cat breeder forgetting her inhaler, I would have missed out on the opportunity to care for the poorly cat and I'd have missed out on such a brilliant review. The more we give freely without expectations of return the more we receive back; when we are in the flow things happen that may seem negative but turn out to be extremely positive. It's best not to sweat the small stuff and trust that the universe has a plan, even if you can't work out what that plan is.

Chapter 6

Dating

It was half-term week, so I had my two youngest kids, Beatrice, and Leo, come to stay with me at my parents. It was so lovely to see them, and we did all our usual things; Monopoly was a big favourite of ours and we would play as soon as everyone was up and out of bed. My mother was a big fan of scrabble, so she'd organise an afternoon game with them. The three of us also went off and explored Dorset; I took them to the city centre and whilst we were looking for treasures in a charity shop Beatrice came over to me with her latest finding, there in her hand was a computer game called 'Emily Archer and the Curse of Tutankhamun'. Emily Archer was one of the main characters in my book, written twelve years ago and here was Emily Archer in a new computer game where she battles in Ancient Egypt! And to top it off, as we left the charity shop and crossed over the road, we discovered that the local museum was currently having an exhibition of Ancient Egypt and Tutankhamun! It was another remarkable coincidence, but what did it mean? What was I supposed to do with this information? I was trying hard to understand, but my senses told me that I needed to wait for more signs to make sense of all these coincidences. The connections to ancient Egypt, like ancient Greece would continue to build slowly over time.

I was ready to explore the world of online dating for the first time. I chose a dating app and took some new photos of myself, wrote a profile and answered questions about the things I liked, my hobbies and interests etc. I started getting a few likes and matches, I didn't know quite what I was looking for except that I wanted someone who would understand me and offer some kindness and support. It felt like the last few years had been one long struggle; with my businesses, my health, the breakdown of my relationship, and the unintended consequences of manifesting my book into reality and becoming a shaman's apprentice!

I matched with a woman called Sarah who lived near my parents in Dorset, we chatted for a couple of days, and I decided to see if she wanted to meet up. She agreed, so I asked her to choose a location somewhere between us both, and she chose the Trumpet Major pub in Dorchester. The name of the pub instantly got my attention, as I'd written that very day about my characters being assigned to their drum major in the army, and here I was going to the Trumpet Major pub. Whatever I was writing about always seemed to manifest into my life somehow, even if it was in the simple name of a pub.

I turned up a little while before Sarah and looked around the pub for signs whilst waiting for her to arrive. When she did, I knew immediately that I wasn't attracted to her; she looked so different from the photos she'd posted on her profile, they seemed like a decade out of date. I was disappointed, but sensed I was there for a reason, so I'd be polite, chat, listen and enjoy lunch with her. I knew I needed practice in the realm of dating, so I thought I had nothing to lose by testing out my dating skills. We ordered some food, and she had a glass of wine whilst I had some water. She worked in administration, and we had absolutely nothing in common. In future I needed to be more discerning in my choices, or I'd waste a lot of time and money on dates. I thought about how I could change my approach as she chatted about difficult customers, and her teenagers' college days.

After the meal I said I had to go, and she was clearly disappointed. On our way out she gave me a big kiss on the cheek and the twinkle in her eye suggested she would be keen to see me again. I smiled and politely said goodbye. I'd learnt my first online dating lesson - be prepared for old photos and get to know them more before meeting up in person. Later on that day I set my location on the dating app to Worksop to see if I could meet someone during my stay in the Midlands. I sent Sarah a message saying that I'd enjoyed lunch, but didn't feel a connection. I never heard back from her.

Jo sent me the first trial section of my novel she'd rewritten, it was from early on in the book, she had a different style from me, and it added a woman's touch to the novel. I was impressed by what she had written and sent it over to my son Leo to see what he thought. I told Jo I was pleased and asked her how much she'd charge to rewrite a few sections of the book for me, she said she'd think about it and get back to me. She was thrilled that I was impressed with her work.

I woke in the early hours of that night with my intuition telling me that I had to open the dating app, so I trusted my instincts and sure enough I saw that I had a new match, her name was Gemma, she was an attractive blonde lady with long curly hair and beautiful eyes. I read her profile and sent her a message saying how lovely it was to connect with her. I was surprised that she replied almost immediately despite it being 3 o'clock in the morning. I commented about what she'd written about herself, she'd mentioned she couldn't be trusted near a buffet, and I told her I couldn't either. We made an immediate connection; within minutes she was making me laugh out loud with her slapstick humour. I told her about my nomadic lifestyle and she didn't seem to be put off by it, although she didn't completely understand it either. That was okay, I could work with that, it all seemed positive, and I was hopeful that I would meet her when I arrived in Worksop. Our messages continued pinging back and forth for hours, it was fun and seemed so easy. She was a security guard, so she was glad of the company so late into the night and over the next few nights I stayed up late chatting to her.

It turned out that Jo had met someone online too, and his name was Ben. We were both experiencing the same thing; the giddy excitement of connecting with someone new; we were hopeful, we were vulnerable, and we were seemingly in sync.

At the end of the half term, I drove my children back to their mother and continued up to Worskop in the Midlands. I'd asked the homeowners if I could have a couple of friends over to visit whilst I was there, and they'd agreed, which I appreciated. I found the hidden key and let myself in. The home was, homely, and comfortable, and once I'd unloaded the car, I looked around the house to find the cat; she was very timid and decided to hide under the sofa once she'd had the initial opportunity to sniff me. I decided I'd let her come to me in her own time, I was keen to crack on with the rewrite as I was making good progress but was aware that very soon my two characters were heading off to war and I didn't quite know what that might mean for Jo and I. Both of us had tried to get answers through our guides, but kept getting the same guidance, only that the book was important, and it contained a prophecy. But what did that mean? And would we be walking into some kind of war like the characters in my book?

As I sat down to write I looked up and noticed a large arrow on the wall, a real arrow from a native American bow which was in a glass case. It was as symbolic to me as the doctor's mask in Edinburgh at the last house, after all my main characters were called Archer! The arrow wasn't the only significant item in the house; my bedspread had a tree full of birds, which was another connection with my book and the time portal, and it would be the first of three bedspreads with trees and birds imprinted on them that I would sleep under in the next few houses.

That night, I lay in bed chatting on the phone to Gemma and invited her to come to the house so we could finally meet in person. Gemma lived in Sheffield and said she would need to organise babysitters and catch a train but she was up for the adventure. We were both excited to meet. I said I'd cook for us, as it would be a chance to show off my cooking skills and hopefully impress her.

The following day I drove to Lincoln to spend the day with Jo at her place, we'd work together on the book and pop out for lunch in the old town. I'd given her the assignment of writing a new future for Tom, it seemed appropriate as she was seemingly playing out his story through her experience in real life. I wanted to give her the opportunity to write his life as she wanted her life to be. We wrote together, and I enjoyed the company. Over lunch we made sure not to talk about any spiritual matters, just about dating, and reworking the storyline of the book. We chatted about our potential dates, and shared the other sexes perspective.

I felt so relieved that Jo was working on the scene where Tom had been killed in the book, once that had been rewritten that I felt that whatever magic was playing out in our lives should be mitigated by the new narrative. I didn't know what else I could do; I was currently rewriting Emily's battle with the plague and adding extra scenes involving healing in her dreams. I concluded that manifesting from the book didn't necessarily run in sequence, things would just happen when the opportunity arose.

I headed into Worksop with my camera, as I needed to get some ingredients for the meal I would be preparing for Gemma that night, and I wanted to find a barber to get a trim before she arrived. I didn't know what to expect of our evening together, I was nervous and excited all at the same time. We'd had some great conversations and had been chatting on the phone every day since we'd first connected, she really was the funniest woman I'd every spoken to.

I'd decided on a mushroom soup to start, followed by poached salmon, dill and baby roasted potatoes. I also baked a camembert with fresh rosemary for nibbles to get us started. The station was just a few minutes away, I arrived to pick her up just as the train pulled into the station. We gave each other a big awkward hug and got into the car, and I immediately noticed she'd gained a fair bit of weight since her profile pictures were taken, a good 10 kilos! As we made the short journey back to the house I was staying at, she got straight to the point with some tough questions.

'So, tell me about your spiritual path. What is this big purpose you have? And what does it have to do with your last relationship and why you ended it?'

This was a lot in one go and I felt a little blindsided, they were questions I was afraid of because I didn't have all the answers. Or at least I didn't have acceptable ones that would make sense to a 'non spiritual' person. The spirit world had advised me to leave Gabriella to explore my freedom so I could learn what they needed to teach me. I was on this incredibly strange journey, the shaman's path, and had been guided to write a document about an evolved society and still didn't know what I was supposed to do with it. Now I had to explain all of this whilst I was driving, on a first date, to a lady that didn't believe in spirituality. Suffice to say, it was only a five-minute drive, but the date was a train smash before we'd even got through the front door.

I struggled to be anything but honest, and answered the questions as best as I could. I told Gemma that I was on a spiritual path and felt I had something important to do in the world, I told her I spoke with my spirit guides regularly, and would allow their guidance to lead me in making major life decisions. And once inside the house I could tell by Gemma's body language that she wasn't happy with my response. It was clear she was uncomfortable, and that was making me uncomfortable too. I felt vulnerable, so I went about serving up the delicious camembert cheese. We spoke about my book, and I showed her the big arrow on the wall and told her about all the incredible coincidences that were happening in the houses I visited. I shouldn't have, I should have just kept my mouth shut and turned all the attention onto her and her life. I assume she must have sent the S.O.S text whilst I was cooking, because within five minutes someone called her to say that there was an emergency, and she was needed back home in Sheffield immediately as her child was sick.

It was 45 minutes before the next train, so we quickly ate the food I'd prepared, which she at least said was delicious. She told me about her ex-husband and the challenges they'd faced together. I saw repeating cycles in her life and mine; in her ex-husband and me. That was something that would be repeated over and over again on my dating journey; the synchronicity between me and their ex-partner which often related to my shadow side. It was the part of me I needed and wanted to explore, which had been repressed until it came to the surface on my dating adventures.

I drove Gemma back to the station as the train was pulling up, and we said a quick and somewhat uncomfortable goodbye. I wasn't sure whether the S.O.S call was legitimate or not, but I knew that would be the last time I saw Gemma. I reflected on what had happened that evening long into the night, I couldn't see how anyone would accept my life and how I was living it. I'd been chosen by the spirit world to become a shaman, but I was from Oxford, one of the world's centres of academic learning that definitely wasn't famous for its spirituality. I felt like a lonely old soul that was misunderstood and out of step with the rest of the world.

The next morning, I woke up to find a message from Gemma on my phone.

'Ben, thank you for the lovely food, you really are a great cook. I've been thinking about what you said yesterday and your views on the world, and I've concluded that you're bat shit crazy and I urge you to seek medical help. Please don't contact me again, goodbye Gemma.'

Some days you wake up to bad news and it ruins your whole day, and this was one of those days. I felt crushed, sad, defeated and above all I felt totally undesirable. She had stuck the knife in deep and crushed my confidence. I went downstairs to make a cup of tea and as I opened the fridge to get the milk, I saw a magnet on the fridge door which read, 'Undesirable Number 1 – Harry Potter.'

I laughed spitefully out loud and said to my spirit guides, 'Yes, very clever. I don't know how you're getting all these symbols to show up at the exact moment that's significant, but you are, and I'm impressed. But maybe instead of being so smart with the signs, you can send me someone to love instead!'

I stirred my tea, and felt an anger rise up inside me. Who would want to date me after I'd been through all of this and seen through the veil of reality? I was seeing the world through new eyes, and when I explained to people how I saw it, and what was currently happening in my life, they either acted like I'd gone completed mad, or immediately shut me out. In that moment, standing there in a stranger's kitchen, it just seemed as if there was no place for me; I felt like an outcast. I would later read that it was a common experience of the shaman, throughout history, to feel alone and disconnected from mainstream culture.

I replied to Gemma with a heavy heart, 'Thank you for your honesty, I'm sorry you feel that way. Good luck finding the right person. I hope I haven't put you off of dating. I'm not crazy by the way.'

I got no reply.

I was low and feeling vulnerable; I'd been knocked down and felt like I needed help to get back up. I was the type of man that was happiest when I was in a committed and loving relationship, it was natural for me to be supportive, thoughtful, and loving, and I gained strength when I had a woman standing beside me. I hoped my destiny was not to be single, no, I was determined to find my life partner; I knew she was out there somewhere. I would find the love of my life, and together we would help each other find wholeness. I knew she was out there, she had to be. I turned inwards and connected to source through meditation, and was guided to go out with my camera to the nearby town of Rotherham.

The weather was gloomy, it wasn't the type of day that I would normally go out to take photos but I followed the inner wisdom anyway. I parked at the top of a hill in Rotherham, and found my way down towards the town centre. I scoped out the coffee shops as I walked, looking for options to sit during my break later. I heard a busker singing outside the train station nearby; she was singing a song about faith and allowing God into your heart. She had a lovely voice, I admired her confidence and fortitude so I put a pound coin in her collection box and sat nearby to hear more. But instead of singing another song she walked straight towards me, I thought she was coming to say something to me, but her stuff was close by, and she was packing up for the day.

'Thank you for the song, it really touched me.' I told her.

She forced a smile and thanked me; I could then see she had tears in her eyes and was visibly upset.

'Are you okay?' I asked.

Sometimes the kind word of a stranger can open something up in us.

'No, not really.'

A tear ran down from her eye, and she wiped it away. I just wanted to give her a big hug.

'Do you want to talk it through with someone?' I suggested.

She nodded with the trace of a small smile of gratitude.

'Okay, then let me buy you a coffee and some cake.'

I smiled, and she smiled back, she was a similar age to me, with a kind, attractive and natural face.

'I'm Ben by the way. Do you know where we can grab a good coffee around here?' I asked.

'No, I don't know the town. I've just come up for the day on the train. I'm Abbey,' she said introducing herself.

I'd seen a coffee shop at the top of the hill near a church, so we walked their together. I helped her carry her gear, and she started to tell me why she was feeling melancholy. It turned out she felt guilty for having sex with a man outside of marriage and had decided to end the relationship even though she really liked him. She was broken hearted and stricken with grief. I struggled with the concept, as my understanding of God and the spiritual world didn't adhere to this no sex before marriage ideal.

We got to the café, and I told her to choose a piece of cake to go with her coffee, so she picked a big piece of coffee cake, which did look delicious, so I joined her, after all I needed cheering up too. She told me she was religious and had invited God into her life; and in doing so she no longer felt alone. She told me how much love she felt for God and how he radiated through her in everything she did, including her singing. The man she'd fallen in love with wasn't religious at all and so in her mind she couldn't be with him. I could see she was clearly so bitterly torn between God and the man she loved. I felt sorry for Abbey, I couldn't help but think her religious beliefs were stopping her from finding the happiness she deserved. I thought about how the spiritual teachings I received from my guides differed so much from her belief system; guilt and shame just didn't come into the equation for me. My guides often taught me that sacred lovemaking was a way to strengthen my connection with the divine; like in the teachings of Tantra, I was taught that sacred sex could bring us powerful energy and help us to become more whole within ourselves.

This wasn't a chance meeting; I knew that deep down; I knew I was here for us to share our stories and learn from each other. I tried to find the words to connect with her, using her language and perspective; I told her that I didn't believe that God would want her not to be intimate with the man she was in love with, that I thought that God would want her to be happy. I spoke about the possibility of opening up her heart chakra, and as soon as she heard the word chakra, she immediately tensed up.

'I'm not interested in anything involving the occult,' she said sternly.

I then realised she was completely blocked off to anything outside of her religious perspective, so I listened instead, knowing my understanding of the universe would be lost on her and unwelcome. I was still curious as to what I could learn from her, and by the end of our coffee and conversation I'd learnt, or rather been reminded, about the controlling nature of some religions regarding all things spiritual. It made me sad as I knew of the incredible wisdom we could tap into by exploring spiritual and religious practices from all perspectives across the world and throughout history, as to widen our minds and our possibilities. Through Abbey I was seeing anew the influence that some religions had on the way we experience the spiritual world, and how some people accepted the doctrine without questioning the teachings, and then suffer the consequences.

Once I was back in Worksop, I gave Jo a call and told her about my train smash date with Gemma, which she'd been excited to hear about. She said her heart sank for me and told me how sorry she was. She then affirmed that I was desirable, and the only issue was that I didn't fit into the average woman's view of the world. I asked her if she wanted to come to the house and eat with me that evening, and she said she'd be happy to. After our chat on the phone, Jo immediately sent me a lovely message saying how lucky any woman would be to have me in their life; that she didn't know anyone as self-aware as I am and that I would find the perfect woman for me without a doubt. Her message was just what I needed, she was offering me such incredible support and I knew how lucky I was to have her in my life.

I decided to rustle up something special and delicious for Jo for dinner, so I set about preparing various Spanish tapas for our meal. As I was cooking, I managed to burn my arm on the oven, leaving a burn mark the size and shape of a leech. When I saw it, I immediately thought about Emily in the book, as I was currently rewriting a section where she'd been burning off leeches on her body that the doctor had put on her to help bring down her fever. Another scene was playing out in front of my eyes, and this one hurt!

As I waited for Jo to arrive, I put some music on and browsed through the bookshelf. I was drawn to a copy of the Wizard of Oz and started thinking about Dorothy and the three characters she travelled with. The book represented a journey to another dimension where these characters were each on their own hero's journey; facing their weaknesses and fears in order to grow. The scarecrow had to find his heart, the tinman his brain, the lion his courage and Dorothy her home. It felt symbolic; I was having to find the courage to be my authentic self, I was having to connect deeply to matters of the heart in order to draw in my true soul mate, I was letting go of a mind filled with old, programmed beliefs to see the world from a new perspective, and like Dorothy, I had no home whilst traveling on the hero's journey. Samuel Russell, the antagonist in my novel showed up three times, and each time he tried to kill Arthur. Maybe that meant I'd have three battles to overcome too; the scarecrow representing my heart, the lion my courage and the tinman my mind. I would soon discover that my suspicions were correct; that was exactly what was going to happen.

Jo arrived and we chatted over the leftover camembert about the possibility that what we were experiencing was an inner journey of self-discovery; where each challenge the characters in my book faced, was a challenge we would have to face in order to grow. Like the metaphors in the Greek myths of old, we were in our own story facing our own inner demons. We both decided the theory was a good one and made sense; we were being challenged and we were learning and growing as a result.

Jo then told me her news; her date with Ben had also taken a turn for the worse. We'd both allowed ourselves to get really excited about potential new partners, and both been disappointed. The similarities were growing, our stories were matching, it seemed what happened to me was also happening to her. The coincidences were stacking forever higher. We also both had noticed that strange signs involving World War 2 kept revealing themselves to us.

Jo had rewritten the scene in my novel where Tom had originally been killed. In her new version he had defeated the enemy, Samuel Russell, who'd then escaped into the woods. I felt relieved that story had been amended, as I was getting so worried that something terrible might happen to Jo. I was mistakenly of the view that we could undo what had already been written, but all we were effectively doing was adding more to manifest, not removing what had been already been written into our future.

We had a lovely evening together; we chatted, we laughed, and we tried to figure out what was happening to us. What could we write into the new version of the book that would improve both of our lives? Could they find money? Could they find love? Of course, anything was possible, so we chatted about how it would all fit. In the original story Arthur would fall in love with Caroline a young woman he'd meet in Gloucester, but he would end up leaving her back in 1643 when he eventually time travelled home, back to his old life in the future. There was no mention of a girlfriend in the book for his friend Tom, so Jo had taken the liberty of writing one in for Tom, by repeatedly speaking to Arthur about his girl back home. We spoke about how we could one day write a book about the rewriting of Arthur Archer, and the ordeals we went through whilst reworking the book, it seemed like a great idea for a future project.

We both made a deal with each other to not give up and get dating again, so we reactivated our apps and giggled whilst showing each other the other side of the dating world. I showed Jo how women presented themselves, and Jo shared with me what my competition was up to. It was eye opening for the both of us, we laughed and shared a fun evening together.

Chapter 7

The Frenzy

I'd been chatting to a woman called Tali for a couple of days on the dating app, she lived between where I was and where I was headed, so we decided to meet for lunch on my way to my next pet sit. I arrived at the pub in good time, so I sat down with the menu waiting for her to arrive and studied the art on the walls, checking if there were any messages or signs to guide me, and there were plenty of trees and animals on the walls to decipher. Tali arrived with a big smile on her face, she was a teacher who taught at a local primary school. She was short with black hair worn in a bob. She looked lovely and as we started getting to know each other, she told me with passion about the children she taught; it was obvious she loved what she did for a living.

As our conversation opened up it became more and more interesting; Tali told me that whilst she was living in Germany, she'd twice ended up in a building the day before a massacre had occurred in that very same place and what was even more fascinating was that both times she had felt the energy of the massacres before they had actually happened. My heckles were up, I suspected that this was by no means a chance conversation. I was looking for meanings in everything nowadays, and whilst waiting for her to join me at the pub I'd done a Google search of her name, and discovered that Tali in Hebrew meant dew. I'd written a character into my book with the name of Dew. My character Emily had met Dew inside an oak tree, and here Tali was in a pub named the Royal Oak. Tali was telling me about a massacre, and in the book, Dew told Emily about how Arthur was stuck in the middle of the Civil War and was in great danger. I was convinced I was being given clues as to something, but I still didn't have enough pieces to put it all together. Maybe it was simply another manifestation from my book, but my senses told me it was more than that.

We both ordered food, and chatted about dating. We were getting on, it was easy, and she was fun. Before long, our lunch was over, so we both sipped our coffees slowly to make our time together last a little longer. I was in no hurry to leave; we were having a lovely time, and it felt good to feel connected to someone. But time was ticking, and I had to get to the Forest of Dean, which was still a couple of hours away. We said goodbye, and both left it open as to whether we would see each other again.

I drove to the Airbnb, in the heart of the Forest of Dean, where I was staying for one night until I could move into the pet sit. It was dark when I arrived and was met by the couple who owned the property. They were friendly, very welcoming and showed me to my room that had an ensuite. It was a comfy room; there was a sofa bed, and a few books on the bookshelf. They recommended a local country pub just a short walk away, as there were no cooking facilities available at the Airbnb. I looked for signs in the room; there was a book on the history of Jerusalem which caught my eye, it seemed that every house I'd stayed at so far had a book on either Jerusalem or Israel. I'd just had lunch with a lovely Jewish lady, and so far there had been considerable links to Judaism on my journey as a shaman. I wanted answers, I needed to understand what all these connections meant. I picked the book up from the bookshelf and asked my guides to explain what the significance was. I channelled into the book as I would the dictionary, closing my eyes and opening the book to a page which read '1099 the 6th of June The first massacre of the Jews and Muslims by the Crusaders'. And then my inner knowing suddenly kicked in, was this a repeating cycle? Could the death of the Jews and Muslims in 1099 be the first cycle, and World War II the 2nd cycle? And there were the two massacres Tali had told me about, at lunch. I sensed there was to be a third cycle, was I being warned about something terrible that was about to happen in the world? Is that what this was all about?

I needed a beer. I'd gone without drinking for a while, but this shook me up, so I decided to take myself down to the local pub for some food and a pint. Off I went with my phone torch leading the way, as the roads in the forest were pitch black. I found the pub; it was a typical old English country pub and it felt cosy and warm. I tried samples of the local beers and chose one I liked, settling down with the menu and my phone. My dating app was buzzing with new likes; it seemed that whenever I'd arrived in a new part of the country my profile would attract attention from the local women in that area. I ordered a beetroot burger and chips; I was still avoiding meat but occasionally having a little fish. The burger was hard to eat, falling apart as I tried to eat it; it was disappointing and tasteless so I gave up and settled back into my chair looking at the women that had shown interest in me on the dating app. I sipped my local ale feeling content and relaxed after a long day.

Felicity, Elizabeth, Hannah, and Laura had all pinged up on my phone. I read through each of their profiles, and they all seemed interesting and attractive, so I swiped right and matched with all of them. It felt like something was shifting; perhaps now I could find a woman to bring into my life and put the disappointment of what had happened with Gemma behind me. I always felt more complete when I was in a secure relationship; my heart yearned to be close with someone, to be in love and feel supported once again. I didn't want to do this journey on my own, I wanted to dance with someone in the kitchen whilst cooking delicious food, with belly laughs and sacred intimacy that was more than sex but a connection of souls.

I began a conversation with Elizabeth, she was a lab technician with curly brown hair and a nice, kind face. Our conversation was easy, and we found plenty to talk about. She had mentioned on her profile that she was interested in learning about tantric sex, I was also keen on exploring tantra, and it was important to me that I found someone who wasn't embarrassed about their sexual side, or talking about physical intimacy. I believe that sexuality is a big part of who we are, it's natural and a powerful aspect of union, and if we want to feel whole and connected to source, then being in a close an intimate relationship with a partner contributes a long way in helping us find that wholeness and happiness in our lives. I found it refreshing that Elizabeth could chat so openly about that part of her life right from the first conversation.

Just then I received a message from Jo.

'What date did you go through the time portal? I feel like the date has an important significance somehow.'

And then another text message from Jo,

'You are such a gift to any partner. Your self-awareness is tenfold higher than 99% of the rest of the planet. Reread that, as this is such a unique gift that you provide to any future love. It allows for open honest communication, to reach higher levels of intimacy and spirituality and bypasses the fights where you trigger each other's past traumas. Don't ever forget what you have to offer Ben.'

It was the nicest thing anyone had ever said to me, and I immediately sent her a message back thanking her. It would have been so much easier if we'd have found each other attractive; we could have potentially made a great couple.

I wasn't sure if I'd be able to remember the exact day I'd experienced my shamanic journey into the tree, when the birds called from the dictionary and the white van pulled to a halt on the verge right in front of me. Then I remembered, I sold a photo that same morning of a white van, I just needed to look back through my photo sale records online and I'd find the date of my shamanic journey as Jo had requested. I logged into the picture library and found the date, the 6th of June 2021. I felt like that date was something I'd just read about, and it was; earlier that evening I had discovered the date of the first massacre in Jerusalem was on the 6th of June 1099. Jo was bringing this to my attention, within two hours of me discovering the very same date in a book at a pet sit. Things were speeding up; things were unfolding so quickly I was struggling to keep up with the meaning of what was being revealed to me. It was becoming overwhelming. I sat there staring at the huge clock on the wall and felt time ticking away.

I sent Jo a message about the 6th of June, and the repeating cycles with 1099 and World War II, but she couldn't follow the significance. She couldn't see anything there; she wasn't seeing the links and synchronicities like I was. I started to realise that I was operating at a heightened sense of awareness, and had to accept that others wouldn't be able to keep up with me.

So much was happening, I had to make sure I kept tabs of all of it, so I set up my laptop and tried to write down as much as possible. It all felt relevant and important; there was just too many connections popping up. I was relieved to get it out in writing as I couldn't keep all the synchronicities and signs in my head, there was just too much of it. Then I realised, in my book Emily kept a journal, it was called the 'Diary of a Queen's Maid', I'd just reached that bit whilst editing the book. I needed to write down as much as I could about what was happening to me. Emily felt it would be important somehow and so did I.

I tried to sleep, but it was hard, the huge clock on the wall ticked loudly and there was no way to stop it. The bed was also very uncomfortable and my mind was spinning with all the messages I was receiving. I tossed and turned, and tried to make sense of my life. I only managed to get a small amount of sleep and could feel it was the beginning of my insomnia returning, and me losing control of what was happening to me. I imagined a surfer riding the crest of a huge wave, doing his best to stay on his surf board.

The following morning, I woke early, I got out of bed and gazed out the window in perfect time to see the sun rise over the Forest of Dean. It was spectacular, full of pastel shades of orange, reds and blues over a lush countryside of rolling trees. I reached for my camera and took some photographs, but I already knew that no photo could do the scene justice.

Whilst showering I helped myself to the guest shower gel which resembled green slime, and as I rubbed the green slime all over my body, I chuckled, realising that the day before I'd been writing about my character Emily looking at her naked body covered in green puss; the impact of the plague on her young body.

I picked up the phone and called Jo, we chatted whilst I dressed and packed up my stuff.

Jo told me she'd be rewriting the forest scene later that day, where Arthur and Tom find their way from the battle at Roundway Down to a shack in Kingswood, where they get kidnapped by a madman who poisons Tom and tries to perform experiments on both of them. She'd decided she would rewrite the journey to the shack, and instead they'd be foraging for food when Tom falls and badly hurts his leg. We'd both decided it was safer to make the scene less traumatic and easier for the characters to find a way out. Although our efforts would make no difference to the eventual outcome in our lives.

I loaded up the car and went to say goodbye to the lovely hosts, when the husband interjected with a warm smile,

'Would you like to join us at church this morning? We're doing a reading for Remembrance Day?'

I didn't have time, I needed to be at my next house for the handover before they headed up to Scotland for their holiday. I thanked him, declined politely, and said goodbye.

I'd forgotten it was Remembrance Day, the day when the country paused to reflect and remember those lost in the world wars. Here I was again, being reminded of the repeating of cycles. I got in my car and picked out a cd, it was one I'd made twenty years before and I hadn't listened to it for many years. Before leaving Dorset, I'd found it in a box of old things at my parents' house, it had the words Pink Floyd written on it, I'd been drawn to it that morning and popped it on now. The first track that played had air raid sirens and bombs going off, it was 'Goodbye Blue Sky'. It sent shivers down my spine, and my hairs on my neck stood on end. I suddenly had the feeling of impending doom. The synchronicities were flying at me like bullets, and all I could do was observe them and write them down. The next song was 'The House of the Rising Sun,' and whilst it played, I drove past a pub called the 'House of the Rising Sun.' Even a simple car journey of just thirty minutes had signs and meanings, everything was talking to me. I felt like the world was suddenly more like a dream, and my energy was like a magnet to the inconceivable. I was scared, I was overwhelmed.

I pulled up in Lydney, a small town on the west bank of the River Severn, I'd made it in good time. The house was neither modern nor old, but it was large. I knocked on the front door and was greeted by a lovely couple. They were behind on their schedule, Jane, was still busy vacuuming the house to leave it nice and tidy for me. As she cleaned, Mike showed me around and gave me my instructions; the cats were normally free to come and go, but he preferred that they were kept in whilst they were away. He'd locked the cat flap with some parcel tape. He seemed to be a cautious man, and clearly the cats were loved and he didn't want to risk losing them. Two of the cats were pedigree, a brother and sister, and the third was a regular old moggy who didn't like the other two posh cats one little bit. Mike explained that I would need to segregate the cats whilst I was there. He told me I was allowed to let the two pedigree cats out the back door but had to make sure I'd got them in if I went out. He assured me they'd come with a simple call. But the moggy still needed to be kept in at all times, which meant I needed to keep the windows closed. I felt sorry for the moggy not having the same freedom as the other cats, but it was there house, and I would do exactly as instructed.

Mike then showed me around their large garden; he was a keen gardener and had vegetables growing, ready to eat.

'Whilst you're here Ben, you're welcome to help yourself to anything. You can have food from the pantry, and you can forage in the garden for anything you want – in fact I encourage you to do so.'

Immediately I realised the significance of his words, I was to forage here in the Forest of Dean, at the same time as my characters were also in the Forest of Dean foraging for their meals in the section of the book I was currently working on, which meant I'd caught up with my book, and was in real time. As Jo and me worked on the rewrite, things that were happening in our lives were matching exactly the part of the story we were working on.

Mike introduced me to the cats.

'Here they are, this is Leopard, Bear and Owl.'

The three spirit animals that joined me on my journey were the owl, the leopard and the bear. I was heading to the section of the book where Tom and Arthur were tortured, experimented on, and seriously tested by a mad man. And here I was with my spirit guides telling me they were right there with me to help me through what was coming. Yet another remarkable coincidence. I was truly amazed by the details the spirit world were putting on for my benefit.

The couple left a little flustered, and I unpacked whilst I brewed a coffee. I called Jo and updated her on what had happened. She told me she'd cut her leg on a walk in the woods, which matched Tom's experience, only thankfully less severe. She was also now in real time with the novel's events! It was unnerving as the characters were about to be captured by a madman. Jo emailed me the latest part of the book that she'd worked on, I thanked her profusely, and then roamed around the big house looking for messages hidden among books and pictures. The place was a treasure trove of signs. Me wandering around the house for signs, reminded me of the ancient shamans who would read messages in the clouds, or the flight of birds, or even the entrails of dead animals. Now, in a very different modern world, the universe was still able to communicate in all kinds of weird and wonderful ways, but how many people were aware enough to even notice the signs they were being given? People continually ask for answers but are oblivious to the fact that they're being provided with answers that they aren't opening themselves to see. The house was full of Second World War pictures and books, the hallway had Lancaster Bombers framed all the way up the stairs. And at the top of the stairs was a picture of Doctor Who's time-traveling Tardis, flying through the streets of London!

The bookshelf in the large sitting room was also full of significance, each book seemed to have a meaning, many connecting to the world of magic. A rare old copy of Thomas Hardy's the 'Trumpet Major' stared out at me, and I'd just finished the section in the book where Arthur had left his drumming major and escaped the battle scene. I needed to end this rewrite so I felt a little safer going forward. I'd let the universe throw my life into chaos, but I needed to feel a bit more in charge of my destiny. So, I decided I would quickly rewrite a new ending to the book, pulling Jo and I out of the rabbit hole we found ourselves falling deeper and deeper into. I brewed myself a second coffee and set up my computer up, and aimed to finish the new ending during my week there in the Forest of Dean.

I was naïve to think it would make any difference. Every crazy and extreme experience I was going through was part of my shamanic training to prepare me for what was to come next. And here I was in the middle of it, struggling to keep my perspective in check. Events were happening so quickly, and just to process all that was going on was exhausting and exhilarating all at the same time. I felt like I was living in a lucid dream in the waking world, I was experiencing life out of the ordinary. The events coming up in the rewrite of my novel included the death of a friend, torture of them both and the both Emily and Arthur almost losing their own lives. Was all that what I was heading towards?

Elizabeth, the lab technician with curly brown hair, sent me a message; she was free that evening and asked if I wanted to join her for a meal. I asked her where she lived, she said Gloucester. I realised that in the book, Arthur met and fell in love with Caroline whilst he was in Gloucester, and I was just about to reach that part of the book in the rewrite. That felt exciting, positive, could Elizabeth be Caroline from my novel? Was I about to fall in love with a strong-minded woman who was into me, who took the initiative in the relationship like Caroline had, when she'd kissed Arthur for the first time?

I decided that before I met Elizabeth that evening, I'd rewrite a quick happy ending where Arthur, Emily, Tom and Rebecca all had long, happy and successful lives. I'd then close the book, leave it be and stay well away from the sequel. The last thing I wanted was to experience Roman slavery, being left for dead twice and taking on the might of Rome on the back of a chariot with just a bow and arrow!

Of course, what I wanted, and what the spirit world had planned for me, were two different things. A shaman doesn't choose to be a shaman, the path chooses him. The shaman doesn't get to decide that it's too difficult and say, 'Thank you spirit world for all the effort, but please can someone else take my place, as this is not everything it's cracked up to be.' And then happily go back to their ordinary life and live out their days. Nope, sadly it doesn't work like that. The spirit world is an all-powerful relentless master that will get its way in the end, or the shaman's life will simply cease to be.

I tried to write but felt utterly exhausted, after being sleep deprived from the loud ticking giant sized clock the night before. I had a date with Elizabeth later and it was quite a long drive to meet her, I needed some beauty sleep first, so I closed up my computer and lay in bed. But I was too tired to sleep, so I mediated for a while then got up and had a shower to freshen myself up. The two posh cats had gone outside, I'd need to get them in before I left for our date. I called Jo to ask for some advice, as I felt like I wasn't handling this whole dating thing effectively. I was hopeful that this one would go well, but I'd felt the same with Gemma, and she ended up telling me I was mad and should seek medical assistance.

I tried to get the cats back in, I used the little squeaker Mike had been given me which he assured me always made them immediately come home, but the little buggers didn't come back. The garden was big, and I wandered around with a torch in the early darkness of the evening. Thankfully I found Leopard hidden under a rhubarb plant, and Bear chilling out in the wooden shed. I got them both in and drove to the restaurant, Elizabeth was getting out of her car just as I arrived, and I must have given her a strange look as she immediately asked me if I was okay?

'I'm fine,' I said, 'I just didn't sleep last night, so I'm tired. But it's lovely to meet you.'

The restaurant was old fashioned and quiet, we were sat in a section on our own which had very little atmosphere. We chatted and spoke about our lives. Elizabeth recounted a story from her travels to Australia when she was in her twenties; she told me she'd been caught in a riptide and sucked out to sea, that she was about to die but the ocean gave her back her life and spat her out onto the beach. Here we go again, I thought, now what's the meaning here? She went on to say that this moment had caused a huge impact in her life, that she was convinced she was supposed to die that day, and because she didn't, she had sunk into a deep depression. She told me that she yearned to return to source, to go to heaven, but knew she had an unknown role to play out in her life first. I thought about my book and knew there was a connection. I remembered, in my second novel the only other person to travel through time in the tree, was Mr Bloise, a history teacher; he'd gone back in time and saved a woman from drowning, someone he'd end up having a relationship with. The conversation, and my thoughts, also took me back to the moment when I walked into the North Sea and spoke with the spirit of the ocean. Had Neptune travelled through time to save Elizabeth, so she could play her role in the prophecy written within my novel? It was all too surreal, but then so was everything that was happening in my life.

As the evening came to a close, we settled the bill and walked back to our cars. There in the car park lit up by the moonlight, and just like in my novel, Elizabeth leaned in for a kiss, and I accepted it. It was soft, romantic, and sweet, and we looked into each other's eyes and said goodnight. On the drive home I replayed that kiss a dozen times; the taste of her mouth, the fullness of her lips, and the way she had held me. But despite that romantic embrace, I wasn't sure she was the woman for me.

I got back to the house exhausted, and checked my phone to find a message from Felicity who I'd also recently met on the dating app. She'd come across my website, read my blogs on the environment and wanted to say well done for being such a powerful eco-warrior. The compliment felt good, it made me proud and massaged my ego considerably. We had so many similarities; she was fascinated with ancient spiritual practices, had a passion for the environment, practiced shamanism and was also a spiritual life coach. She had vast knowledge of ancient Egypt and symbolism. We decided we definitely needed to meet up, and I suggested she pick a location between the two of us. I felt a connection to her, but I'd also just had a really lovely night with Elizabeth, I felt drawn to both of these women; like each of them had something to share with me, even if it wasn't romantic. I needed to find a way to just let everything play out. I decided I'd go on a couple of dates with each of them and go from there.

Despite the continuing insomnia, I felt slightly more rested the next morning and started the day with a run. Whilst on my run I'd received a message from Felicity to say she'd be thinking about me all night and couldn't sleep, that she'd tapped into my sexual energy. Elizabeth messaged me to say she had enjoyed the kiss and couldn't wait to see me again. And finally, another woman I had previously matched with, Laura, messaged that she wanted to meet me in person, but she didn't drive so I should come and meet her in Bristol.

It was a welcome distraction from my troubles, my shamanic training, and my fears. Perhaps one of these ladies would be the one I was searching for and lead to something meaningful? Could one of these ladies be my Caroline? What I didn't realise at the time was they all would play a role in my story.

Elizabeth, who I'd kissed in the car park the night before, agreed to meet up again before I left the forest. I suggested she find some time in her diary and I'd do my best to make sure I was free.

I took myself out into the forest and walked for miles through the tall autumnal trees. It was so cleansing, and I needed it; I needed to ground myself and clear my head. I had the forest to myself as I so often did and wondered why I didn't meet more people on my country walks. The air was fresh, and I tried to clear my head by breathing it deeply into my lungs.

Once back at the big house I spoke with my guides through a shamanic journey, and they gave me instructions to cleanse myself; they wanted me to fast, and they wanted me to have a bath and take all of my crystals in the bath with me. So, I filled the bathtub and placed twenty or so of my crystals into the water. As I soaked, I felt truly relaxed for the first time in days. The bathroom was full of house plants which created a nice natural ambience, and I almost fell asleep. After a little while I pulled myself out the tub and wrapped myself in a warm fluffy towel. I noticed there was some black gunk at the bottom of the bath and knew it had come from within me; that the crystals had somehow sucked out a black tar like substance from my skin. It was bizarre, it was gross and I was glad it was out of me. I put the crystals on the windowsill to recharge. I followed my guides suggestion about fasting, and stopped eating, realising that where I was in the rewrite of the book was when my characters were starving in the forest.

It was all connected.

That night I couldn't sleep again, but just as I was about to finally nod off, the cat called owl decided to climb on top of my chest and make his bed there. I'd been warned about him wanting to sleep on me, but it felt comforting, so I left him there. I just didn't have the heart to move him. He slept on me for a couple of hours before I eventually put him outside the room, so I could actually get some sleep. I realised later that even that moment with the cat matched the scene in the book that I was working on; Arthur was tied up and couldn't move or sleep. The cat had played his role too.

The following day I was checking out the map to see where I actually was, and discovered I was actually in a place called Kingswood, and my characters in the book were also in Kingswood! I was exactly in the location where I had got to in the rewrite; it was an incredible coincidence and it was taking me to the edge of reality, which instinctively I knew was where I needed to be in order to understand what it meant to be a shaman. I asked for some guidance through the dictionary, and the answer I got was that I was at university. I was learning how to be a shaman and this test wasn't for the faint-hearted, it was pushing my boundaries of what I believed to be possible. The guidance told me I was safe, but I could also fail, I needed to keep going, I needed to ride the wave. There was no giving up.

Jo called me, she was in a dark place. Her life was mirroring the place in the book where Tom was poisoned, tied up and in big trouble. I tried to lift her spirits; I told her it would pass, that we just needed to get through this section of the book. I needed to finish editing the ending of the book in the hope that would bring an end to it all, but the universe was keeping me so busy and distracted. I was deeply concerned about Jo, so I checked in on her throughout the day, but she ignored all my messages. I managed to rewrite the scene in the shack to make the escape simple; instead of burning buildings and being chased by angry dogs!

The following day I went to see Maggie, my friend I'd previously stayed with on my way to Glastonbury. It was a short drive to Bath from where I was, and we'd arranged to spend the day together. I hadn't slept well for days and must have appeared a little spaced out. She listened as I shared my adventures, learnings, and theories on what was happening to me. After lunch we sat with a coffee in her lounge and she offered to do a healing on me. I gladly accepted and lay still as she shone divine light through me. It was wonderful to have my friend do some healing work on me, and it wasn't long before I drifted off to sleep. It was the first time I'd slept peacefully for days; her house was a sanctuary for me in the midst of a whirlwind of craziness.

We walked into Bath and wandered through the old streets and then visited the cathedral. I sat and enjoyed the energy of the sacred place and prayed for support and guidance. We went for a drink afterwards, and all over the walls of the pub were pictures of soldiers matching the battle scene that Tom and Arthur had just experienced in the book.

On the way back to Maggie's we passed a shop selling handmade wooden animals and drums; we both bought lots of things in advance for Christmas presents, and I was drawn to a new drum for myself. It was bigger than the one I already had, and I just knew I had to buy it. Later my guides told me the new drum represented my promotion as a shaman, which matched Arthur's promotion in the book, by Sir William Waller. I was pleased, it felt like I had been given a pat on the back, I was staying on the surf board, but only just.

That evening I spoke with Hannah for the first time, I had attracted a lot of attention on the dating app since my arrival in the forest and was struggling to keep up. Hannah lived in Oxford and she told me she'd just ended a difficult marriage, and that they were sorting out the details of separation and divorce. I'd been there myself, so I could relate, they were dark days to get through. She then randomly asked me if I was Marc's little brother? There I was in the middle of the Forest of Dean, talking to a stranger I'd met on a dating app that knew my older brother! I told her that indeed I was his younger brother, and she told me she'd been one of Marc's school friends back in the day. She even remembered me as a ten-year-old boy! She told me she'd once been to my childhood house when I was at home. And then I remembered exactly who she was.

Hannah had been my first ever crush; the friend of my brother's that had come over and I was instantly enamoured with. As my powers of manifestation had increased, somehow I had been able to pull her back into my life. I remembered being back at Cutteslowe Park, watching her and her pretty friends sitting on the swings. It was the time of big hair, Bananarama and Human League. I remembered her and her friends were dressed up with bright makeup and short spiky hair. Like the bizarre coincidence of Jo's father happening to live on the street where I'd grown up on, now Hannah had entered my life again, with an even more powerful connection of being my very first crush. Immediately I knew we were supposed to meet, but I didn't know where it would lead me. She was now working for charity combating pollution and doing some great work globally; she matched with the type of partner I wanted in my life. I asked Hannah if she wanted to meet, and she said very much so. We arranged to meet on my way back from The Forest of Dean, we would have a drink together in a pub in Oxford.

Laura was a drama teacher who lived in Bristol. She had invited me to her city to have lunch with her. She'd seemed really sweet in our chats, she was a mother of two teenagers, living a good life and supporting her community. She was passionate about the environment and open to walking a spiritual path. We'd agreed to meet in a couple of days and, yet again, I also had no idea where it would take me. I was just trying to let the universe guide me, to be in the right place at the right time.

Elizabeth, who I'd kissed under the moonlight in the car park, sent through her suggestion for our second date; she wanted to go for a morning wild swim in a sacred lake she knew about. Of course she did! In my book, Arthur, Tom, and Caroline went skinny dipping in a lake and I'd just rewritten that section the day before, so as it was in the book, I knew I had to honour it. The idea of swimming in a freezing cold lake in England in mid-November did not appeal to me at all though, and it was also the same day I was meeting Laura for lunch in Bristol. I could go from one date to the next as it wasn't far out of the way and conveniently saved some driving time, so I agreed to both. But before that I still had my date with Felicity, and I had the forthcoming lunar eclipse to get through. It was all becoming too frantic; it was like I was driving a car on full throttle without ever considering taking my foot off the accelerator.

I broke my fast with food I'd foraged in the garden, I found beetroot and onions and fresh herbs. I cooked a beetroot soup which would last me a few days; it wasn't my finest work, but it fed me. That night, I slept badly, again, I sweated profusely all night and kept having to get changed, I must have drenched through three or four sets of clothes. I was so glad to see the morning. I was tired but felt sprightly enough. I took a shower, put on some clean clothes, and brewed a big pot of coffee. I sent Jo a message, and she replied saying she needed some space from me; what we had been going through was taking its toll on her, she was suffering from headaches and sickness and felt like she was heading towards a darkness that she couldn't avoid. As Tom was fighting for his life in the book, Jo was also fighting and she was shutting me out.

It was the night of the lunar eclipse, and everything felt more powerful, I was still experiencing a state of heightened awareness and didn't know if I would remain like this or if it was only for a short period of time. It was disorientating, it felt like I was connected to a deeper knowledge; like I had tapped into the energy and wisdom of the universe, like I had accessed a hidden part of our existence that a tiny few had access to. I could see and understand life, and myself, in a way I'd never experienced before. It felt amazing, enlightening, confusing and painful all at the same time. I needed to connect with my guides to get some guidance on everything that was going on, so I did a shamanic journey to the Upper World inside my mind. I was met by a guide I'd never seen before, he appeared to be a Native American; he was wearing the typical attire of a warrior and held a small tomahawk in his hand. We walked together in a forest, and he told me he was one of my guides but had only come now as I'd reached a new stage in my maturity and was ready for his teachings. I asked for his name, and he told me I could call him after his weapon, Tomahawk. We had a clear channel, and I felt comfortable and at ease in his presence.

'Can you tell me about Jo? I'm deeply concerned about her?' I asked him.

'Jo has played her role in your life for now. She needed to go through this experience with you. She will put this period down as an unfortunate adventure and shut the door on your relationship until she too has reached maturity on her path. Jo can become a powerful shaman if she wishes, but for now she wants to focus on herself and finding a partner so they can start a family.'

'Is there anything I can do for her?'

'Not now, but if she chooses to rekindle your friendship in the future, you can both begin again with a blank canvas and a new relationship. At this time, you're both actors in the story; both playing characters, and she played her role perfectly.'

'Can I also ask you, which one of these women I'm dating is the right choice for me?'

Tomahawk smiled and slapped my back jovially.

'Now where would the fun be in telling you the answer to that question? Just enjoy the journey and remember, try and stay up on that surfboard you're riding.'

And with that last comment he was gone.

I met Felicity at a pub at a mid-way point between us. I was looking forward to finally meeting her. We'd both driven an hour to get there, and the pub was on the outskirts of Chippenham. She'd arrived a few hours before me, and was working from her laptop on some copywriting she was doing for a client. She'd found a cosy spot in the corner of the old pub. She looked lovely; she had a radiant smile and her energy seemed to make her glow. We chatted easily and spoke of our interests in spirituality, ancient civilisations, and ancient wisdom. Her knowledge was greater than mine and I thoroughly enjoyed the opportunity to learn from someone who was walking a similar path; the fact she'd been on the path longer than I meant there was such a beautiful depth to her knowledge. I soaked up her wisdom and her company.

I couldn't help but notice the picture opposite me, above Felicity's head. It was an old photograph of a Victorian hot air balloon in a market square, with men in flat caps standing all around it. I also noticed a second photograph had been exposed over the top of it, I knew the technique from my college days. The image exposed on top was of a coastline with waves lapping along the beach. It looked like the ocean waves were lapping over the feet of the cloth-capped men standing by the hot air balloon. I pointed it out to Felicity and told her I thought it was a sign; that I believed we were there at this exact spot for a reason, and it had something to do with water rising and natural disasters.

She turned and studied the photograph too, and agreed with me.

'Look at what's written on the balloon, it says eclipse!' She pointed out.

The day after the eclipse, there's a message in front of me about rising tides, I put two and two together and read it as a warning that the eclipse was going to trigger some kind of natural disaster which would cause mass flooding.

We chatted more about it, studied the other pictures around us, and both agreed what we were seeing was a message. I was in my heightened sense of awareness, and it just felt true. I was enjoying Felicity's company, and the food was incredible; the best meal I'd eaten for some time, the fasting had certainly increased my appetite. I looked deep into her green eyes, leant across the table and we kissed. My heart skipped a beat, I liked her, there was something different about her. She was free, she was like me, we seemed to be kindred spirits. Our dinner drew to an end, I paid the bill, and I watched her from behind as we walked outside. She had auburn wavy long hair, and her pretty dress was thin and clung to her hips. I was momentarily mesmerised.

We walked back to her campervan, holding hands loosely. As we stood by her van on that dark country road, she pressed her body against mine tightly looking at me deeply, and then put her fingertips to my lips and touched them gently, as if studying them, before kissing me. Then without saying a word she opened the back of the van and led me inside; a little light came on inside to reveal her cosy nest. It was dark but the little light there lit her face perfectly, she had a strong nose with a light sprinkle of freckles dancing across her face. There were no expectations, no promises, just two souls in complete union with each other in the here and now. We snuggled up to each other, the heat from our bodies keeping each other warm and talked late into the night about our dreams, hopes and aspirations. I drove back to the forest late at night.

It had been a lovely evening but I was troubled by the signs I had seen in the pictures on the walls. I got back and plonked myself down on the comfy sofa, and saw on the wall opposite a huge piece of wall art which was a map of the world made out of triangular shapes of metal. As I studied the map I wondered if there was a message there too? It looked as if the west side of the world was facing the east in battle; North America was shaped like a rocket facing east, and the lamp by the sofa reflected light onto the artwork like a nuclear bomb hurling towards Eastern Europe. Could this be connected to what I'd seen with all the signs about war and the repeating cycles from Jerusalem? Or was I starting to read too much into everything?

The following day I took to the country roads and ran, and after a quick shower I was ready to get back to the rewrite of my book, I attempted to spend the rest of the day writing and adding more detail. I tried, but I was fading, although I'd slept a little the night before it definitely wasn't enough. The day flew by in a sleepy, barely productive, haze, and my thoughts were clouded. Felicity was on my mind; she'd made it clear she didn't want a relationship, just something light and casual, maybe I wouldn't even see her again. I knew not to get my hopes up. Dating was proving to be a rather complicated affair.

Chapter 8

The Long Night

That night all I wanted to do was fall into a long deep sleep, but I couldn't find any comfort in my bed. My body ached, and the pillows were either too soft or too hard depending on whichever way I rearranged them. I tossed and turned and knew the clock had passed midnight when the unexpected occurred; I was visited by a spirit. Without the need for me to do a meditation, a shamanic journey or go into a trance, I could hear it talking to me inside my head. It was same voice I heard when I listened to myself think, yet it wasn't me, it was more powerful and assured, it spoke with complete confidence and I understood that the intelligence behind the voice was coming from somewhere outside of me.

My awareness was already heightened, but this felt different, like I'd reached a new level; my connection with the spirit world had opened up even more, and I was about to spend the night having an extraordinary conversation.

'You can ask me as many questions as you like,' said the voice.

'Ok, I'm not sure what to ask but perhaps it will come as we speak,' I replied to the voice inside my head. There was obviously no need to speak my thoughts out loud, the intelligence could hear me perfectly.

'You've been noticing repeating cycles recently, haven't you?' The voice asked.

I will call the voice 'he' as it was using my own voice to communicate with me, although I know it had no obvious gender.

'Yes, I have been noticing cycles. As I experience something in the present moment, I recall a past incident that matches it. It flashes up in my head like someone showing me an old movie reel. But I also get a knowing that things I experience will play out again in the future. It has led me to question whether negative experiences in my past will be repeated somehow in my future? I also see my repeating cycles matching those of my father and both of my grandfathers,' I said.

'The experiences that were presented to your ancestors and their choices of what to do with those experiences were their own. And now you are getting to choose how you act with each repeating cycle. You need to follow your intuition each time, and not look to copy anyone or act the way you feel you 'should'. If you knew all the stories of your great grandparents and their parents, you would see repeating patterns and cycles there too. Yet in these times you live in, most people do not pay much attention to their ancestors so the wisdom they can gain is lost,' he explained.

'Do not be fearful of future events playing out. What is the point in worrying about what may never happen? You already know the power of thought; that you give energy to what you think about, and what can happen as a result. So trust in your path; trust that your guides will give you only the experience that is for your highest good.' He continued reassuringly, 'See the cycles as ripples in a pond. You may be in a ripple that had begun long before your birth, which increases in significance with each new ripple. Or you may be experiencing a new ripple for the very first time. The ripples can go backwards in significance as well as forward.'

It was mind blowing stuff and somehow, I felt I already knew the wisdom he was offering to me, but that I'd forgotten, and he was using words in my head to help me remember the truth that I already knew.

'I see that you have great concern about the plight of many of the species on the planet,' he said.

'Yes, I am, is there anything we can do?' I asked.

'Well, humans can do plenty, but they are not ready to act. There is not enough appetite within the people of the world to install the leaders to make the changes that are needed. You face mass extinction, and only the strongest species will survive on this current trajectory,' he paused for a moment to make sure I was keeping up, and then continued, 'The world is in a state of chaos, and it's begun to move towards a new epoch. This period of history will be painful, yet so is any profound stage of growth. Like within so without, I believe that is one of your favourite quotes, isn't it?' He said warmly, and I agreed.

'Well, just as you're having to let go of your old way of life in order to transform and grow, so is humankind needing to change. You may have accepted your fate, but the humans have still not found the willingness needed for their survival and evolution.'

The lessons went on throughout the night; Occasionally I would ask if I could sleep but I was told I didn't need to. I was taught how to manipulate time and how to expand it in order to gain as much time as I needed. He explained that the way we measure time influences how it works for us. However, time can be altered if we don't pay attention to it. It can be accomplished by switching off our phones, taking away clocks and our watches, and hiding any reference to time, including watching the sun move across the sky. If we didn't observe time so much then we wouldn't be governed by it; therefore, time would expand and shrink as we needed it to. The spirit asked me if I had noticed that I always arrived on time wherever I went. And yes, It was true; If I was ever late for any occasion, the person I was meeting was also late, and they would arrive apologetically, just after me. I was told this was because I had already been working with time. That was also the reason why I didn't wear a watch and I didn't even like a ticking clock.

The spirit taught me about our ancestors and the importance of respecting them by remembering and honouring them. I was also shown how important it was to respect our elders; we had reached a time in our civilisation that many of our elders were losing their place in the hierarchy of society. Instead of being respected for their wisdom and experience they were placed in care homes, deemed worthless to society, and left with little quality of life. I was told that I needed to listen to my elders and to respect their opinions; even if I didn't agree with their point of view, I should politely nod and simply not follow their advice rather than trying to prove them wrong or give them my opinion. This would be the way to improve my relationships with my elders and offer them the respect they deserved. Besides, by being receptive to their opinions I might actually learn something new. He went on to say that we try too hard to keep the elderly alive even when they have no quality of life.

The lessons became increasingly more complex as the night wore on; it was proving to be the most intense and interesting night of my life. As I just lay there in the dark, I was taught about astrology and how the position of the planets affected different aspects of life just like colours influence people. Apparently, colours have an energy that when combined with words, they have different impacts on peoples' choices. For example, if white is inside red in a brand logo, then it will have a different impact and energy than if it is the other way around. This, in some way, matches how the position of the planets work, in astrology; if one planet is surrounded by two others, its impact in astrology will either be mitigated or enhanced. Quite incredibly, colours worked the same way. I needed years to study what I was being taught in one exhausting night.

I returned the focus of the conversation on me as I needed further understanding of the situation I was going through at that time; it simply felt more important to me than how colours worked in certain combinations. I asked the reason why certain events had happened to me. I and was immediately shown some repeating cycles in my life as flashbacks.

I was told that I had experienced them in order to form my character or that they were small ripples to events which were yet to unfold. The spirit spoke of my car accident in Spain when my ex-wife had been driving and the car had rolled on the motorway. It ended up upside down in a ditch with us still inside. He said that the reason I was saved that day was because I had an important purpose to fulfil in my life. I found this interesting as it was at that point in my life, after the accident, that I began to have my first spiritual awakening which would lead me to leave my photography business and start building supportive communities.

I asked who it was I was speaking with. The answer he gave was that I could call him what I wanted: God, spirit guide, higher-self, an angel. It didn't matter as everything was all interconnected. We are all part of the same thing, a universal energy.

It was only when the sunlight came in through the window that I realised I'd been conversing all night with this guide. Morning had arrived, I hadn't slept but, surprisingly, I felt okay. I got in the shower, freshened up and threw a batch of laundry into the washing machine; I had sweated through most of my tee-shirts and was running out of things to wear.

I tried to make sense of what had just happened, it reminded me of the story of Solomon when he was visited by an angel in the night who imparted wisdom onto him. A lot of people throughout history talk of divine inspiration when they get new ideas that help transform the way we see the world. Perhaps this is how we discovered fire, how we discovered how to craft tools, plant seeds, and study the stars. Perhaps people of the ancient world had been visited in the night by the spirit world and were taught lessons that helped humanity move forward. Yet now, we may consider these moments as mental breakdowns or delusional behaviour. It is believed that we need to protect people and shut them off, from these rich, powerful and enlightening experiences by numbing them with medication.

I finished my coffee, packed my shorts and a spare set off clothes into a bag and headed off for my double header - a date with Elizabeth for a wild swim at the lake, followed by a date with Laura in Bristol. It didn't cross my mind to cancel the dates because of the extraordinary events of the night before. I had let go, I had allowed the universe to flow through me and as a result I was having the most extraordinary time. I was living every moment in the present; I was living a lifetime of deep rich experiences in one single year. I put on some driving music and headed out on to the open road, fully expecting something else incredible to happen next.

Elizabeth and I parked up alongside a country road near enough at the same time, we gave each other a hug. The last time I'd seen her we'd exchange a kiss in the pub car park illuminated by moonlight. She'd brought some fresh raspberries to nibble on, and a hot flask of tea for us to drink after our wild swim. As we walked towards the lake along a muddy nature trail, she told me that she didn't want me to skinny dip in the lake, and her comment caught me by surprise, as I had absolutely no intention of skinny dipping. But I did instantly remember that the characters in my book had all taken their clothes off when they'd bathed in the lake. Maybe she sensed that somehow? I told her that I hadn't planned to be naked, but was curious why she'd said it. She shrugged and said,

'I just had a feeling you would.'

She told me that she'd been to the very same lake the night before with her friends, and that they'd performed a ceremony to cleanse the lake. She told me how the lake was sacred and that at the end of World War Two the Americans who were stationed near there had dumped all of their old military vehicles into the lake, contaminating it. I listened carefully, trying to decipher the meaning of it all.

We found a spot near the edge of the water; it was definitely a cold

November morning as there was steam coming from the surface of the lake and our breath as we spoke to each other. She asked me about my plans after I'd finished rewriting my novel, I told her about the document I'd written and hoped one day to be able to share it with people and see if it could make a difference, somehow. She changed her clothes behind a tree, mirroring the passage in the book when Arthur looked the other way, and I did the same. I removed my clothing leaving just my running shorts on, like the day I'd walked out into the North Sea.

'I feel like I'm a character in one of your books,' she said giggling like a teenager.

I smiled and thought to myself, 'That's because you are'. It was strange, she'd suggested the activity, she had picked the spot, she was playing out the role of one of my characters and all I was doing was allowing it to happen. But if I told her about all the synchronicities, she would think I was crazy. So, I marvelled in the synchronicity alone, in the repeating cycle and the miracle of life when you see it for what it really has to offer. We were also in the same geographic location that my characters were having their swim.

I walked to the edge of the water and balanced myself along a fallen tree that was stretched out into the lake. I was cold, I didn't want to do this, but I knew I had to. She stood behind me watching me from the riverbank. And then, like the day in the North Sea, I knew what I was there to do; I was here to offer my cleansing of the lake. I stared into the lake, connecting to it and then without thinking about it I took off my ring which had been a gift from an ex-girlfriend who'd had it made especially for me in Canada. It had ancient sacred geometry carved across a silver band, and was something I treasured, but I instinctively took the ring off and hurled it into the water, offering it to the lake to help cleanse and protect it.

I watched the ring splash and disappear whilst I said a healing prayer quietly under my breath, and hoped it would make some kind of positive difference. I walked out a little further along the tree, it was slippery and damp, and I almost fell in. I looked out at the lake, it was so beautiful. I connected to my spirit animal the salmon and without too much thought I dived into the ice-cold water. Immediately I realised it was a lot colder than the North Sea! I swam out into the lake and tried to gain my composure, but I was shivering and could feel my body was in shock. Elizabeth watched on from the side and seemed to be laughing in delight at my misfortune.

'It's freezing, are you coming in?' I called out. She dipped her legs in and didn't look very keen, but nonetheless she was brave and joined me, gliding far more graciously into the water than I did. She had been here just the evening before, so she knew the iciness that was coming. She swam out towards me and we both swam to the centre of the lake.

'Your lips are turning blue. We should get back and warm up,' she laughed.

'You go ahead. I have something I need to do first,' I replied.

She turned and started swimming back. I spoke to the spirit of the lake and thanked it for the experience; I apologised for the dumping of the vehicles and swam back to Elizabeth who was now sat on the log wrapped in her towel. I was still in a heightened state of awareness, and even though I didn't fully understand what I instinctively wanted to do next, it felt important to connect our energies and to the lake. It felt like an integral part of the cleansing, so I asked her if I could connect to her energy, and we held hands with our legs in the water whilst we sat on the fallen tree. I moved the energy around our bodies through a visualisation, and allowed the energy from the both of us to flow into the lake. Afterwards we dried ourselves, got dressed and drank from the warm flask of sweet tea that Elizabeth had thoughtfully brought with her.

I told her I'd enjoyed myself, although I wasn't sure I had as it felt more like a freezing cold ordeal I'd had to endure. We chatted over the tea, and I noticed she kept looking at me in a strange way.

'I'm sorry but I'm just going to say how I feel,' she said uncomfortably.

'Go on.' I said, not knowing what was coming next.

'I think you're really interesting, although a little strange. But strange can be good, right! And even though I'm trying, I'm just not feeling it. I can't see us in a relationship. I'm sorry,' she said honestly.

I wasn't feeling it either, but had known she had brought me there by instinct, to fulfil the prophecy contained within my book. She had played her role perfectly and now she was bowing out, and handing the baton over to another.

I drove to Bristol to meet Laura, the drama teacher, and found a spot to park my car. All the recent events were really starting to take their toll on me, and I was tired and cold. I called Laura, she was already at the restaurant and she told me the directions so I could find my way there easily. I arrived a little worse-for-wear and unfortunately, she was seated at the only table that had been available which was outside on the terrace with an outside heater. It wasn't ideal, I'd been freezing in the lake and needed some warmth, and something hot and tasty inside me; I would have much preferred to be sat by an open fire, and not dining alfresco. We ordered scrambled eggs and coffee. I looked at her, and noticed she resembled a former girlfriend of mine called Kate; she wore the same style clothes, she had the same shoes and then as she described her life it reflected Kate's too. The family issues matched, and I was able to empathise with her because I'd lived through a similar time with my ex. I was transfixed by how similar their lives had been.

After lunch Laura walked me around Bristol; we went through quaint markets and listened to buskers and enjoyed the street art which gave the city its unique charm. I realised I'd been on the same route around Bristol once before, with my ex, Kate! I saw the repeating cycle and somehow it warmed me. In the street outside the cathedral was a bride laughing joyfully as people called after her in excitement taking photos. We went into the Cathedral; it was beautiful, timeless, and serene. My intuition then took hold, it told me that this was no chance visit. I saw my marriage to Maria in Spain, in Toledo. Laura took my hand, and as we walked up the aisle, I felt goose bumps all over my body. As we walked hand in hand, I saw my ex-wife's father walking beside us! He had died the previous year, but it appeared to me that he was not here as a spirit but incarnated in the flesh! He was literally there walking by us. Was I hallucinating? The man had his face, and he walked alongside us on the same side he had done at my wedding. I narrowed my eyes in fascination and watched him. Had I fallen off the surfboard at last? Was I losing touch with reality completely? I just stared at the incarnated man who I hadn't seen since my divorce. I had loved him; he had been a kind and generous man. I was sure that I wasn't hallucinating, and to this day I still believe it was him.

He walked off and I told Laura what I'd just seen, although it probably wasn't what you want to hear on your first date. I have no idea what she must have thought about me in that moment, but she was kind and didn't make me feel awkward at all. It wasn't the first time I'd seen him since he'd died; I'd seen him in a dream, waiting at a train station with other men, waiting to cross over. We left the cathedral and went for a coffee. I was trying to make sense of what had just happened to me, a preoccupation of an apprentice shaman I suspected. We chatted and despite my odd behaviour the date was going well; I'm not actually sure how I managed to hold it all together considering the current craziness of my life. I told her about what I had seen with Felicity in the double exposure photo on the wall of the pub, with the waters rising, as it was playing on my mind. I wanted to talk it through with someone who was objective and had a sympathetic ear, and that seemed to be Laura. She listened, and again she didn't judge me in anyway.

After our coffee we wandered through the streets of Bristol, and I started seeing the street art as messages and translating them for her. Each one was so rich in meaning, and so I began to I tell her a story using all the art work we came across, and they matched perfectly with the story I was creating. It was fun and we laughed, we'd had a charming day. Afterwards I realised this too was a scene from my book, Arthur being fascinated when he reached a 17th century market and marvelled at all the things everyone else saw as normal, and Caroline couldn't understand why he saw them as out of the ordinary, but it made her laugh too. Laura was now playing the role of Caroline, an ever-changing role. Everything was moving so fast and I needed to rest, I needed to sleep. I needed it all to just stop for a little while.

Our date finally came to an end; it had been enjoyable and eventful. I gave her a hug and thanked her for meeting me and headed back to the Forest of Dean. I got straight into bed and tried to sleep, but once again sleep didn't come. As Arthur and Tom were being tortured in the shack by a madman in my book, I was being tortured too – through sleep deprivation and experiences that were making me question my own sanity. So, I got up and looked around the house for more clues in the books, and kept seeing signs pointing to natural disasters. I was convinced something was coming, only I didn't know what or when. What should I do, should I warn people? Wouldn't they think me mad? I asked my guides through the pages of the dictionary and the message was clear, I had to tell my family, I had to warn them. I sighed deeply; I didn't want to tell them. I didn't know if I was right, and I really didn't want to make a fool of myself, especially to my family. I helped myself to a pie from the pantry as the sun was going down, it was my last night in the Forest of Dean, and I was ready to leave. I wanted to escape this crazy scene, just as Arthur did. I hoped I would get at least a little sleep that night, but sleep continued to elude me.

That evening I played my father at online chess. I was seeing the world with different eyes and as a result, even the chess board seemed different. Having lost the previous seven times to him without much of a fight, this time I'd been able to beat him effortlessly in just a handful of moves. He was caught by surprise and so was I; I wasn't just seeing signs clearly. I could actually play a game of chess better than I'd ever played before. I was a different version of myself. I was still in a period of heighten awareness and wondered whether I'd stay that way forever. I suspected this was part of the new me, and my life would never be normal again. But how could I sustain such a pace?

I called Jo to see how she was doing; she said she was still in a dark place and was really struggling. My sense was that we were moving through the uncomfortable scenario were almost out of it. However, after my characters had escaped the madman they went to the lake, which I'd already done, and they ended up being chased by other men also out to kill them! That's when Arthur's friend Tom met his fateful end, whilst Caroline and Arthur were spending the night out in nature. And that part had happened with Felicity in her campervan. It seemed that despite us writing a different ending, the book was still playing out in our lives. Jo told me she was taking some time off work, and just needed to be alone.

I was worried about the impending disaster I felt was on its way; my sense was it would be an earthquake triggered in Turkey, it was a leap, but that's what I was sensing. Although I was getting more signs about a war than anything else; everywhere I went there was a picture of a world war bomber, or another war sign of some sort. I decided to just tell people what

I'd seen and then update them if anything else came up. And then as I picked up my phone to call my brother, I received an email from myself; it contained an image of a huge wave and in is centre was the face of Neptune looking angry and fierce. I had seen the image a few years ago, it was on the news, and I'd forwarded it to my friend Maggie. Here two years later, at this exact moment in time, it had come back to me undelivered. It could have represented the metaphor of the wave I had fallen off, but I hadn't considered that then.

I pulled out my address book from my bag and as I did a piece of paper fell out. I looked at it; it was something I'd written a year before when I'd been teaching Beatrice about our ancestors and our family tree. Were my ancestors telling me to warn their descendants? I was left with little doubt that I would have to share my insights, regardless of how I felt, or if it made me sound like a crazy person.

I spent the morning calling my relatives. I told them that I'd seen something; I told them what I'd seen and that they needed to be safe. What I didn't know at that moment was that I was making a terrible mistake because I would be wrong, and word would get around that I'd completely lost my mind; everything was about to come crashing down around me.

I cleaned the house and started getting myself ready to go to Oxford to meet Hannah, I was looking forward to seeing my very first childhood crush after all this time. As I cleaned, I kept getting text messages from my relatives; people were becoming concerned about me, especially my ex-wife. They were chatting about me between themselves, and no one quite knew what to do. Word was spreading, had Ben actually lost the plot? My reputation was in freefall!

I wanted to write one last thing in the novel before I packed up, to add a little more protection to the story, and as I opened the book on my computer two words were randomly highlighted on the screen, they spelt out the words 'your face'. It made me stop dead in my tracks; two simple words but they contained so much meaning for me. In the midst of all that was happening, it was my grandfather's catch phrase, he'd said it over and over again 'Your Face.' And here he was with me just after I'd found the piece of paper containing my family tree, and a day after I'd seen my father-in-law in the cathedral in Bristol. I felt my grandfather's presence; I was close to my ancestors and even the ancestors of my ex-wife, I was close to the veil and crossing between the two worlds.

I was running late; the day had gone by so fast, so just like when I had first arrived to find the home owners vacuuming the house, they returned from their holiday and found me vacuuming too. I was feeling muddled and flustered, my life resembled a whirlwind and the weather outside matched my inner turmoil. I left soon after, heading off to meet Hannah, glad to put my experience in the forest behind me. It was raining, the sun was shining and in that moment on the country road, a rainbow appeared in the sky and shone in through the window of my car onto the passenger seat beside me. The end of the rainbow. Another miracle. I would later read in a book about rainbows finding shamans in such a way.

Thirty minutes later I got a call from Mike to say I'd gone off with the house key. So, I had to drive back and return the key to them, which meant getting to Hannah on time was going to be a stretch. As I started my journey to Oxford once again the navigation system in my car started to play up, and instead of taking me the more sensible route on main roads, it took me along dark narrow, winding country lanes. There were no streetlights, and I needed to concentrate hard, and then a deer ran out into the middle of road in front of me. My heart stopped in my chest as I swerved hard to miss it and smashed into the raised earth bank on my left.

The deer ran off unhurt, but my car was damaged, and I was bruised and badly shaken. I swore out loud. I needed to gather myself, I needed to calm down. I took out my shaman's blanket and wrapped myself with it as I stood at the side of the road; I felt angry, I knew I was being tested and I wasn't happy about it. The spirit world was creating scene after scene that pushed me to my absolute limit, and I felt like too much was being asked of me. I was exhausted and annoyed.

'This is your fault,' I shouted into the night sky at my spirit guides, 'You did this!'

I called my stepfather and asked him for his help, I needed to know how far I was from the nearest town because all I knew was that I was stuck on a dark country lane in the middle of nowhere. He worked out that I was only a ten-minute drive to Ross on Wye. I asked him to book me into a hotel there. I would see if I could drive the car there in one piece, and if it wasn't possible then I'd call the roadside breakdown service. He kindly booked me into a hotel, and I drove my damaged car timidly into the little town and sighed a huge sigh of relief as I pulled into the hotel carpark. I checked myself in; I was shaken but managed to get myself up to my room. It took me ten trips to empty my car, I'd packed terribly as I was in such a mess and must have looked that way to the receptionist too. I could sense the hotel security guard watching me like a hawk. I felt like I looked like a criminal, and then I realised, of course this was all from my book again; Arthur and Tom had been chased and Arthur had to lose his white horse, my little white car. Tom was shot, Arthur and Caroline were hiding but suspected of committing a crime, Arthur's reputation had taken a downturn just as my family was currently questioning my sanity. Books didn't come to life did they? No, unless of course you're a storytelling shaman!

I lay in my hotel bed, and wrapped myself up in my shaman's blanket, in the small but cosy room full of messy bags. I was hurt, my body ached after the accident, I was freezing cold, and I was shaking. I only then remembered that I was supposed to be on a date with Hannah. 'Fuck!' I called her straight away, she answered and said she was on her way home from the pub; she'd had a drink by herself at the bar and was cycling home.

'I am so sorry Hannah, I got into a car accident on the way to you. I'm now at a hotel in Ross on Wye.'

'Are you okay?' she asked sounding genuinely concerned.

'I'm okay. I'm a little shaken and now I'm stranded here in Ross on Wye. I should have called you sooner, but I was shaken up and lost track of time. I'm really sorry,' I said, and I meant it.

'That's okay, I had a good time. I was sat at the bar by myself, I spoke to a few people and then after my drink I headed home. I've never been stood up before, it's new for me,' she laughed.

'And I've never stood anyone up before. I feel so guilty,' I said apologetically.

'Don't worry, sort yourself out and we can arrange something the next time you're in Oxford. I hope the car's not too badly damaged.'

'I think it's a right off.'

'Shame, well I better get on, it's cold outside and I have a long cycle ahead of me,' she said, and we ended the call.

At least I hadn't completely blown it with Hannah. I needed to eat, I needed to rest, and I needed to ground myself. I had a hot shower and headed down to the hotel bar where I grabbed myself a beer and ordered some food from the menu. I had a steak pie with chips, and I savoured every mouthful. I sat at the bar for a while watching people and noticed how different I was, how sharp my mind had become. It was as if I could recall every memory I'd ever had, everything I'd ever seen or done before; it seemed like I suddenly had a photographic memory. I relaxed at the bar, exploring my mind and its inner workings; I felt like I could recall the knowledge from every book I'd ever read. Now I don't know if it was true or not, but that's what it felt like as I sat there in the bar and remembered parts of my life I'd completely forgotten about. I was able to match up the repeating cycles and find the meaning in things. I played with my memories and unpicked them in my mind. I saw them from new perspectives. After I'd finished with my meal I headed back up to my room.

But before I slept, I picked up my novel and flicked through it; I concluded that the rewriting hadn't helped to change the events from playing out, it had only added extra scenes to the story. We hadn't stopped what I'd written before from manifesting into reality. I wanted to read what was coming next, so I could at least know what to expect to unfold in the next few days or weeks. I found the point in the story where we had reached; Tom was dead and Arthur was in a terrible condition; Jo had disappeared from my life completely and my current state was terrible too. Arthur had walked back to Witney where he would find his sister Emily waiting for him; I hoped that was me going back home and re-joining with the people I loved. Or perhaps Arthur represented my spiritual side whilst Emily represented my logical side, and it could mean I would be able to regain control of my life. Or did it mean fully uniting with my higher self? Or was it a journey back to wholeness? I didn't know, but it sounded much better than what I'd been going through; a journey back to wholeness sounded just what I needed next. Perhaps the second part of the book would flow at a much slower pace, perhaps it would take years to play out each chapter, rather than hours or days. I didn't know. All I knew was that the end of the book would leave Arthur in hospital with a bullet wound and close to death. What crushed me was that there was no Tom in the story anymore; instead of having a close friend to share the adventure with and stand by his side, Arthur would proceed alone and have to prove himself to the people that didn't trust or believe him anymore.

I woke shaking, cold and soaked in sweat. I stripped off my wet clothes, stepped into the shower to warm up, dressed in some clean clothes and got back under the blankets until I was warm enough to head down for breakfast. I would need to call the insurance company and report the accident and sort out where I was going next, but first food. I ordered a fresh coffee, a pot of tea and eggs Benedict. The food was delicious and nourished my shocked and suffering body. The music that was playing in the restaurant seemed to match every thought I was having, and it was unnerving, the messages still seemed relentless.

After breakfast I went out to my car and inspected the damage; it wasn't looking good, I'd lost the bumper, you could see into the engine and brake fluid had poured onto the driveway. I'd been lucky to get it to the hotel in one piece. I went to the hotel reception desk and asked if I could book the room for another night, then called the insurance company. They couldn't tell me much; I'd just have to wait for a call. I needed to rest, I needed to heal, but first I needed to organise myself.

I was trying to understand why I was so different. Although my body felt weak, my mind had seemed to have had an upgrade; I had endless answers to my problems, of which there were too many to sort through. However, I knew I was vulnerable; my battery was running on low and I had to keep myself warm. The hotel was old, and we were in a cold snap, so I asked for a heater to be delivered to my room. In the meantime, I wrapped myself up in my blanket and got under my covers fully dressed until my shivering stopped. I meditated and tried to sleep. Once the shivering abated, I looked at the chaos of my things scattered all over the small room; it was time to tackle the mess. I started with my food, everything came out of the bags and was re-packed in a far more organised way. I loved my food, and took a variety of herbs, spices, oils, and tinned pulses everywhere I stayed. Once the food was organised, I went back under my blanket to warm myself up again. I continued systematically working my way through all of my possessions, stopping in between to get into bed and warm myself up again. I couldn't remember ever being so precise with my organising before; I'd become a meticulous version of myself that seemed to be explaining to the normal version of myself what I needed to do. I was talking to myself, explaining things – I had to put my car keys in my left jacket pocket, my wallet in the right, my phone in the inside pocket; I was always to stick to this simple routine, then I wouldn't have to search through my pockets each time I needed something, which was an inefficient use of my time.

Next was my suitcase, I took all my clothes out and divided each corner of the case into different sections; one corner for my loungewear, pants and socks, another corner for my smart clothes, another corner for my casual clothes and the fourth corner for my jumpers. The zipped pockets would contain all of my paperwork, each zipped pocket had a different purpose. I'd arrived in chaos, but would leave with military organisation. And then I remembered something, I had read about this technique in a book, years ago but never put it into practice. My mind was recalling this knowledge from that book now when I needed it. I had seemed to have total recall.

The rest of my day continued in the same vein; I literally organised every aspect of my life that I could from that little hotel room. I went through my emails and archived or deleted anything I didn't need; I cleared out hundreds of them. When the heater arrived, things started to improve. I had avoided checking what the time was, and had closed the curtains to work with 'time' as I had been taught. I was experimenting with losing track of time, losing sense of what time was. It had been explained to me that when I paid attention to time I reset it to that point and lessened my ability to stretch it.

Jo sent me a message; she'd decided she needed a complete break from our friendship; she needed to get back to normal life and I couldn't blame her. I'd already seen it coming; we had both been through a lot together in a short space of time. Tom and Arthur split in the book exactly where we were right now. She'd be okay, Tom's death would perhaps represent a rebirth for her, a chance for huge spiritual growth. Sadly though, I lost her when I needed her the most, when I needed a friend to offer the level of support that she had given me before. I was saddened by the message, but right now I needed to focus on myself and getting back up onto my horse, or surfboard, or whatever it was I was supposed to get back onto!

In time I would feel let down by Jo, for her refusal to talk through what had happened to us during that extreme period; I would try a few times over the next year to rekindle our friendship, but each time she would close the door in my face. She had played her role in the drama that had unfolded both as characters within my novel and in her own life. I later concluded that she had blamed me for the darkness that had followed for her. I wanted to understand what had happened to her during those days when I was in Ross-on-Wye, but we never did have that conversation.

Progress was slow with the insurance company, so I booked another night in the hotel and started calling around to the family members that I'd alarmed with my warnings about natural disasters and the car accident. I told them all that I no longer saw anything happening this year, I'd seen something but couldn't be sure when or where; I told them to keep an eye on the news and offered an apology for my strange behaviour. It was humiliating and humbling at the same time, made worse by not knowing what had been said behind my back, or how far the word had spread about my demise. I took comfort in the fact that Arthur, the protagonist in my book, recovered quickly and had some good moments to look forward to; he was reunited with his sister, Emily, and they were looking out for each other once again. I was hoping things would start looking up for me soon too.

I got a message from Felicity and as I started to read it my heart sank; she'd loved our time together in her campervan, but she'd decided she wanted to get back with her ex-boyfriend. She said they had unfinished business. It wasn't unexpected but I still felt a tinge of regret and disappointment running through my veins. I'd manifested these women into my life to seemingly play out a role in my book. I hadn't done it intentionally; I longed for a partner, I wanted someone to hold on to and to help me heal some of the pain I still carried. I wanted someone to wake up with, someone who would pull me out of the rabbit hole and once out, stop me from sliding back in again.

I had productive day and decided to find a quiet cosy pub in the picturesque Herefordshire town I had found myself in. It was freezing outside, and I didn't have a clue which pub to go to, so I settled on a small one at the edge of town which once inside was the size of a large sitting room. Local friends were chatting together, and I sat at the bar alone, until a middle-aged woman sitting with her friends, got up and offered me a friendly welcome. It turned out she was the landlady, and I asked her if I could try a local ale from the area. She poured a little in a glass for me to try, it was good, so I asked for a pint. It was good to be away from that small hotel room, as I listened to the chatter and laughter, I took out my phone. There was a message from Laura, the lovely drama teacher from Bristol. She told me she wasn't interested in pursuing a relationship with me; like Felicity she was gentle and polite. I replied saying I wished her well. I could have avoided so much rejection if I'd just stayed in and tried to sleep instead of going on all those dates, but there had been an unstoppable pull, like a moth to a flame, to meet these women. I hadn't even considered not exploring where each path might take me.

I took a swig of the local ale to console myself. 'The only way was up, right?' I thought to myself and decided to focus on what I was grateful for. I started writing a gratitude list on my phone: I was alive, I was healthy, I'd gained knowledge that had changed my perception of reality, I had wonderful children, I still had some of my savings, great friends, and loving family members. I reread the list and relaxed, things could be much worse. I sat reflecting on my gratitude and finished my drink, and made a decision; I'd stay off the dating apps and enjoy the quiet life... or so I hoped.

I woke up to a cold room, and a song immediately popped in my head; it was Soul II Soul's, 'Back to Life, Back to Reality'. It was a clear message that the chaos was over, the heightened sense of awareness and incredible knowledge I'd been experiencing had gone. I could feel it; I was back to normal, or at least my new normal. I would have to figure everything out by myself, rather than having all the answers at my fingertips. I laughed out loud, it felt good to be back in the driving seat again, although it would take a little adjusting. It was time for me to get out of Ross-on-Wye and head down to Dorset, so after a tasty breakfast I walked to a car hire outlet at the edge of town and rented a car. I was leaving a different man than the one who'd arrived. My car was due to be picked up that day and I wouldn't see it again. I grabbed a coffee and hit the road, I felt ok... just about.

Chapter 9

Grounding

I pulled up at my parents' house in Dorset, I was just stopping for a night before heading to my next pet sit in Newbury. I needed time to ground myself and get back on my feet, I needed to reflect upon and understand, what had been happening to me. The extreme experiences of the past few days had felt like I'd been in the eye of a tornado.

I was greeted with warm hugs and relieved looks, and it felt so good to be back. My heart was warmed by the love I received; there's nothing like family to make you feel like you belong. As Arthur was reuniting with Emily in my novel after his traumatic ordeal, I too was reconnecting with family after my traumatic ordeal. I was told that I'd lost a lot of weight, and I had, which also made me feel good, because despite everything I was looking good. I unloaded the car and asked my stepfather, Graham, if he wanted to come on a walk with me. It was cold, but I felt like I had some explaining to do, and I wanted to put his mind at rest.

My stay with my parents was brief, too short, but I had my next pet sit to get to. What I needed most of all was to see my children, and thankfully I would be able to in the coming days. But for now, I was on the road again, heading to a small cottage on the edge of Newbury. I pulled up to the quaint cottage, found the key they'd hidden for me and let myself in. There was a huge drum in the front room, it was a step up from the one I'd bought in Bath, but almost identical aside from the size. I took it as a sign that I had earnt another promotion as a shaman, I'd taken the extreme test and made it out the other side. I needed to put the novels out of my head and just focus on getting myself back to a normal; I'd been through such an ordeal, I'd completely lost touch with normal life and now it was time to reconnect to the non-shaman part of me. I'd organised for my ex-wife to meet me in Newbury the following day with the children, so we could all spend the day together.

I woke up to find snow everywhere, and my ex-wife Maria, was nervous about driving in such conditions. But thankfully the weather cleared, and we all met up as planned in the centre of Newbury. It was wonderful to see my children, I gave each one a big hug and we went Christmas shopping in town. The market square had a huge Christmas tree and a farmer's market that was selling quirky Christmas gifts. For lunch we went to a little tearoom down a quaint alley. My children seemed well, happy and they were all getting along. However, Maria told me she wasn't happy with me driving the children; she said I'd been acting way too strangely of late and then there was the car accident as well, so I could only have the children if someone else could drive them for me. I felt deflated, helpless, and gutted. I needed her support, and I needed to see my kids. But I also accepted that I needed some time to transition back to normality and reflect on what had happened to me; I thought that perhaps the spirit world had orchestrated her decision, giving me the time I needed to recover.

I wasn't due to have my children that Christmas; Maria was planning to take them to Spain to see family. I would ask my stepdad to pick them up when they were coming to my parents for our pre-Christmas celebrations. It would be humiliating for me to ask, but I didn't have any fight left in me regarding Maria, I just wanted to enjoy my day with the children without any drama. After we'd finished shopping in Newbury we headed back to where I was staying, and I cooked a meal for everyone in the little homely cottage. Then we all cuddled up and watched a movie together before they headed back to Witney. I was only in Newbury three nights, but it gave me the chance to spend a couple of days with my children and get some much-needed rest.

Once I was back in Dorset I searched for a new car and luckily, I was able to find a similar car to the one I had written off. I had sorted out my car issues, but now I needed to plan how I was going to earn a living; I'd lost all of my coaching clients by this time. I made the decision to switch off from my communication with the spiritual world, that I needed to put some boundaries in place between me and my guides. I needed to find a new way forward, so I put the dictionary out of sight, and also stopped reading my cards. The safest way forward was to listen to my inner voice, not the external influence of my spirit guides, I would follow my intuition alone.

I then got a message from my local doctor on my answer phone; both my ex-wife and Gabriella had apparently been in to see her out of concern for me after my premonition about the Turkey earthquake. They had told her about the things I had said and how strangely I had been acting. My doctor wanted me to book a time to see her, but it was the last conversation in the world I wanted to have. How could I explain what I'd been through? How could I explain a deeply spiritual shamanic experience to a Western doctor who, I assumed, would consider my ordeal to be some kind of psychotic episode? Perhaps I had misjudged her. I didn't know what to do or say, so I decided to ignore the message for now and think about my response carefully; I'd need to be careful or I could end up in trouble.

I called my good friend Tony and told him about the message I'd received from my doctor and asked his advice. He told me not to speak with her. She wouldn't understand the journey I was on. I also called my dear friend Maggie and talked it through with her too; she echoed Tony's view, which was also mine. So, for now I'd leave it, and wait until I felt a little more comfortable having that conversation.

The pandemic was still causing major problems with schools;

Beatrice's school had a shortage of teachers due to sickness and so she was given the week off. I offered to have her in Dorset at my parents' house for the week and Maria accepted. I was so excited, it would be wonderful to spend some quality time with my youngest. It would be the first time that I would have a whole week with Beatrice without any of her other siblings. She'd recently turned ten and was changing fast. Maria was also now willing to let me drive her, which was progress. When I fetched her, Beatrice thought my new car's heated seats were the coolest thing in the world, especially as the weather had turned and it was really cold. She sat in the front passenger seat and was in charge of keeping the seats warm, but not too hot that our bottoms melted!

Our week together went by so fast, as we filled it with stuff that made us both happy. Beatrice would be the first person to hear my new version of Arthur Archer and the Tree of Time, the new name for the novel. I had given up on a quick simple ending and decided to do the book justice and finish it properly. I felt I just needed to see it through to the end. I now knew that I couldn't avoid manifesting the book in my life regardless of adding new parts or editing old ones. I just wanted to have the new book ready to publish and sell. Besides, I'd been told by two psychic strangers in the past month, in the dating world, that it would be a successful book, with one person even saying it would be made into a movie! I'd spent too many hours rewriting it and it had cost me dearly, I now had to see it through to the end. So, in the mornings when we first woke up, I would read a couple of chapters of the new book to Beatrice and then she'd do a little homework next to me whilst I carried on writing. Those were priceless days for me, and at the end of the week I picked up my other two children so we could all spend the weekend together as part of our early family Christmas, before they headed off to Spain.

There were six of us that weekend, myself, my stepfather, mother and my three kids. We feasted, played games, went for walks, and watched movies. It was dark and cold outside so we rarely left the house. We opened the presents we'd bought for each other, and Sara, my eldest, gave me a beautiful painting of a stag which I absolutely adored. Beatrice had bought me a beautiful drawing of a bear with a butterfly on its nose, and Leo beat me at chess for the first time, which caught me by surprise. On the Sunday afternoon I took them home. I had one last pet sit of the year to complete, a long journey up to Sheffield to look after a cat, where I hoped to finally write the ending of the rewrite of my novel. I was getting close to the finish, it would need a good edit of course but I was making great progress at last, and it felt right to finish the ending before the new year began.

Before heading to Sheffield there was something I had to take care of, and that was my first date with Hannah. We had been chatting via text message, and occasionally spoke on the phone when she went for her evening walks. We had a fair bit in common; we'd gone to the same schools, we knew some of the same childhood friends, she was passionate about the environment and networked throughout Oxfordshire, which meant we knew a few mutual connections in the grown-up world as well. She didn't have any children and had thrown herself into her career. She was a high powered, elegant, and successful woman, more at home in the boardrooms of corporate London offices, negotiating investments in her various projects than the country lifestyle I was used to. She was interested in hearing about my life and asked all sorts of questions about my work and my family. We were getting to know each other and it felt promising.

After dropping off the children back in Witney, I did the 20-minute drive to central Oxford to finally meet her. I was meeting Hannah in a Thai restaurant that she had chosen. It had a great reputation and she'd said she wanted it to be somewhere special for our first date. I arrived before her and sat quietly at a secluded table in the back of the restaurant. I saw her approaching from the street, she had an umbrella up and was wearing a long raincoat. Her hair was tied up on her head and she looked beautiful.

I got up and met her before she reached the table, I smiled broadly, told her she looked lovely and gave her a big hug. She gave me a big smile back and a delicate kiss on my lips! It was welcome and caught me by surprise. As we sat down, we met each other's eyes across the table, and it just felt good. We chatted easily. The waitress came to take our order twice but we kept sending her away as we were too busy talking to look at the menus. We spoke about my children and my brother, sharing stories about him when he was younger. I found a new photo of him as she hadn't seen or heard from him in over 30 years. As the evening progressed, I decided to gather up some courage and see what she was feeling.

'So, tell me, now that you've met me in person, what do you think? Do you think you'd like to see me again?' I asked as casually as I could.

'Yes, I'd love to see you again. I love how different you are to most other people,' she replied.

I leant across the table, she met me halfway, and we kissed softly in that quiet corner of the restaurant. It was tender, it was delicious.

As the meal came to an end, we ordered another drink and flirted with each other. We laughed about our experiences in the dating world, and I was careful not to sound too hopeless. She shared a hilarious story of a professor with strange fetishes that made improper suggestions to her.

As she'd come to the restaurant by bus, I offered to drive her home on my way back to Dorset and she accepted gratefully, she lived a twenty-minute walk from the city and it was pouring down with rain outside. As I pulled up outside her house, she leant over and we kissed again.

'Would you like to come in?' She asked.

'I would,' I said smiling into her eyes.

Hannah lived in a cosy flat alongside the old canal in Jericho. We went up a narrow staircase and she was greeted by her black cat as she was switching on the lights. She put some treats down for him, asked me to choose a record from her vinyl collection whilst she poured us both a glass of red wine. I chose one by Sade. We stood in the kitchen, and each took a sip whilst staring expectantly at each other. Feeling the sexual energy between us I put my hands either side of her face and kissed her whilst gently pushing myself up against her warm body.

I was lustful and losing myself to my desire for her, my hands were exploring her body as hers were exploring mine. I gently bit her neck as she unbuckled my belt and unbuttoned my trousers. I could feel her exploring hand as I hardened to the touch. It was so welcome, it was bringing my body back to life. I clumsily undid her bra. I felt I was totally out of practice in the art of lovemaking, 'I want you,' she whispered breathlessly into my ear. 'I want you too,' I replied eagerly and I did. I pulled her dress up, revealing her slender frame. I slid her panties off and lifted her up on to the breakfast bar. She opened her legs invitingly and my excitement reached fever pitch. With her hands around the back of my head she held my hair tightly as I worked away finding the spot which I could feel was giving her the most intense pleasure with my tongue. She let out an exquisite moan of pure delight. She led me to the bedroom, took off my clothes and we fell onto her bed. I teased her until she could take it no longer. The night had been quite spectacular and had ended in a very unexpected way. Despite the many hours we'd spent communicating before we'd actually met, neither of us had expected us to connect so passionately.

I awoke the next morning initially unsure of where I was, until I heard Hannah's gentle breathing next to me. I checked my phone; it was a little past 6.30 am. I knew she was working that morning, but I wanted to show my gratitude for the incredible night we'd spent together, so I snuck out of her bed and went downstairs to make her breakfast. I couldn't find anything so I walked to the local bakery and picked up some freshly baked croissants.

Spending time with Hannah, connecting with her the way I did both mentally and physically was exactly what I needed. Our intimacy had grounded me back to earth; it had pulled my energy back from the clouds a little and given me strength and a feeling of wholeness.

After our breakfast we said a really sweet goodbye and I drove back to Dorset with a giant-sized smile on my face. I felt like I'd met someone who desired me the way I desired her, and we'd had an incredible evening together. We made plans to see each other again soon after Christmas, when I would in Oxford. I felt like I had at last found a little happiness outside of my time with my family. I'd just spent the night with the first girl I had ever had a crush on, when I was 10 years old. It felt like I'd turned a corner; I'd survived the tough spiritual training that my spirit guides had subjected me too, and now I was putting my life back together.

The following day I tackled the long drive up to Sheffield, it was my last pet sit of the year on a steep hill full of rows of terraced red brick houses. Isabel welcomed me into her home; she wasn't leaving until the next day and had cooked a meal for the both of us which smelt delicious. I unpacked my car and joined her in the kitchen as she talked through the instructions for her cat Hermon. He was a much loved long haired older cat with arthritis who needed daily medicine and grooming. Isabel was a book editor, and as we chatted over dinner. I asked her some questions about the grammar I'd be struggling with in my book. She was pleased to have a writer in her home; she told me she'd had a long list of people wanting to stay and had selected me over many other candidates, because she'd looked into my background and read my blogs on the environment and politics. We had a really lovely evening together, and the next day she left whilst I was having breakfast.

The weather was cold, but it was a blue sky and cloudless day. I'd checked the forecast for the week and this was apparently the only nice day I was going to have, as the rest of the week promised rain. So, I decided I'd spend my first day photographing the city; I took a long walk through Sheffield and attempted to capture the feel of the place through my camera's lens. The festive Christmas markets were on and their shining lights sparkled making it feel like the whole of Sheffield was ready to have a wonderful Christmas.

My focus was on finishing my novel, I had a quarter left to rewrite, and as I found my spot in the old-fashioned front room and rewrote the scene where Arthur Archer hunted wild boar with Prince Rupert, I noticed at my side there was an ancient tapestry of an archer shooting at a wild boar. In every house the paintings and other artifacts always seemed to match what I was doing whilst I was there. When I was writing, the décor or artwork of the place I was staying in would match the scenes I was writing, and if I wasn't writing they'd match what I was doing or thinking about. Not for the first time. The world isn't how we are told it is after all; it's far more complex than we could possibly imagine. When you can learn to let go and allow the universe to guide your path, you start to see little miracles everywhere and see how we're all interconnected; here to play out the synchronicities in each other's lives. I wondered about the tapestry and how it had found its way to be there beside me at that precise moment in time. Who made it? How many people had it belonged to over the years before it found its way here to Isabel house in Sheffield?

Behind where I was sitting was another tapestry that widened the scene, it was a medieval hunting party in a forest. Arthur was also involved in a hunting party, so both pictures matched perfectly what I was writing. I searched the house for more signs, and noticed I had yet another duvet cover with a tree full of birds; representing the tree of time in my book. And the hallway and landing had historic images of Oxford University scattered throughout, and in my book, Emily was working in that very same university at the part of my novel that I was currently working on.

It was during those days in Sheffield that I received the call from my doctor. I was nervous about it; I wasn't sure how to handle the conversation. We had plenty of history together through my work as her family photographer, and her as our family doctor. To ignore her call completely would have been disrespectful, and as much as I wanted to, I just couldn't do it. She called back soon after I had left my message for her. She was genuinely concerned about me and asked me some challenging questions that made me feel very uncomfortable. She questioned me about seeing my dead father-in-law and being able to recall everything I'd ever learnt in my life, and she asked me about my perceived superpowers, which is how Maria or Gabriella must have described it. I told her about my insomnia, and that I'd put the whole thing down to lack of sleep. She reluctantly let it go. She told me to get help if anything like that happened again, and I promised her that I would. I was deeply embarrassed by the phone call. Later that day I would reread a scene in my book where Emily was rejecting the help of her doctor, as he tried to cover her in leeches to help her with the plague. Emily thought she knew what she needed, and so did I.

The week flew by. I didn't want to face the cold and just wrote my way through the week, with the occasional chat on the phone to my kids or Hannah. I was so ready to head back to Dorset and enjoy my Christmas break; the year was drawing to an end, and I wanted to put the whole crazy experience I'd endured behind me. On my last full day in Sheffield, I was thrilled to finally finish the rewrite of my novel; I'd set out to achieve the goal of finishing it by the end of the year and I'd done it. I'd started working on the book in mid-October in Scotland, and by the 20th of December I had rewritten a 100,000-word novel; I was immensely proud of myself. I hadn't just written the whole book, I'd lived it as well, which was a rather unique experience! When I put my mind to something, I always saw it to its conclusion, no matter what obstacles are thrown at me. I would take a break for Christmas and then begin the editing process.

I started to question everything in my life. It felt like I was on a soul-searching exploration, now that I was safely away from the chaotic adventure I'd been experiencing. I needed to understand my life and where my path was leading me. I didn't buy into the Western world's view of how the world worked; I'd seen too much that opposed those beliefs. I'd experienced and seen things that the Western world's view couldn't explain or even comprehend; like the spider that had climbed into the drawer in my office and crushed itself inside my cheque book exactly to the shape of my signature. I'd given myself the name Bear whilst becoming a druid, only to discover that the name Arthur I'd used for the main character of my book, also meant Bear. I'd lived on the same street that I wrote about in my book, 10 years after writing it, and I hadn't chosen that house, Gabriella had. And then there was the visions I'd seen, and Jo disappearing from my life just at the point when I'd reached Tom's death in my book. And of course, discovering my publisher's name Janus, meant the god of time travel. Then there were the lyrics to the Nick Kershaw song, The Riddle, playing in my head the day I supposedly when through the time portal in the tree. I knew what I'd seen was real and true, but I still didn't understand what it meant for me and what I was supposed to do with it all. I was way too stubborn to give up my beliefs and put it all down to mental illness, that would be the easy way out. I wanted to understand my experience and learn how to work with it all, to gain insight and fulfil my life's purpose. That was the curiosity of the shaman within me, the desire to understand the mystical side of life and integrate it into my day-to-day existence and help and guide others on their path.

My trip in Sheffield came to an end, I'd finished my book, and it was time to head back down to the south coast of England. I went back to my parents' house and we had a quiet family Christmas, just the three of us. On boxing Day, we were joined by my stepbrother Christopher, he arrived with his arms full of gifts and a big smile on his face. I didn't see Chris very often, only once or twice a year. My mother as always made sure Christmas was special; she filled the house with love and made time for all the little festive details she deemed important. My parents gave me some money for my Christmas gift. I would need to address my income in the new year, and had decided to turn back the clock and revisit my life as a professional portrait photographer. The world had opened up again and I needed to put my best foot forward and try and find a way of earning enough money to support myself and my children.

Over the Christmas period I started reading up on rewilding; it was an area of conservation that fascinated me; the idea that nature would be better off if we just left it alone. I immersed myself in my studies and dreamt of a future where I was part of a rewilding project in the U.K. By connecting to the spiritual world, I'd also connected far deeper with nature; the two were interconnected, inseparable, part of the same thing, and now my long-term dreams were becoming very focused on the preservation of nature.

I still kept an eye out for natural disasters, half expecting something bad was going to happen. I was hoping I'd been wrong, but I couldn't help but think there was a chance I'd been right all along. I'd have to accept that either I'd had a premonition about something that would happen in the future, or I'd simply misread the warnings, or been tricked by my guides in order to fulfil a part of my book; the part where Arthur's reputation takes a downturn. I suspected all of this might actually be true.

As the new year began, I was back in Oxford staying at my cousin's house, which gave me the opportunity to spend more time close to my children, who'd just arrived back from their holiday in Spain. Hannah and I had set aside a day together which I had been looking forward to, we'd been chatting and texting over the Christmas period and we were really starting to get to know each other.

I picked Hannah up from the train station. She jumped into the car with a huge smile and a bottle of wine. When we got back to the house we started chatting and I poured her a glass of wine. But both of our minds were on one thing and one thing alone. I put my hands on her waist and kissed her lips. I found myself even more aroused than the previous time. I felt more comfortable with her now. I could taste the red wine on her tongue. As the kissing got increasingly more passionate, I led her to my bedroom full of sexual desire. Our breathing quickened as I started to undress her. She looked stunning in her dress that I easily zipped down. It fell to the floor, and she stepped out of it revealing red and black underwear. She looked exquisite, I just couldn't wait to be with her again. She undressed me quickly, as if we only had moments to spend together, her womanly desires seizing hold of her. She was even more daring than the first time. I quickly took off her underwear and we climbed on to the bed. We were both lost in the freedom of the moment. She let out a moan of pleasure, and then took my hand and showed me what she desired most. I understood. I moved my mouth closer to her breasts and kissed them gently. She let out a gasp. 'Bite harder. I like it,' she said biting on her lip as if struggling to contain her pleasure.

With my adrenaline taking over, I could delay no longer. I caught a scent of her, and it excited me even more. I watched the pleased expression on her face, she bit her lip again in anticipation of what was to come. I couldn't wait any longer. She let out another moan of intense pleasure and arched her back. I noticed how her breasts moved as she did so. I reached forward and caressed one of her breasts again. I watched her as I built up my momentum; her face was red, she looked at me intensely and she could no longer control the sounds that escaped her mouth. She grabbed the duvet tightly and screamed out a long low moan of intense pleasure as I felt her legs tighten around mine. She had climaxed. I let myself increase my speed, and I too let out a sound of intense satisfaction. I collapsed beside her. I felt incredible and by the look of her face, so did she.

After our love making, I made a simple lunch, a Greek aubergine pilau. We chatted whilst I prepared the food. I had high hopes for the two of us. After devouring the meal, she looked hungry for me again. I could see it in her eyes and it was extremely welcome. We kissed passionately, and soon afterwards we went to my room again and made love. She had swept into the house full of desire and lust and left satisfied with a cheeky smile across her face. That evening, on my own again, I was full of hope. I'd found someone I wanted to be with; she was intelligent, successful, and sexy. The tide had turned for me at last, I could rebuild my life from here, I thought. However, the universe hadn't finished with me yet. I had an unfinished journey to complete which I apparently wouldn't be able to do in a happy fulfilling relationship, at least not yet. There was still plenty of magic in my novels left un-manifested and my happiness made no difference to how the story was unfolding.

The following day I received a message from Hannah saying she was pulling the plug on our fledgling romance. She said it had got too serious too quickly and she didn't want to be emotionally entangled; that she wanted something light. I'd told her that I could see myself falling for her and that was her red flag. She told me I was lovely, and I would make someone very happy. As I read the message I was crushed, I simply didn't want to feel the pain or frustration. I knew I was already vulnerable and dwelling on this loss was not good for me at all. I'd got such a high from our connection; I didn't want a huge low now that she'd disconnected or untangled herself from me. I took a deep breath, grabbed my coat, and headed straight for the forest; I needed to be connected with nature and ground myself. I surrounded myself with the trees, and in my mind, I took myself outside of the situation with Hannah and saw it as an observer; she'd been a wonderful gift for me. She had been the perfect interlude on my lonely path, and I'd been shown the power I had by being able to manifest my first crush back into my life, sharing something that was amazing, even if it was fleeting. I would be thankful to her for what she'd given me, recharged my battery and replenished my soul and made me feel desired for the first time in many years. And I decided to look forward to the time when I'd meet the right person for me... surely there was someone out there!

I received a message from a man called Brian, he reached out to me to see if I wanted to look after his two dogs in a village Buckinghamshire for a month in February. I had a house sit in the Lake District in Cumbria before, and this house sit would give me accommodation up to March, it was a good fit. Brian's dogs were large Mastiffs, and they weren't socialised, but he told me I'd be fine with them. I told him that during the February half-term I'd love if my children could come and stay too, and he said they were most welcome as the house had 7 bedrooms. I decided that in these next coming months I'd get back into my portrait photography, to start earning more money again. I knew I'd need to start all over again; I'd need to go out on the streets to attract new clients and I wanted to focus on the Oxfordshire area where my kids lived. Brian's house was only forty-five minutes' drive from the edge of Oxfordshire, so it made sense to do the house sit.

I left my cousin's house and moved on to my friend Tony's; he was away for a couple of weeks, and I was grateful to be back there. Not for the first time, I lost myself in editing my book; I edited all week, sat at the kitchen counter with the occasional interruption from Tony's cat. Tony returned from overseas with a warm manly hug and a big smile, happy to be back with his cat and to see me.

I received a message from Gabriella; she had decided not to go back to Italy after all. She wanted to talk to me, there was apparently unresolved feelings we needed to work through. It caught me by surprise. It was nice to hear from her, as I'd missed her and the security we'd had together, and she told me how much she'd missed me. We agreed to chat on the phone that week, after I'd arrived in Cumbria. The conversation had been a complete surprise and I was still recovering from the disappointment Hannah had caused me. It was a welcome distraction.

I said goodbye to Tony but before I left, he shared a last story with me; it was another part of my book playing out. He told me that his friend Susan, who often stayed over at his house was complaining that I'd been staying in her room. He thought that was strange because it was his room, in his house. Then it struck me, in my book, Arthur stayed in a house in Oxford, Just like I currently was, and he had to share the room with someone who didn't want him there. It all matched, I too was staying in Tony's bed and having other people complain that I was there. My involvement in the first book was still happening, whether I paid attention to it or not. It was a long drive up to Cumbria and the weather was moody. When I arrived at the cottage, just outside of Cockermouth, I was tired and hungry. Dave and Jenny welcomed me into their home and introduced me to their cat. Jenny had cooked a vegetarian lasagne, and Dave opened a bottle of wine. We shared a delicious meal together with sticky toffee pudding and ice cream for dessert; It was such a lovely and warm welcome to Cumbria. They told me about the pet sitters they'd had in the past, how they'd really enjoyed their company and always found them interesting. They invited me to have a listen to their cd collection while they were away, which was extensive to say the least. I would spend the week editing my book, listening to great music and when the sun came out, I'd go to the lakes with my camera. I was excited and glad to be there; I'd been to the Lake District once before and had always vowed to go back, but I hadn't expected to be spending it on my own.

The following day Dave and Jenny left early, when I came into the kitchen that morning after they left, I discovered I had the most spectacular views of the rugged Cumbrian landscape and a garden that was full of wild birds. They fed the birds daily and as a result they were treated to the most incredible variety. I took a moment to take in all of the beauty I was seeing and felt truly present in the moment. I was so grateful to the universe for providing me with such a wonderful place.

That afternoon I went to Loweswater, one of the beautiful local lakes. The weather wasn't great, it was cold and threatened to rain, but I was still game. The rain poured and I didn't care. I took some moody wintery photos and then made my way back to the warm house. That evening with an open bottle of wine, I chatted to Gabriella on a video call. She was staying with a friend in London; she looked great, I could tell she'd made a real effort for the call. I had been thinking about her all day; I had felt like this journey hadn't been of my choosing, that I'd been pushed out of the relationship by the spirit world and although I could understand there had been issues in the relationship, I hadn't been given a choice to work through them. I wanted to take control of my life again, I wanted to choose who I would be with and if that meant Gabriella, surely that was up to me.

'So, how have you been Benjy.'

That was a term she'd call me when she was being playful.

'It's been one heck of a journey, that's for sure. I'm still trying to figure out exactly what has been happening as it's been a very surreal time. What about you? What made you decide not to go back to Italy?'

'Well, I did go back but quickly fell back into my role as the youngest in the family, and I hated it. Sometimes you don't realise what you've got until you don't have it anymore, and other times you realise why you left something behind. I've been doing a lot of reflecting of late,' she said openly and honestly.

'That's true. I know that feeling. What are you doing for work now?'

'I'm working in marketing, as a temp. It's okay, I have money coming in at last, and I can work remotely and there is the potential for long term work with the company,' she said.

'I wanted to see if you'd like to explore a conversation about us getting back together?' She continued. 'I'm lonely, there's a hole in my life that you used to fill. You were going through some weird stuff and perhaps you're through all of that now?'

Although she hadn't been particularly romantic in the suggestion it was still an inviting offer; especially after being rejected by both Hannah recently. I felt like I was standing halfway up a snow-covered mountain freezing and scared and was being offered a warm blanket to wrap myself up in, with someone saying, 'You don't have to go up there you know, you can come home with me.'

'Okay, let's explore it and see what that looks like,' I said hopefully.

And immediately something happened inside of me; I could feel a warm fuzziness filling my body. I could leave my spiritual path. I could play out a smaller life and concern myself with human pursuits of security, overseas holidays and growing old in front of the television with a well-kept garden, homemade cookies and a house filled with grandchildren with snotty noses that sat upon my knee. The thought of that felt safe and warm.

Over the next week Gabriella and I spoke every night, and as the days passed in Cumbria, we were rapidly rekindling the spark between us. I hadn't told her about my adventure with Hannah. I decided that my dating journey needed to be kept away from her right now. I was feeling lost, and just wanted to be saved; I wanted someone to close my novel and stop it from manifesting in my life. I knew the spirit world had told me I was to become a shaman and that Gabriella wasn't right for me, that I needed to embrace my freedom; but all that seemed to have done was bring me fast paced adventure, loss, and plenty of solitude. Yes, my spirit guides had told me a life with Gabriella wouldn't make me happy, but I was feeling so vulnerable and I just wanted to be rescued by someone who could help me find my way again. I wanted to wake up with someone and be able to hold them tight. I knew Gabriella was far from perfect for me, but I'd been searching for someone else and got repeatedly rejected. I was confused as to what I really wanted.

I continued to edit my novel whilst there in Wales. I was reworking a section where Emily was chatting to a friend, and I randomly wrote that a red squirrel had run out in front of her, and she commented to her friend that she'd never seen one before. I'd never seen a red squirrel either, but it was an animal I'd always wanted to see in the wild. The following day I headed off to Lake Buttermere. The weather was perfect for photography, and I was excited to get the chance to be out and about with my camera. As I was driving towards the lake, I saw a sign by the side of the road warning drivers to be careful of red squirrels crossing. I thought of what I'd written in my book the day before, and at that exact moment, to my utter amazement, a red squirrel crossed the road right in front of me! I couldn't believe it. I'd written it one day and then manifested it the very next. I finally got to see a red squirrel just like Emily. I would seriously have to think about the potential I was wielding with my writing.

I arrived at Buttermere, parked my car and walked through the village. The scenery was spectacular, and the light was just right for photography; so I spent the next few hours making my way slowly around the lake taking every opportunity to take as many beautiful photographs as I could. It was a rare day to be surrounded by so much beauty and have all the time in the world to capture it.

I spoke with Gabriella each day after she'd finished work; we explored aspects of our relationship and it felt like she was already setting up way too many rules and regulations of how to proceed together, it all felt unnatural and awkward. We couldn't live together for at least a year, we'd have to start our dating from scratch like we'd just met, and I'd need to see a psychotherapist to find out why I was acting so unconventionally. She thought my illness had caused some kind of mental condition, and I was increasingly feeling that this wasn't a good idea after all. I was not having mental issues; I was just able to see the world from a new perspective and a higher sense of awareness than before.

On my last evening in Cumbria, I spent the evening chatting to Gabriella, she told me she loved me and that she had fallen out of love with me whilst we were together; she blamed it on her focus on her business. We discussed the possibility of her coming to stay with me at my next pet sit in Buckinghamshire; my birthday was soon approaching, so we were thinking of having a celebration there with my children. Deep down though I wondered what the spirit world would make of all this; would I be allowed to simply go back onto my old path again? Was it dangerous for me to go against the will of the spirit world? I already knew Gabriella would never accept me as a shaman, so it would have to be one or the other, but not both.

Chapter 10

Leaving the Path

The weather took a turn for the worse, and as it was my last morning in Cumbria. I cleaned the house from top to bottom, fed the birds and left some food down for the cat. I took in the view of the gorgeous landscape out the kitchen window one last time, and then headed out the door with my car packed to the rafters. I had my camera equipment, my laptop, my clothes, four bags of food, my coaching cards, and my spiritual items. My first stop was Ennerdale, to check out a rewilding program that was close by. I pulled up and parked the car, it was bitterly cold and looked likely to snow and I was feeling a little nervous about the weather, with such a long drive ahead of me. I walked to the lake and read all the information that showcased the great work they were doing and headed back to the car and set off for Buckinghamshire. I'd be on the road for at least five hours, so I filled the car up with fuel and drove through the hilly landscape, enjoying the scenery. My mind felt crowded with thoughts of Gabriella, and whether it would be the right choice or not to get back with her. Somehow it didn't feel right.

In 2008, I was on holiday in Spain with my wife, and our children. Sara was three and our son, Leo was about to turn one, Beatrice hadn't been born. We'd borrowed Maria's sister's car and were out for the day visiting landmarks, between Madrid and Toledo. On our way back to Toledo, after a visit to some natural caves, Maria lost control of the car on the motorway. Thankfully Sara had been travelling in the car in front of us with her auntie and uncle. But Leo was in the back of our car strapped into his car seat when Maria lost control of the car. The car swerved to the left of the road, from the passenger seat I grabbed the steering wheel and tried to get us back in the middle, but the car went too far to the right too quickly, it flipped and rolled across the motorway. It was a terrifying experience that will live long in all our memories. After rolling on the motorway, the car ended up upside down, in a ditch at the side of the motorway. I looked behind me to see my small boy looking startled but unhurt and looked next to me to find my wife in shock but seemingly with no physical injuries. I had whiplash and a couple of broken ribs, I was sore, but regardless of the pain we'd escaped in what was later described by the ambulance crew as a miracle. That moment changed me, I think I left a part of me behind on the motorway that day.

As I passed through Pembrokeshire, on my way back from The Lake District, the heavens opened and down came a heavy downpour of snow. Just before the snow started there'd been rain, so the driving conditions quickly became icy and dangerous. It was bitterly cold, there was ice and snow all over the road and the visibility was terrible. I was still a long way from where I needed to be, and I couldn't postpone the journey. I had two choices; to find a layby and wait for better driving conditions, but the weather could get worse and I could end up getting stuck in the layby, or I carried on and hoped that the further south I got the better the weather would be. I made the wrong choice; I was nervous but continued on the road ahead of me.

I was concentrating so hard, but still I felt the car skid towards the middle of the dual carriageway. Oh no! I was losing control and with it I was immediately taken back in my mind to the car accident in Spain as the memories flooded my mind. I was in a repeating cycle, only this time I was alone, and I was terrified. I tried to steer the car back to my side of the road, but as I did, I swerved too far and the car swerved completely off the road. Was I going to die here on this road? The car went up a steep bank, and as

Arthur and Emily were travelling back in time through a tree in the midst of a storm in my second book, I was smashing headfirst straight into a tree at the side of the dual carriageway.

I sat in my car shell shocked, my car rammed into a tree and the snow suddenly stopping as quickly as it had started; like it had been sent solely to cause my accident. Somehow, almost impossibly, I was unhurt and let out a huge sigh of relief when I realised this. I was seriously shaken, but I was able to step away from the car and thanked God I'd get to live another day. My life still felt out of my control. I'd survived the car accident, and though I was physically sound, I felt like it would have a major impact on my state of mind. I was cold, I was shaking, and I was being tested yet again.

A lorry pulled up and two Cumbrian men got out to see if I was okay. As soon as they saw I was, they wished me well, and then drove off and just left me there. I looked at my car, the front was crumpled into the tree, the impact had been significant. A police officer arrived on the scene, he parked his car and put cones out on the road. I was so relieved to see him.

'Are you okay? Have you been hurt?' he asked sympathetically.

'I'm okay.'

'I'm sorry to have to ask you this, have you been drinking or eating, sir?'

'Yes,' I said.

He looked disappointed. 'What have you had?'

'A salad,' I replied.

He looked relieved and smiled.

'That should be okay!' he laughed. 'But let's get you tested anyway. Please can you blow into this tube.' I held the contraption to my mouth and did as I was told.

The breathalyser test came out negative, and next we planned to get the car towed away, but I couldn't get hold of my insurance company, so I took the policeman's offer to get a local company to collect the car and take it to the nearby town. Two tough looking men pulled up and put my car, with all of my things, onto the back of their pick-up truck and drove me into Pembroke.

I was cold and seriously shaken, on the short drive to Pembroke I called Brian, the man with the two dogs who I was on my way to, and told him I'd been in a car accident and once I'd figure out what to do I'd call him back. We pulled up at the police depot and I was in shock; I was so glad to be alive and amazed that I wasn't injured, but I was overwhelmed by what had happened and I was struggling to think with a clear head. I had all my stuff in my car that was now a total right off, and I had to get to a remote hamlet somewhere between Milton Keynes and Buckingham.

'Right, you've got five minutes to take what you want from the car. We need you out of the depot as we're an emergency service and need to lock up so we can be ready for the next emergency.' A man said, with a gruff Scottish voice, in an unfriendly manner.

'I'm sorry, but I need more than five minutes to think through what I need to do. I have all my stuff in the car and where I'm staying. I won't have any transport and it's in the middle of nowhere. I need a little time to think,' I replied.

I needed my mind sharp, yet I didn't have access to it. My words were met with an icy stare.

'You're not listening to me, are you? That's not my problem, it's yours. You've now got four minutes to take all you can carry, and get yourself to the train station. Everything else will be safe, as it's in a Police lock up.'

'I'm in shock. Can you please give me the time I need to figure out what I need to do?' I said with a raised voice.

'Hurry up, or you'll be leaving here nothing!' she said, we were not seeing eye to eye.

'Please have a little understanding; you need to be compassionate when people have just had a car accident,' I persisted.

I couldn't understand in that moment why I was being treated so badly. Later on I would realise, it was all in my second novel! Arthur and Emily had travelled through the portal in a storm only to be met by complete hostility. This man was just playing his part in my second book, but of course in that moment feeling freezing cold, overwhelmed and in shock, I was unable to see it. Not that it would have helped if I had realised.

I clearly had no choice; I took all I could carry and stood in the freezing rain whilst I waited for a taxi to take me to the train station. Had I not been so rushed into a decision, I would have picked up a hire car, transferred my possessions over, and continued my journey. But that sensible choice had been taken away from me. I arrived at the train station, bought myself a ticket, and after an hour of waiting in the cold, still shaking slightly from the shock, I boarded my train and called Gabriella. I told her about the accident and what I'd been through, I just needed some support and understanding, but all I got was accusations about the state of my mental health.

After a few hours on the train, I was met at the station by Brian and his wife Cathy. The house was in the middle of the countryside, a long walk from any nearby town or village. They showed me around beautiful modern house and I unpacked. That evening we shared a meal together of pan-fried duck breast with mash potatoes, and it was superb. Dessert of chocolate mousse followed, whilst they spoke about all the things I needed to do in the house. The house appliances were all top of the range, so they explained how everything worked and I was doing my best to take it all in, but my mind was spinning after the accident. I was emotionally exhausted; and just relieved to be alive. The last thing I wanted to do was be polite and professional. I didn't know whether to be thankful for the spirit world for saving my life, or to be mad at them for bringing the freak storm that made me crash into the tree in the first place. I felt both.

I said goodnight to Brian and Cathy, and their two large dogs, and took to my bedroom. As I closed the curtains I stared out at an imposing full moon. There was a king size bed, and the ensuite bathroom was huge; you could have fitted four people into the tub. Once I was warm and cosy in the big comfy bed, I saw a message from Gabriella asking me to call her, so I did; perhaps now I'd get the support I so desperately craved after my ordeal, maybe she was just so worried about me earlier and that caused her to snap. I wanted to hear a loving voice saying that I was lucky and it would all be okay from now. Instead, she told me that the crash had proved to her that I wasn't mentally stable, and she didn't want to continue exploring whether we could get back together after all. I felt a deep emptiness inside of me. She continued by saying she didn't want to talk to me for a while, that she needed to move on with her life and put down the phone.

I was at the very peek of my vulnerability and here she was kicking me while I was down; she couldn't even wait to share her thoughts until the next day. In that moment I just thought she was heartless, and I hid myself under the covers; I felt like I was underwater, I was drowning. My guides had been right, she wasn't the one for me; when the shit hit the fan, she'd proved that she didn't want any part of me and my crazy life. It had been a bad day, a very bad day, and as Emily was sinking in the river, drowning and giving up, in my second book, I was sinking under the covers of the huge king-sized bed.

The next morning, I tried to put on a brave face and took the two large, and relatively unsocialised dogs out for their morning walk whilst the couple got themselves ready to leave. I didn't actually walk the dogs, they walked me; I felt like I was on a sledge being pulled by huskies. I was pulled through farmer's fields; it was muddy and the wind bit hard around my head so I pulled up the collar of my coat to protect my ears from the bitter cold air. It was bleak, and I was feeling bleak, as I reached down with a bag to pick up a giant warm stinking elephant size poo. I felt as low as I could feel, like I'd reached rock bottom. I hoped this was the bottom as that meant the only way was up from here. I loved a walk in the countryside, but being pulled by these two dogs through muddy fields in the rain and wind on a cold February day felt like torture.

Brian and Cathy drove me into town to buy enough food for a couple of weeks, as I didn't have a car and they lived a 40-minute walk from the nearest shop. I spent a small fortune as I didn't want to go without anything, and I was feeling very sorry for myself. When I got back to the house I noticed a huge blank canvas on an easel, as I stared at it I couldn't help but see the symbology behind it; I'd been through a death and rebirth of late and now it was my time to begin again, I had a new clean blank canvas to paint a new chapter of my life when I was ready.

There was another sting in the tail from the car accident to deal with; Gabriella had called Maria and told her what had happened. Maria had then sent me a message telling me that my children couldn't spend the week with me for half-term after all, and in fact they couldn't get in a car with me ever again! I couldn't believe that Gabriella had contacted my ex-wife, and now I'd have to work really hard to rebuild my relationship with Maria, in order to have time with my children.

Maria continued messaging me, she said she'd got legal advice and if I wanted to see my children I would have to appear on foot, and could only take them for a walk near her house. The message blindsided me and I was livid, so when I picked up the phone to speak to her all of my emotions exploded. A culmination of the shock of my accident, Gabriella throwing me under the train with my ex-wife and being stuck with two dogs in the middle of nowhere got the better of me and I was anything from calm and assured and reassuring. I got angry with Maria, bringing up the car accident in Spain when she was driving, and she hung up on me. I was powerless, she held all the cards.

Before I knew it, it was time to take the dogs out again for their second long walk of the day, back in the rain and bitter wind. Again, I was pulled through muddy fields, across roads and over more muddy fields, swinging stinking bags of fowl smelling shit. That evening with a slobbering dog's head on my lap I decided I needed something to help me get back on track, I needed a distraction. This wasn't the time for calm contemplation, or deep reflection, I simply wasn't capable of it. I needed a lift, something to help me through this; I was going to open myself up to dating again, I needed something or someone positive in my life. I was near Milton Keynes for a month, so perhaps I could meet someone around the area in that time. The universe didn't want me to get back with Gabriella, that was absolutely clear, and if I went against the guides instructions clearly bad things happened.

The house I was staying in was very luxurious; with a grand open plan lounge and kitchen, an office that doubled as a gym, and another beautiful lounge area downstairs for entertaining, that was strictly off limits for the dogs. They wanted me with the dogs as much as possible and the dogs seemed to need constant attention, wherever I was sitting Kyle, the alpha male dog, would put his head on my lap and if I moved his head, he would put it straight back. He was so full of drool that it made my trousers soggy and wet, he also had a very strong dog smell; it wasn't pleasant. I was struggling to bond with them, they'd been spoilt; I'd watched as Brian fed them duck breast he had prepared for our meal. So naturally, whenever I went to cook, I was accompanied by two huge dogs expecting their share of whatever I was eating. It was a very different experience from the low-level work needed when I looked after people's cats. It would take some getting used to.

That evening whilst I was watching a movie with a dog's head on my lap, my dating app pinged, and I saw that an attractive lady had shown an interest in me. We got chatting over texts and I learnt that her name was Adele; she was a South African living in the UK as a carer. She had no children and was quite a few years younger than me, she was also a fellow nomad, moving from house to house looking after elderly women. She was open and honest and told me she didn't know if she was available for a relationship, she'd just felt compelled to join the dating app on the day I'd decided to switch mine back on. Was there fate at play here? There usually was. I got the feeling from her messages that she felt lost; she was looking for something but didn't know what. I was drawn to her, she seemed so sweet, kind and innocent. We agreed to have a first date when she was in a gap between assignments. She sent me a link to her social media page, where I discovered that she used to be an actress and a model. I watched her show reel, she wasn't just talented, she was hot! As our conversation continued, I could tell that, like me, she was in need of someone to help her find a bit of stability.

Tony heard about my accident and offered to come up to where I was staying, and take me out for dinner so I didn't get cabin fever. He was a great friend; the only male friend I had that would always check up on me and offer support. We went to Woburn Sands and found a country pub with an open fire and good food, and it felt so good getting out of that house. Without a car I felt stranded; there were no shops, coffee house or anything close by, just muddy fields and country roads.

Tony and I chatted over beer and laughed at my misfortune and apparent bad driving. I told him about Gabriella, and how she'd dropped the idea of us getting back together as soon as I'd had the accident. I also told him how she'd been in touch with Maria and now, I couldn't see my kids and would spend my birthday on my own. Tony was always on my side; he told me how Gabriella had been in touch with him too and had suggested I was going through a mental breakdown. He joked about my mid-life crisis, but he knew enough about spirituality to know that what I was going through was very different to any midlife crisis or mental breakdown he'd heard of. Tony knew me too well; he knew I couldn't be stereotyped or pigeon holed in anyway and he too was annoyed at Gabriella. It felt good to have at least one person on my side.

Tony told me he'd recently joined the apps too and had a really bad date; so bad that he'd never go on another date again. He sounded like he meant it, and I admired how he didn't need a woman in his life; he was content and in harmony with himself. Tony had great friends and he was close to his family; he always had so much time for those he cared for, and I was privileged to be one of those people.

The following morning, I decided to get myself organised, so I set myself some goals for the month I was there. Firstly, I needed a new car, but I was still waiting to hear back from my insurance company. Until I found out if my car was repairable, which I seriously doubted, I needed to wait. I'd managed to carry my suitcase, laptop and camera on the train, but everything else was still in my crashed car, sitting in a Police lock up in Pembrokeshire, along with four bags of rotting food. Second on my list was to focus on rebuilding my photography career, look for an agent for my rewritten novel, and I was going to get fit whilst eating healthily. I planned to put grit and resilience back into my life. Yes, I'd been through an ordeal, I had to accept that and be kind to myself, but I also couldn't use it as an excuse to give up. Now was the time to use all the wisdom I'd learnt in all the self-help books I'd ever read. I'd hit rock bottom, so now I had to get myself back up, wipe myself down and keep going, and there was no better time than the present. I could hear the Rocky music playing in the background to my life.

I set myself goals for each area of my life and I would do all of it without the help of my guides, or my readings, or magic. I was turning my back on shamanism, taking hold of that blank canvas and starting to put my life back together; the universe could do what it wanted to me regardless.

Next, I set about making a plan for each aspect of my life. I was not beaten; I refused to be beaten. I was motivated, and totally ready to reclaim my life. 'You can't keep me down!' I thought. I was the boxer that repeatedly keeps getting up off the floor. It's not about how far you fall but how far you bounce back afterwards. For my photography I planned to canvass with examples of my portraiture on the streets of busy towns within the boundaries of Oxfordshire; that way I'd find leads for people wanting family portraits and find a whole new audience for my work. As a young man I'd built my first business doing exactly that. The only thing that could stop me was myself, or so I thought!

I decided to mothball my coaching; I was done with my guides and their lessons. I just felt it was too dangerous for me to be in regular contact with them. Yes, their lessons were incredible, but they were also relentless and came at a cost. I needed some wins, I needed to make some visible progress and I needed the outside world to see me getting back on my own two feet again. I set myself up with a fitness programme; I had access to my own gym in that big house and I had to take the dogs out for two long walks every day.

I took the long walk into the local town and found a car showroom and found a white Astra; it was similar to the previous two I'd owned and the price was okay. I was pleased I had an option here within walking distance, it meant I could sort my car situation out without the need to ask anyone else for help. I found a barber and I didn't have to wait long for my cut and shave. Afterwards I felt like a new man; I was well groomed, I looked sharp and had an action plan to follow that should guarantee me success. I was back on track, less than a week after my car crash and being rejected by Gabriella.

I got into a rhythm of walking the dogs, cleaning up after them and editing and working on the photographs I'd been taking on my trips across Britain. The weather was atrocious, so most of my walks were wet, muddy, windy, and cold. As the first week came to an end, the farmer's field had turned into a quagmire, and boy did I grumble about those walks to anyone who would listen. On top of that the dogs were becoming more and more anxious about being away from their owners for so long. Kyle would chew his bed unless I stayed with him most of the day, and I struggled with the neediness, as I currently needed to give myself and my new life most of my attention.

The news finally came through that my car was a right off, and the insurance company transferred the money for the car into my account. My things however were still in the old car, and nobody could tell me where it was now. I didn't want to think about it. I had the cards I created in there, 2500 handwritten cards that had taken me months to make. No, I wasn't going to think the worse, my old car and its contents would turn up eventually. I put it out of my mind and went to buy myself the new car I'd found.

I took the white Astra for a test drive. 'It'll do the job,' I thought. Unfortunately, I was unsuccessful at haggling the price down and by the end of the conversation with the car salesman, I was lucky to pay the asking price! But as the first week in Buckinghamshire came to an end, at least I was finally mobile again. I could now drive to Oxfordshire and start finding photography clients and come back to Buckinghamshire in the afternoon to take the dogs out for their second walk of the day. The only problem was the weather, nobody would want to stop and talk to me on a cold, wet, miserable day like the ones we were having. Besides it was the last thing I wanted to do, stand out in the cold annoying people who didn't want to be annoyed. And so, I waited patiently for the rain to stop.

That evening I chatted to Adele, the South African carer. She told me that she was upset; the woman she was looking after had dementia and was giving her a really hard time, shouting at her, and making her feel worthless. I listened, holding space for what she was feeling. We were connecting, and I could feel myself becoming more and more drawn to her. She was so appreciative of the time we were spending together. It was nice to focus on supporting someone else and take my focus off of my problems.

I returned from walking the dogs in the heavy rain, cold winds, and mud. Once I'd got the dogs in, dried them down and fed them, I realised I'd lost my new car keys. I only had the one set and I thought they must have fallen out of my jacket on the walk as I was being pulled and jigged along. I was angry with myself and could hardly believe my luck. The walk was long, and the keys could be anywhere. I was dreading the idea of having to go out there again to retrace my steps, so I searched the whole house but they were nowhere to be seen. I had no choice, with the look of an old grumpy man I put my waterproofs back on and disappeared out into the rain to do the walk all over again; but this time without the dogs. I retraced my steps, cursing my bad fortune, feeling frustrated with myself, and keeping my eyes glued to the ground. When I was five minutes from arriving back to the house with still no car keys, wet, downtrodden and unbelieving of what had just happened, Adele called me.

'Hello handsome, how are you?' I could immediately tell that the brightness in her voice was an attempt to put on a brave face but really, she needed to offload about the difficult client she was looking after and her terrible day.

I stopped in my tracks, pleased for the welcome distraction, and as we spoke and her voice warmed me, I looked over to my right and there behind a tuft of long grass was my missing car keys! 'Oh my God!' I thought to myself as she talked to me about her difficult client. Had she phoned a moment before or after, I wouldn't have found my keys. That was divine intervention as far as I was concerned; I believed her guides were working through her to help me and offer what I needed in my moment of desperation.

I picked up my car keys and got myself back in the warm house, dried myself down and made a coffee whilst still listening to Adele and the ordeal she was going through. What I didn't realise was I'd just lived through another section of my book; before Emily had been taken by the Roman's and sold into slavery, she had fallen into a river whilst being chained and was drowning, until a Roman soldier dived in and saved her. The Roman soldier was called Lucan, and he had a powerful crush on her. Lucan had to search for the key to unlock her chains, and miraculously he'd found it just in time to save her and bring her back to the surface. Adele, who I hadn't yet met in person, had reached into my life and helped me find my key exactly when I needed. So maybe she was the one I was looking for? Maybe she would be the bridge back to solid ground for me, and I could do the same for her in return. It was a powerful metaphor and I was taking notice.

Whilst chatting Adele told me that her diary had opened up, and that she was now free that very evening if I wanted to meet her for a meal in Hitchen. Hitchen was about an hour's drive from where I was, and I didn't even need to think about it, I jumped at the chance. I couldn't think of much else as the day went on. So, I finished work early, had a work out in the home gym, took a long hot bath and meditated, to try and calm my nerves. Adele had told me her favourite colour was blue, so I picked out a light blue shirt, with a smart blue blazer, some dark blue jeans and my tan leather boots. I was about to leave the house when I realised that I couldn't find my wallet. Here we go again, I thought. Surely my wallet hadn't fallen out of my jacket on the walk too? After a thorough search of the house my wallet was nowhere to be seen. So, all of the good work I'd done bathing, meditating and relaxing, getting prepared for my big date, had been seriously undone. I had to call Adele.

'Hey, I was about to leave the house to come meet you. I don't know what to say, except that if I come, I'll have no money with me, as I've lost my wallet somehow. I think it must have fallen out on my walk with my car keys when the dogs were pulling me through the mud. I won't be able to search the fields until morning as it's pitch-black outside and it could be anywhere.'

'I don't care about you having any money,' she said. 'Just get yourself to Hitchen and I'll pay for the evening.'

She was already on the train, if I left now, I'd only be a little late, so I went for it. I got the dogs settled, jumped into my new car and headed out into the storm and darkness. I was nervous, the winds were really strong, and I hadn't driven my new car. I was still recovering from the shock of my last accident, and now I was going out in a storm, and the car would be blown all over the road. Plus, I had no money with me should there be any problems. This was the only night Adele was free before her next assignment, and sometimes you just have to go with the flow and accept the moment as it presents itself to you.

I joined the motorway and kept my speed to fifty miles per hour, clinging to the slow lane. Even at that speed the car seemed to skid and slide in the wind as I kept replaying the recent car accident in my mind. I tried to push the thoughts out of my mind; the last thing I needed was to manifest another crash, I knew all too well about the power of thoughts. I took a cd from a case that was randomly sitting on the passenger's seat; I grabbed it without taking my eyes from the road and put it into the cd player. I was relieved to hear Sting's voice eager to calm my soul; it was exactly what I needed, and immediately helped me to settle into the drive.

I was getting closer now. I felt a jolt in my stomach, butterflies; I'd found someone I cared enough about to fear losing and messing it up all over again. Cars overtook me as I thought about Adele and our forthcoming dinner together. I turned off the motorway, and to my relief I found myself on a quiet country road that was now protected from the elements. The car in front of me suddenly pulled out onto the other side of the road. And before I could fully comprehend why; I saw a fallen tree right ahead of me. In the split second I had to respond, I swerved, following the car in front. I knew I'd been lucky again, had I not been fully concentrating, or had a car been coming from the other way, my new car would have hit that tree in the road and I didn't want to consider the outcome and all the explaining that would have laid ahead of me.

I pulled over to gain my composure and sent a text message to Adele, telling her I'd be ten minutes late. As I started driving again, she called me.

'Hi, I've just arrived, I'm walking into town now. There's a pub restaurant called the Old Mill House; I'll wait for you inside.'

I already loved the sound of her voice with her South African accent; there was something musical about it, the tone was melodic and pretty. I couldn't wait to meet her in person, but what must she think of me after losing my wallet just as I'm leaving the house for our first date? I guessed she might be on her guard, thinking I was a catfish; someone who dates to get money. How would I put her mind at rest without having a single penny on me? It didn't matter, what mattered was meeting her; everything about her was like a magnet pulling me in. I hadn't even seen her in the flesh yet, but I could feel the infatuation already building inside me.

I pulled into the car park at the Old Mill House. My excitement rose and my nerves jangled, and there was a fine line between where those two feelings met inside me. I checked the mirror at the entrance of the pub and put my hand through my short greying hair. I was no longer a young man, but I was far from an old one too.

As I walked through the busy pub, manoeuvring myself around people sat at large wooden tables, laughing and chatting, I soaked up the wonderful atmosphere, it was light hearted and jovial. After all the people had been through recently, they had come here together like people had been doing after tragedies for centuries. They were successfully putting the events of covid and two lockdowns behind them. And I realised that's what I was doing too, putting it all behind me; I could feel the strong winds of change that were blowing through the world.

'Are you looking for a woman?' Asked the barman, noticing I was looking around for someone.

'What an insightful comment,' I laughed to myself.

'Yes I am.'

'Well, there's one sat alone around the corner there.' He pointed and sent me a knowing smile, like he knew it was a first date.

Adele was tucked in behind a table in a small side room containing maybe half a dozen other tables. Adele stood up and walked around the table to greet me; we looked into each other's eyes and both smiled broadly, before giving each other a warm friendly embrace. Her friend had done her hair for her, and her face was glowing with excitement, intrigue and wonder; she looked absolutely lovely. There was a sparkle in her eyes, and I could tell she was as nervous as me. She was shorter than me by a good, few inches, and I liked that. Her hair was long and straight, dark brown with highlights, her skin was fair and she had beautiful blues eyes.

She was in her early forties yet looked younger still.

'You look smart,' she said sitting down again.

I sat opposite her and I looked at her lovely face, it matched her sweet-sounding voice perfectly. Despite being a former actress, she didn't come across as confident as I expected. She'd been through a rough time with her divorce and moving to a new country, and somewhere amongst those two things she'd lost her path and was searching for a new one. She told me she was a spiritual person looking for a spiritual man, that her ex-husband hadn't taken spirituality seriously and that led to issues within their marriage. Although we were both spiritual, Adele's idea of spirituality was different to mine; for her spirituality was about her religion, for me it was about the universe, my path of discovery, energy and connection to a higher self. Her parents, now in their eighties, were devoutly religious, and Adele had followed their wishes and followed their faith.

The waitress arrived.

'Can I get you a drink?'

'I'll have a glass of red wine please.'

'And I'll have a ginger beer.' I said, the waitress smiled and left us.

'You don't drink?' Adele asked.

'I love a drink, it's just that I have a new car and I'm a little nervous driving since my recent accident.'

She seemed disappointed to be drinking alone; I wished I could have had one too, it would have helped to settle my nerves.

The waitress came back and asked for our order and suddenly the big table opposite burst into song, 'Happy birthday to you, happy birthday to you...'. Adele and I joined in, and when the song finished everyone applauded. Adele told me how much she loved celebrating her birthday, and how she'd be going home to South Africa later in the year to celebrate with her family. It was her mother's birthday around that time too and she really wanted for them to celebrate together. I could see how much her family meant to her, and it was a good sign.

I was attracted to her, there was no doubt, and I told her as such. There was always a chance that there would be no chemistry between us, but there in that small room, it felt more like a science lab with explosions going off left, right and centre. I was mesmerised by her; she was so full of smiles, letting her stressful day drift away to be replaced by something new, me. She told me she needed me in her life right now, and the excitement that came with me. I leant across the table and planted a kiss on her lips. It was the perfect kiss. Even more so, as she hadn't been expecting it.

After the meal was finished and the table cleared, I moved around to the other side of the table and held her hand. She noticed a little red patch of skin on my hand caused by eczema, and she touched it gently. That simple gesture really moved me; to be cared for in such a small and gentle way had been missing in my life for as long as I could remember. She didn't realise it but that little action alone, was a green flag signalling a woman who was compassionate, gentle, loving and caring; everything I'd been craving for. I felt like a wilting plant finally being watered. She was filling me up and it felt wonderful. We kissed again, only longer this time, completely oblivious of the other people sitting in the small room with us.

The evening was coming to an end, and there was no question whether we wanted to see each other again, the question was not if, but when. We were the last to leave the pub, and a group of staff sat together drinking in the corner as Adele paid the bill. I drove her to the train station, not knowing when I'd see her again.

I arrived back at the house to find two excited dogs who were very pleased to see me. I didn't think the evening could have gone any better, until I discovered my wallet in the downstairs bathroom. How I had not found it there before I left the house was beyond me; I guess that's part of the problem of living in a huge house, it's easy to lose things.

The following day I woke with a spring in my step. The strong winds had given way to a softer breeze, and even the boggy walk was more enjoyable knowing there was a woman in my life again. After our walk, I settled the dogs, brewed myself a coffee and set myself down at my laptop. It was time to look for a publisher.

As the weather improved, I decided it was time to try my hand at street canvassing, to see if I could pick up my first new clients for my portrait photography business. I was going to use the tried and tested technique from my younger days. I would stand on the High street in Bicester, in Oxfordshire and approach people who looked like my target market; women with children that looked like they could afford to spend a few pounds on family portraits. I had a framed portrait I would take with me as an example of my work and had business cards ready, as well as a clipboard to take down their details. I would stand on the street hell-bent on finding clients, and eventually I'd find someone who wanted to have their photos taken, that was the simple plan. There was a part of me that wanted to do this. It was almost like I wanted to toughen myself up again and prove I still had the fight in me, the grit and determination to succeed no matter what befell me. I saw myself as strong and here was my chance to prove it to myself once again.

I arrived in the market town just as it was starting to rain, the weather had turned during the drive. I really needed the rain to hold off as people would head home at the first sign of a possible downpour, and those that would remain wouldn't want to stop and talk. It was feeling cold and damp; a really bad day to start, but I'd driven forty-five minutes to get there and didn't want to give up before I'd began, what kind of message would that send to myself. I found a spot in the centre of town and approached the first lady, she was in her thirties and pushing a pram, seemingly in a world of her own.

'Hello there, I'm sorry to bother you but...' she ignored me and walked straight past.

I approached another lady, she smiled and said no thank you. The next three all told me they'd had photos done by a local photographer just before Christmas. I made a note of the photographer's name. This was my competition, so I'd need to research her. I was getting cold, and the rain was starting to get heavier. I was getting absolutely no interest in my portraits, so after I'd asked the sixteenth person without success, I decided to walk back to the car and call it a day. Just as I was about to leave, I saw a woman who looked like my ideal customer; she was smartly dressed with two children and walking confidently. I crossed the street to speak with her.

'Hello, I'm sorry to bother you. I'm a portrait photographer based near here, and I'm looking for people who might be interested in getting some up-to-date family photos taken.' I said, showing her the portrait that I had with me.

'That's a lovely picture,' she acknowledged politely. 'But I've just had some photos done, so perhaps later in the year?'

I grabbed my pen and wrote down her details. I said I'd call her towards Christmas, and then headed back to the house feeling a little more hopeful. I had approached seventeen people in ninety minutes and on a cold wet miserable day; I had passed my first test. I was up to the task. What I wasn't sure of is whether the people of Oxfordshire would want my services; had the world moved on whilst I was pursuing other avenues? Had the competition taken the industry to a new level and left me behind?

My birthday was fast approaching, and I'd planned to celebrate it with my children, but here I was stuck in Buckinghamshire which was too far to drive to see my kids because it meant leaving the dogs for too long. Luckily though the universe had a great surprise in store for my birthday.

'Honey, I have a suggestion.' Adele said as we chatted whilst I was walking the dogs.

'How about I come and stay with you for a few days? I have some time off in between my next placement and it happens to be on your birthday. I could come to you on Monday and stay a week. How does that sound?' She asked excitedly, knowing how thrilled I'd be.

It was too good to be true. After just one wonderful date we'd be staying together for a week and have the opportunity to really get to know each other. If it was going to work out between us, it would have to be like this as she worked non-stop three weeks out of four, and on the fourth week she was based near London, which was too far away.

'I would love that. Let me ask the homeowners and see if they'll agree to it.' I said eagerly, not wanting to get my hopes up.

I spoke with Brian and told him how my children couldn't come because my wife had dug her heels in after my car accident and wouldn't let me see them. He kindly agreed that Adele could join me for my birthday, and I marvelled at the universe; when I'd first arrived, I was about to get back with Gabriella and my kids were coming for a week; they would have been bored and I would have had to spend the week trying hard to entertain them. Now, I was in the throes of a new relationship and my birthday would be all about romance, passion and exploration.

I picked up Adele on the Monday evening from the local train station. She had a huge yellow and black suitcase that she called 'Bumblebee', and I could see why. We hugged and kissed and both grinned from ear to ear. Once back in the house I prepared us a paella and as I cooked. She poured the wine she'd brought with her and selected the music. Music was important to me and I was interested to see what she would choose from my collection. I had downloaded all of my music onto my computer and she was scrolling through my collection. She chose one of my favourites, Counting Crows. It was a reassuring choice and I knew we wouldn't fall out over music.

That night we snuggled up on the sofa, we drank wine, we chatted, we laughed, and we kissed. For the first night together, we had left it at that, sleeping together in the same bed wrapped in each other's arms. I woke in the morning with the sweet smell of Adele sharing my bed. I lay there, held her gently and listened to her inhale and exhale as she slept, her chest softly rising and falling. It was a special moment after all I'd been through; just a handful of days after smashing into a tree in Cumbria, I was now lying in a king size bed, with a beautiful woman, and the day promised wonders.

When I got back that morning from the boggy fields, with two soggy dogs, I was greeted with the smell of fresh coffee and a cooked breakfast of eggs, toast and smoked salmon. Life was good. I was no longer alone. I finally had someone to share special moments with, I'd turned the corner and the wheel of fortune was turning in my favour once more.

That afternoon was all about us. We were now both comfortable enough to start exploring each other's bodies. I could sense how nervous Adele was, she'd had issues in the past with her lovers and she wanted everything to be just perfect, and so did I, for her more than me. Kneeling facing each other in the centre of the bed, with the sunlight flooding in through a window on to our naked bodies, we started kissing passionately and before long we were hungrily making love. All the waiting had manifested into a deep desire for each other. I couldn't take my eyes off her body. I studied her shape, her skin, her scent. I wanted the moment to last a lifetime. She had little moles on her light skin, her pubic hair was neatly groomed, her skin was smooth and young. We touched each other gently, tenderly until the moment arrived for us to become more intimate. I lovingly caressed her shapely breasts, her hand travelled down and found my penis, her touch sent me tingling with pleasure. It was time to be present and soak up every single moment of the anticipation that had been building between us. I pushed her back on the bed so she was lying in front of me, the look on her face was just beautiful and inviting. I wanted to be inside her, and I felt that was exactly where she wanted me to be. I noticed how her face flushed, her breathing quickened, her little noises increased and got louder and more frequent. She was closer to orgasm now and so was I. I wanted to hold out for her, so we could reach climax together, in perfect unison. She grabbed hold of the bedsheets and clenched them tightly between her fingers as she arched her back and let out a loud groan of pleasure. I let myself go too. We looked into each other's eyes and then simultaneously let out a laugh of pure delight. We were connected, we were having so much fun!

My birthday arrived, and something else happened on the same day; the Russian army invaded their peaceful neighbours in the Ukraine. The previous year my spirit guides had directed me to read all about the Russian government. They'd sent me plenty of signs about a pending war and a mass loss of life. What I didn't know was why it was seemingly connected to me and what I needed to do about it if anything at all? The true impact of this invasion in the U.K would be felt later in the year, when the cost-of-living crisis would pull the plug on my fledgling photography business. I recollected all the signs I'd seen along my journey, about a world war and the earthquakes in Turkey. I'd seen the signs for both, and wanted to believe I was wrong, but this was an unnerving development and so chilling to happen on my birthday of all days.

After I got back from walking the dogs, I took a coffee up to Adele and I found her in bed waiting for me. She'd showered and put on some beautiful lingerie that she'd been saving for my birthday; she looked incredible, especially with that come-hither look on her face. How could I resist? I decided the invasion of the Ukraine needed to be put firmly out of my mind. I needed to be right here, right now, enjoying this delicious birthday treat lying on the bed in front of me. My heart was dancing; here I was, on my birthday, in a luxurious multi-million-pound house, with a beautiful woman who was everything I wanted her to be.

It was then that we connected tantrically for the first time, I'd longed to connect to someone deeply through tantric sex since learning about it through books. I showed her how to bring in divine light through her crown and move it throughout her whole body. I showed her how to circle her energy through her body and into mine and then through me and back into her body again. I could feel her sexual energy enter me and cascade through my chest, and there in my solar plexus her energy filled me with a surge that opened my connection to a higher power; It felt like our union was bringing me closer to the divine.

We lay there afterwards in each other's arms in absolute bliss and Adele told me how I'd officially ruined sex for her from now on, because if it wasn't with me, she didn't want it. It was a lovely compliment, and I was pleased to hear it. The lazy morning was as perfect as perfect could be; I could imagine Simon and Garfunkel writing a song about that morning, describing the beautiful ambient light from the window reflecting on Adele's pale, slender, toned body.

That evening we found a restaurant in a village not too far away, it was a big restaurant and had a great menu. We had both dressed up for the occasion and were welcomed by a friendly waiter who sat us by the bar. The food smelt delicious, and I was ravenous after so much lovemaking. As we waited with our drinks Adele told me more about her family; they were Afrikaans and her parents didn't take kindly to the English, due to the colonial times in South Africa. They were devoutly religious and had been deeply unhappy with Adele when she'd left her marriage and moved to the

U.K. She said she already knew they'd find it hard to accept another man in her life, and I she knew it would be even harder with me being an Englishman.

The waiter brought me a dessert with a candle in it at the end of our meal, it was a banana fritter with vanilla ice cream, and as he placed it in front of me the surrounding tables sang happy birthday. Adele had sneaked off earlier to set the whole thing up. It was a nice touch, and I felt my cheeks redden at the attention I was receiving. I asked the waiter to take a few photos of us, and the meal came to an end, so we headed back, and made love yet again.

As the days went by Kyle, the bigger of the two dogs, was becoming more and more anxious without his owners and had now destroyed two of his beds. I'd given him plenty of attention, but he still wanted more. I told Brian what was going on, and his reply was short and abrupt: 'You're not giving him enough attention!' Adele searched the house and found a sewing kit and went to work at repairing the two dog beds; she did a great job, but it would be a temporary fix as there seemed no way to stop him. We drove into town and in a charity shop I bought Kyle a teddy bear, hoping it might distract him from destroying his bed, and it did for a time. He took it everywhere with him in his mouth and loved chewing on it. But the poor bear lasted until the last couple of days, and ended up as bits of fluff scattered all over the sitting room floor. When we were walking through the town we saw, abandoned at a bus stop a dog's bed. We laughed! The universe seemed to have delivered us what we needed. However, despite the helpful gift I couldn't take it. I thought someone would probably come back for it, or perhaps it had fleas and I'd take them into the luxurious house. Kyle would have to do without.

It was a sad moment for me when our week together came to an end. We'd got on so well; it had been a gamble, but it had paid off. I took her back to the train station with her bumblebee suitcase, and a tear in her eye when I said goodbye. I didn't want her to go, I didn't want to be alone again. I didn't know when I'd see her again. She'd been the catalyst for an upturn of luck in my life; she'd given me new strength and hope of a better future. I held her tenderly in my arms and kissed her goodbye as the train arrived. She climbed on board and waved goodbye, and my heart sank.

When I got back to the house, I received an email from an environmental action group near where I used to live. Their work was to hold the local government and water companies accountable for the pollution in the River Windrush which ran through Gloucestershire and West Oxfordshire. The plight of the river was a problem close to my heart, and I felt even stronger about it now that my connection to Mother Nature had become so more important to me. I knew all too well about the pollution of the river and had written blogs on the subject. The email was outlining a new vacancy for a project officer for the river; it was a job with a modest salary, but the work looked gratifying and challenging. They needed someone to bring about an improvement with the water quality in the river; someone who could work with all the stakeholders, the farmers, the politicians, the water company, local businesses, and the general public. The idea of working on such a project excited me. Could I do it? I would need to fully consider the implications. The job would solve two issues for me, it would give me an income, and it would mean I could be near my children again in a settled job. I would be working at the heart of the community. As a shaman, I felt the job would fulfil the work I was called to do. The only problem was that I hadn't worked for anyone for twenty-seven years.

After giving the job serious consideration, I decided I had nothing to lose by sending in my C.V and applying. I didn't have any experience in conservation work, but I did have knowledge on the subject, plus I had a bucket load of experience leading volunteers, working to support charities and networking at a high level. I knew at least half of the local politicians in the area, through various incarnations of myself, and I knew the local business owners. I had a chance; I just needed to get an interview and make a good impression.

I received an email back from them after a few days telling me I'd made the shortlist, they'd be in touch soon to set up an online interview. It had all happened so quickly and effortlessly, like it was the path I was meant to be on. How would it all fit in with the document I had written and all that I had learnt as a shaman? I couldn't make sense of it all, but in a world that seemed like it was heading for war, a regular secure job was what I needed, even if it was taking me off course.

My month in Buckinghamshire was finally coming to an end. I'd arrived in a complete state; in shock after a serious accident, without half of my things and no car. Thankfully I would be leaving in a much stronger position; I'd started up my photography business again, had a new love interest, a new car and was on the short list for a new job that could establish me in a new career. Things were looking up and I was buzzing with enthusiasm. I spent my last day cleaning and tidying the house; it was a big job and as I cleaned one area Kyle was undoing what I'd just done. I'd swept the floor, and here he was flicking cat litter everywhere so he could eat a recently delivered cat poo, something he considered to be a fine delicacy. Brian had requested I pick up the poo in the back garden so I set about the unpleasant job. The garden was full of the stuff and it took me a considerable time collecting it up in a large sack. Once back inside Kyle tried to jump up on the work surface and knocked a bowl that smashed into pieces all over the floor. I had another pet sit coming up with a dog, but I decided to cancel it, and stick to cats from now on; they were much simpler and caused less stress. The weather had been atrocious; strong winds, storms, flooding and bitter cold temperatures, and taking the dogs out for two long walks every day had left me excited to have my freedom back.

Brian and Cathy arrived during the night when I was asleep, and when I woke in the morning and came downstairs, Brian was in the kitchen with a stern look on his face.

'I see the cat has been using the carpet as a scratching post,' he said accusingly.

'You were supposed to keep her locked in the front room with the dogs,' he continued.

I felt like I was in the headmaster's office and I just wanted to leave; I didn't want a confrontation of any sort.

'I remember you saying that the dogs were to be locked in the front room, and I did that. But I don't remember you saying that the cat needed to be locked in with them,' I replied treading carefully.

I distinctly remembered them saying the cat slept on their bed, but I decided not to bring that up. Brian was tough and he had a way of talking that was aggressive and authoritarian.

I noticed he'd turned a plant pot upside down on the kitchen counter, and had pulled out the dead plant, getting soil all over the floor. I'd spent a long time getting that floor clean and ready for them, and suspected he'd thought I'd killed the plant and was making a firm point about his displeasure, but the plant had been dead when I'd arrived. He was clearly in a bad mood, and I wanted no part of it. I said my goodbyes giving the dogs a stroke and Cathy a hug and shook Brian's hand. I filled up my car as quick as I could and left before breakfast, I just wanted to hit the road and get myself back to Dorset and with it regain my freedom.

I called Adele and she said she had the morning free and asked if I wanted to join her for a coffee on my way home. It would be the last chance we had to see each other for a while. I drove the short distance and found her in a little café; we ordered two huge pieces of cake and sat next to each other holding hands. She told me her new client was called Mrs King and she was very fond of the elderly lady, and I realised that Adele being a home carer, was playing another role in my book, that of Emily's friend Rebecca. Rebecca was a servant to the royal household and here Adele was effectively being a servant to a King – 'Mrs King'. These little synchronicities never failed to make me chuckle and I pointed it out to her. I felt like she was replacing Jo in my life and in the stories in my novels; but where Jo had played Tom and Rebecca, Adele was playing Rebecca and Caroline. It was fitting that she was a trained actress.

We had planned for Adele to join me in Wales later that month, but she broke the news to me in the cafe that it wouldn't happen as she had accepted another assignment and wouldn't be able to see me again for a good, few weeks. I was gutted, it would be weeks until I saw her again. She could see I was sad, and then without thinking she asked if I wanted to come and stay with her in South Africa, in Cape Town, when she visited her parents in a few months' time. She had her own flat there so we would have our privacy, and I had three good friends living in Cape Town that I'd love to see again. I said yes immediately. We had something really exciting to look forward to, just like in my novel when Arthur and his girlfriend, sat eating apple pie talking about how Caroline might be able to come back with him to the future.

We said our goodbyes and I drove back to Dorset, and just as I was getting near to my next house sit Adele called me in a panic; her client Mrs King had gone missing, she had dementia and no one knew where she was. The situation sounded so stressful, and I was full of admiration for the strength, dedication, and resilience that Adele put into her work. I also realised that she was living out another part of the book for me; the king going missing and his servants and guards not knowing where he was and looking for him. It was so bizarre how everyone who got close to me seemed to play the role of a character in my book and play their part in scenes that were written down. It seemed that once they connected to my energy, they connected to the magic contained inside my novel.

Chapter 11

Grit

I arrived in Bracknell during the evening, Max and Elizabeth had waited for me to arrive so they could show me around the house before they headed off to the airport for their flight. The house was a modest redbrick two-bedroom house on a quiet cul-de-sac. They were a young couple with a well-loved ginger cat who adored company; every time you walked into the room he'd wake up, run to the centre of the carpet and ask for his tummy to be rubbed. It couldn't have been a starker contrast from my previous house sit. The house reminded me of my first house when I'd moved out of my parents' home in the 1990's. I'd lived with a friend in rented accommodation, it was poorly decorated and damp, but we didn't care. This place was a little better but not by much. However, I was grateful for a roof over my head and had plenty of things to get on with. I unpacked and got myself ready for an early night as the weather was good the next day and I planned to canvass in the streets of Thame in Oxfordshire, to continue building my database of potential new photography clients.

I knew the historic market town well, when I first set my photography business up in the 1990's I came to Thame canvassing to build my business. It felt like I was repeating the cycles; staying in a similar house to the one I had lived in back then, walking the same streets on a cold March morning with a photograph in my hand, approaching mothers with babies and children. It felt like I was back in control of my destiny, and it would only be a matter of time before I would start earning good money from my photography once again. By the end of the morning, I had four telephone numbers. I had asked twenty-five people just as I promised myself I would, so I treated myself to go to a little chocolatier I'd discovered, that made their own chocolate and gave you scrapings to go with your coffee. It had been a successful start, and I drove back in the warmth of the car feeling two inches taller.

I got back to an email about my job application; I had an online interview at the end of the week; I was excited and nervous. That week I also planned to see my children, continue canvassing, sending submissions to agents for my book, and I'd planned to photograph Wokingham and Reading whilst I was in Berkshire. I had a lot to do in a short space of time, I was going to be very busy.

As the week went on, I noticed that Adele had surprisingly started pulling away from me in our communications; instead of being keen to talk each day she now would take her time in replying and was no longer available for video calls in the evening. I suspected that she was starting to doubt us. I'd have to be careful not to get hurt. I was confused, everything had seemed to feel so good between us, almost magical. Was there something going on that I didn't know about?

I found all of the information I could about the current plight of the River Windrush; I researched Thames Water, their shareholders, the local action group and the work they were doing in uncovering the pollution in the river and the excessive dumping of raw sewage. I spent hours finding out all that I could, including solutions used for other rivers and their success stories. I felt I knew enough to get me through the interview. I didn't feel that my lack of knowledge on the subject would be what stopped me getting the job, rather my lack of qualifications and experience.

On the day of the interview, I dressed in my smart suit blazer and white shirt. I received good luck messages from Adele, Sara, and my mother. I set my computer up and then waited nervously for the video link to accept me into the meeting. If I got the job, I'd no longer need to be hopping from endless housesits and canvassing in the streets looking for potential clients. I dared to hope that I could start again in a new career; I would be passionate about the river and work my socks off doing all I could to restore it to its natural state.

There were four interviewers, three middle aged men and a younger woman; they seemed friendly and got straight in with the tough questions. They asked me what I'd begin with if I got the job, and I said I'd spend time learning what they'd already done and start to build a social media following, to find a wider audience of concerned stakeholders. They asked me what the biggest issues were with the river, and I pointed to the sewage being pumped in by the water company. They asked about my experience in conservation, which was only my independent studying and writing. I told them about what I'd seen with the Ennerdale rewilding project and how I'd love to explore how a similar project could impact the Windrush. After the interview was finished, I realised they hadn't asked me about my relevant experience, or anything about what I'd created with The Oxfordshire Project. I kicked myself, I should have found a way to slip that into the interview. I was happy enough though; I didn't feel out of my depth, I'd answered all the questions thoroughly, and despite not talking about my previous experience I'd done well. I'd have to wait a few days before I found out the outcome.

That afternoon I took my camera to Wokingham and photographed the pretty little market town, which was a lovely surprise as I hadn't expected it to be quite so nice, yet It was a welcome distraction from the interview; I was able to shake off the nerves of my first job interview for over two decades. The following day I drove to Reading and photographed there too.

I'd found that whatever my focus was on at any time, the world around me seemed to match that focus in some way. And Bracknell was no different; as I was focused on the sewage problem in the River Windrush,

I'd managed to manifest a sewage problem in the little house I was staying in. After the first day the toilet had got blocked; I'd spoken to Max about it but he just told me to use the plunger, as apparently this was a common problem for them. I tried over and over again with the plunger, but with no luck. I watched various videos on how to unblock a loo, but nothing was budging it. In the end, I had to drive to a local petrol station every time I needed to go to the toilet. It was incredibly frustrating. I wondered if it was a metaphor for the job I'd applied for; a problem that couldn't be solved by one person despite all their hard work, whilst the water companies were owned by shareholders to make big profits, these problems simply wouldn't go away.

The day I left Bracknell I received an email about the job; I hadn't got it, someone else stood out as being the best candidate for the job and it wasn't me. I just had to let it go and trust that the universe had other better plans for me. For now, I would focus on my photography and the book and put the disappointment behind me.

I'd booked a night in a bed and breakfast in Eynsham in Oxfordshire. It was my daughter Sara's seventeenth birthday the following day and I wanted to be able to celebrate with her. Being seventeen, she had plans for the night before that did not involve her parents, so I got in touch with my friend Neil. We had a meal in the local Indian restaurant, and then spent a couple of hours drinking beer together and playing pool just like we used to in our twenties. I'd wanted to have a few beers to put the disappointment of not getting the job behind me and Neil, like always, was great at coming out for a drink at short notice. It was fun to play pool again and have that tipsy feeling as the alcohol dances in your bloodstream. I told Neil about Adele, about leaving Gabriella and my journey as a nomad, as we hadn't seen each other since. He was one of those friends that I could see every few years and it was as if nothing had changed between us.

When I got back to my room there was a message from Adele, she hadn't heard from me and was really worried I was dead in a ditch somewhere. I sent her a message confirming I was alive and okay. Perhaps I was wrong? Perhaps she wasn't about to dump me after all; she still seemed to care. Adele was a bit of a fatalist, always imagining the worst was about to happen!

The next day was a blue-sky day. I left my little room and photographed Eynsham to add it to my collection, and then drove to Witney to spend the day canvassing. Witney is a Cotswold town I'd lived in for twenty years and knew like the back of my hand. I bumped into people I knew; former photography clients and old friends. After a long day I went to my ex-wife's house and picked the children up, to take them out for a meal. We spoilt ourselves with delicious Italian food, and I left Sara with some money as a gift before taking the long drive back to Dorset.

As I was driving it dawned on me, Adele was repeating her past cycles with men, with me. She'd told me that she'd kept her ex-husband at a distance, she even lived in a different country from him at one stage, and she'd taken on a new partner after they'd split up and had done the same with him. She would push men away from her as if she wasn't able to give up her freedom within in a relationship. Through my dating adventures I was learning about relationships, and seeing how people repeat past patterns; I noticed how people kept bringing situations back into their lives in order help facilitate these repeating cycles. Perhaps, once I understood people's patterns I could decide how to proceed; if I was willing to play my role in that pattern. The pattern that was playing out with Adele left me with a bad feeling. Like with Gabriella I was being kept at a distance.

After a short stay in Dorset which gave me just enough time to reorganise myself, I drove to South Wales for my next housesit. I would be staying in a beautiful house in the small village, which was nestled on the border between England and South Wales. When I arrived Agatha greeted me with a coffee and Welsh cake, and showed me around her beautiful historic house, that seemed more like a hotel. The house was all white, with a huge lounge and a large chess board set up that just made you want to play a game right there and then. Her office contained thousands of books; there was historical nonfiction, a large selection of classics, books on psychology, theology, business and even dating. It was my idea of heaven.

Agatha had two cats; they were fluffy, independent and cute. There was a large modern kitchen, the perfect kitchen to dance in with a beautiful woman, a glass of wine and some romantic music. Upstairs was a reading room which looked out onto a little square courtyard, the reading room had as many books as her office, but this room was full of novels, hundreds of them, organised alphabetically by the authors' last name. I loved the house and knew I would settle in quickly. I drove Agatha to Newport to catch her train, as she was heading off to Ireland to see family.

On my second day in Wales, I headed to Cardiff with my camera. I photographed the castle and then came across a picturesque street full of bars and cafes. It was too good an opportunity to miss, so I took a seat outside a café with a great view of the castle, put my camera away and ordered a mocha. I sat there enjoying the view and watching people passing by. It was late March, and the cold winter days were being replaced with a hint of spring time which was lovely. I dislike the winter; it's when spring emerges, and everything comes to life that I am at my happiest. I was getting used to spending time on my own, being happy in my own skin and traveling around by myself. I had opened the door to many new experiences and opportunities like this one, sitting in this perfect spot in Cardiff with the view of the castle, and the smell of Welsh cakes wafting under my nose from a little shop next door.

I spent hours wandering the streets finding interesting things to photograph, and then with tired feet and a happy heart, I found my way back to the car. But I hadn't finished with Cardiff yet, I drove to Cardiff Bay and took photographs along the seafront and the marina before heading home. Like Edinburgh, Nottingham and Sheffield, Cardiff was a great city, and I appreciated her beauty.

I started the dreaded telesales in the afternoon, calling people I'd met whilst canvassing. I made my first two confirmed portrait photography bookings; my hard work was starting to pay off, I was rebuilding my life and enjoying the process. The rest of the week followed a similar pattern; the weather was great and there were plenty of opportunities to photograph different places.

On the way back to the house, I called into Monmouth. It was another historic town full of character, old buildings, and friendly people. My camera was filling up with photos; it would take me months to process all I'd taken on this trip to Wales. I finished the week with a trip to Ross-on-Wye, where I relived the eventful few days I had spent at the hotel there after my car accident just a few months before. I felt an affinity with the small town, like we had unfinished business, or maybe that I'd lived there in a past life.

The days had been warm and I'd picked up the first bit of sun on my skin for the year, but the night's had been really cold. It was an old house and the windows let out the heat and allowed in the cold. The seasons were changing and the year was moving on. On my last evening in Wales, I chatted to my oldest, Sara; she was struggling with her coursework and her motivation, and she needed me. Luckily my next stop was Oxfordshire and a house in a picturesque village near Thame, not too far from where my children lived. And I wouldn't just catch up with my children, Adele had managed to get a few days off too and she would be coming to stay with me.

I continued to follow my well-thought-out plan. I was focused on all aspects of my life. I was trying hard to build a relationship with a new partner; I was waiting to hear back about my book from the literary agents, and I was in Oxfordshire, not only near my children, but also just a short drive from Thame where I could canvass for more clients and promote myself. I knew I'd be earning money again soon and that really excited me. And to top it all off, the next house I was staying in was spectacular; it was a huge, comfy and set off the road with picturesque countryside all around it. It was a wonderful place for me to spend a few days with Adele, it would be romantic, and I would be able to get plenty of work done too. I felt enormously blessed, and I was so grateful.

When I arrived at the housesit, Nadine the owner was there with her children. She showed me around and gave me all the instructions I needed. She'd made a meal, we sat down together with a glass of wine and chatted about our lives. It turned out that we had a mutual friend, Alan; he'd called me out of the blue the previous week and asked to meet up for a coffee. It was yet another strange coincidence as I hadn't spoken to him for years. He lived in the next village along, and the fact that we knew each other put Nadine's mind at rest. She'd been talking to him that week about a pet sitter coming. It was all rather odd, but odd was the new norm for me, and it confirmed I was exactly where I was meant to be. I was still very much in the flow.

Before Adele joined me, I drove to see my children; I spent time helping them with their homework, fixing up their bicycles and being dad.

I felt willing to gradually allow my spiritual side back in, I'd just needed a break from it whilst I was trying to rebuild my life. The first step in the process of reconnecting to my spiritual side was a book I felt a powerful pull to read; I'd found it on a bookshelf in Wales and it had been calling out to me. It was called 'Conversations with God', and I hadn't been able to finish the book in the week I was there, so I purchased a copy of the book, and it was having a powerful impact on me. The author had been able to converse with the divine, whether that was God or a spirit guide or an angel, I'm not sure, but according to him, it was God. The conversations had reminded me so much of my experience with channelling my spirits and the divine. I remembered being woken up in the middle of the night and writing down my conversations in the same way he had done. On one such night I woke up in the darkness to a voice in my head that said, 'It's 3.21 am, check your phone and you'll see I'm right.' I turned on the light and it was exactly 3.21 am. Nothing surprised me anymore; it was all part of the magic and my shamanic life that I was experiencing. In the dead of the night, I picked up the dictionary and had asked questions about my life and the universe, and my guides would talk to me about religion, the corona virus, politics and the meaning of life. As I red that book many of the conversations I'd had, were repeated in his conversations. It was a nudge for me to get back on my spiritual path, but what I still needed to learn was how to be successful in the business world, whilst allowing myself to fully immerse myself in the spiritual world at the same time. I wanted to learn how to find that balance.

A film crew turned up, which Nadine had notified me about; they were filming an episode of a television show called Mid-Summer Murders in the local village, and Nadine was allowing the film crew to park on her drive. I watched through the window as they set their lights up in the neighbour's garden, but after a little while I got bored and headed to Thame to do more canvassing. I was motivated, working hard and getting results. I returned home that evening to find a bottle of wine had been left for me as a thank you by the film crew.

I still had a couple of days before Adele arrived, and Alan came over to have a coffee with me. I'd first met him as a photographer. I'd photographed his family for twenty years and now his children were at university, and I was beginning photography all over again. He was such a gentleman, the perfect client, and being with him made me feel reconnected to that old part of who I used to be. Somehow, I seemed to be manifesting my old clients back into my life; Alan wasn't the only one, it turned out the family with the Cocker Spaniel that I was supposed to housesit for and I'd tried to cancel, was also one of my old portrait clients. They had managed to talk me out of cancelling the housesit, so I would go there as planned and look after their dog, Maisey. I would give dog sitting another chance and hopefully change my mind about it.

It was the last day of March when Adele finally arrived. I picked her up from the train station, and I couldn't wait to see her. I didn't actually think she was going to come but she did, and here she was with her bumblebee suitcase. The long embrace she gave made me feel like I'd been missed; we did have something between us, there was the chemistry I'd felt before. As we got in the car, she put her hand on my leg and chatted about her journey. I could see that she was worn out and tired, and hadn't been eating properly, due to the stress of work. She needed looking after and I really wanted to do that for her.

I prepared us a Thai meal of salmon with noodles, put on some music and opened the wine the film crew had left for me. Before we were even halfway through the bottle of wine we ended up in the bedroom and made love; it was delicious, she was delicious, and I'd missed her. It was everything I'd hoped it would be, passionate, connected, and intense. We left the dishes until the morning and fell asleep in each other's arms. The was exhausted and I was so pleased to see her.

I woke up listening to her gentle breathing not wanting to disturb her as I knew how much she needed to rest. I slipped out of bed quietly, made myself a cup of tea and fed the cats. As I sat in the kitchen with my tea, writing in my diary, Adele came up to me from behind and hugged me, kissing my neck.

'Come back to bed, Honey,' she said sleepily as I pulled her on to my lap and kissed her.

It all felt so good, our energies were connecting again, and I was in my happy place. We went back to bed and stayed there for hours. Had I been wrong all along, was she actually really ready for a relationship with me?

The week continued in a similar vein; in between our lovemaking I worked, looking for clients in Thame, and had some success. We filled the fridge with the finest ingredients and ate Italian, Spanish and French dishes with good wine. It was idyllic, like something out of a romance novel. One evening we were invited to friends of mine, Ed, and Valerie; it was the first time I'd seen them in a couple of years. Adele was surprisingly nervous about meeting my friends, but she was charming and made a lovely first impression. I was proud of her that night and started to allow myself to see a future between the two of us. Sharing a house, sharing friends, I was starting to fall in love with her; I was risking my heart again. But I should have paid attention to the warning signs; I always fell in love a little too quickly for my own good.

At the end of the week, I made her some chocolate truffles to take away, there were thirty, one for each day until I saw her again. She was touched and seemed so grateful by the gesture. The final morning came and we cleaned the house together, then I took her to the train station,

'These chocolate truffles you made me, who does that? I mean, what kind of man makes homemade chocolate truffles for his girlfriend. Thank you so much Ben, that's so lovely of you.'

I hoped that it would be different this time, that she wouldn't pull away again like she'd done before. We kissed and said goodbye. I'd miss her, I really didn't want to let her go again.

I was on the move again. I knew the drive to Hook Norton well; as it I was in my own backyard. I was on my way to my previous photography clients to look after their Cocker Spaniel, Maisie. Hook Norton is a small Cotswold village near Chipping Norton on the border between Warwickshire and Oxfordshire. The houses are old, made of Cotswold stone, and the terrain is green, lush, and hilly. It's quite idyllic and I was happy to be there. David greeted me at the door and helped me in with my suitcase and bags of food. I met Maisey, their beautiful and sweet natured Cocker Spaniel. David's wife Nicola showed me how clever Maisie was; it was like something you'd watch on Britain's Got Talent as Maisey stood on two feet doing all these cute little tricks and moves; she won me over straight away. I thoroughly enjoyed the show and applauded whole heartedly.

They'd prepared a lovely lunch, a pasta dish with a cream sauce and prawns, followed by a pear crumble. The food was delicious and we chatted about the fact I'd been at the house years before to photograph their children. My portrait photos of the family were still on the walls, and it was like going back down memory lane.

David and Nicola took me for a walk with Maisey; we crossed the road and entered a farmer's field, which led into a stunning landscape of rolling hills, beautiful trees, and wildlife. Leaves were beginning to grow on the trees, and you could feel the sun's gentle warmth on your skin. Maisey was crazy for retrieving balls, so the whole walk was about throwing the ball and her retrieving it and bringing it back to me. She was excited and her enthusiasm for the game was infectious. I really did like this dog.

Nicola and David left after the walk and just out of curiosity I wandered around the empty house looking for signs. In my bedroom I saw something that was quite remarkable, I was definitely back in the book; in my novel Emily and Arthur had a dog, also a Spaniel like Maisey, and he was called Nelson. In my novel, Nelson was constantly in and out of the duck pond in their garden, and here on the wall in my bedroom was pictures of duck ponds and a family portrait I'd taken. As I looked closely at the portrait, I noticed the daughter's face and to my absolute amazement it was the face I'd used for the cover of my book! It was the real Emily! So here I was staying in Emily's bed, with her dog and pictures of duckponds. I'd manifested another scene in the book; I'd manifested the face of Emily, her house, and her dog! It was another unbelievable coincidence. When I had applied for the housesit, I didn't even realise I already knew who they were, and they didn't remember me either. And I hadn't even got the pet sit at first, originally, they'd chosen another candidate, but that person let them down and I was their second choice. I'd then tried to get out of it, after my experience of being pulled through the mud in Buckinghamshire twice a day for a month, convincing them that I wasn't suitable. But they weren't having any of it and had persuaded me to come and stay. Now I knew why, I was always meant to be here to play out this part of my book.

My days there went by quickly; I canvassed for business in Chipping Norton in the mornings. My canvassing wasn't successful. I kept trying as the rain and cold weather swept in from the west, but decided I was wasting my time and took Chipping Norton off my list of potential places to rebuild my business. It was a shame as I'd fond memories from that town; I'd run a successful business network there for close to ten years. I had taken my photographic studio equipment to the pet sit with me, as I had my first photo shoot booked in whilst I was on that trip. But on my last day, the shoot that I'd planned was cancelled; annoyingly the client no longer wanted the photos. Things were changing in the country; I could feel it. The war in Ukraine was beginning to affect people's psyche as the price of fuel and energy was getting more and more expensive.

I headed back to Dorset for Easter. I was having my children come and stay with me at my parents. I was missing them so much, and Maria had at last agreed that I could drive them again. I'd decided not to fight her, we were making progress and I wanted to build on that trust with patience rather than undoing it with a confrontation. On the way back down to Dorset I stopped off in Shipton-on-Stour and Stow-on-the-Wold and took photographs of the beautiful historic little Cotswold towns. I wished I had someone to share those trips with, but I was getting used to being alone most of the time and at least that way I could concentrate on the photography and take my time.

After a couple of days back in Dorset with my parents, it was time to pick up my children in Oxfordshire and bring them back with me. I tied the trip in with a photo shoot I'd booked in, it would be my first since starting up again. I arrived at the shoot; it was a lady called Fran and her three children. I set up my studio in her house and went through my old and trusted routine. I did various poses, connected well with the children, making them smile and ended up with a decent set of photos. I'd done it, I'd got my first shoot under my belt, I was at last a working as a portrait photographer again. It was an easy shoot; it felt like putting on an old familiar pair of slippers, I knew the job so well I could do it with my eyes closed. I left her with a price list, and we made a time for me to come and show her the photos. I felt great about it, it was a huge sense of relief, It was another win!

Chapter 12

A Deeper Understanding

My mother is a wonderful cook, and she loves to make delicious food for her family and her grandchildren most of all. As a result, my children loved to come and stay with me at my parents' house; all their favourite foods would be prepared, and they were absolutely showered with love. It was a sanctuary of sorts for all of us.

The week was filled with love, fun and family. Beatrice, Leo, and I enjoyed playing boardgames together; as a child growing-up I'd spent a lot of time with my family on caravan holidays playing boardgames on wet summer days in Cornwall. Leo was always up for a game and would play anything you wanted, but Beatrice was pickier; she'd only play what she wanted to play. Sara on the other hand would only play scrabble, and usually just to spend time with her nan. Beatrice would always wake first in the morning and immediately come and wake me up too, sometimes we'd be the only ones up before eleven o'clock. That was Beatrice and my special time before anyone else got up; we would eat breakfast together and then play a game, and afterwards I'd read to her. She didn't really like books, so that was very much her making an effort for me.

That week I'd organise one event a day, where we'd go out somewhere and do something; it might be a walk-in nature, a trip to the beach, or a Dorset town where we'd grab a hot drink and pop into the little shops looking for books or clothes. Whilst out and about with Beatrice and Leo, I felt it was time to tell them about Adele. I'd already told Sara and she'd kindly kept it quiet for me until I was ready to share the news with my youngest two. So, on a morning when it was just the three of us in a café with hot chocolate, I decided to broach the subject with them.

'So, I've got a little news I'd like to share with you.' I said, I could tell they weren't expecting news of any significance.

'Go on,' said Leo.

'Well, I've started seeing someone. She's very sweet, her name is Adele and she's South African. She's a bit like me, she's a nomad of sorts. She travels around looking after people, whereas I look after their pets.'

Beatrice shuffled in her seat and frowned a little.

'So, you're moving on with your life then.' she said in a matter-of- fact kind of way.

She'd loved Gabriella and was loyal to her, and I could see she wasn't ready to let someone new into her life. I hadn't planned for them to meet yet, I just wanted to prepare the ground so they could meet in time.

'I'm pleased for you Dad,' said Leo.

When he wasn't sure about something, he played it safe and said very little, he was the perfect diplomat.

'Do you have any questions? Is there anything you want to know about her?' I asked.

Both of the children gave me a blank look, so I left it there. I could see they weren't sure about the situation. They both knew me well and didn't quite know how to react to my new nomadic way of living; it was hard for them. I wanted them to be happy for me because I'd met someone, I wanted them to be interested in her, to ask me questions about how we'd met and what she was like. I got none of that, but then there was also no hostility or anything negative.

That week Leo and I had started running together. He was a fit 14-year-old with an athletic body, so he'd have to run at a pace that was too slow for him in order for us to run side by side, but eventually he'd run ahead and we'd meet at a halfway point. Whilst I was gathering my breathe and taking a short break, he'd continue to run across the fields to wear himself out a little more. We'd then run again together for a while on the way home before he'd eventually race on back to the house without me. I remembered running with my father at the same age; we'd raced short distances around the streets, but for Leo and me it was more of a measured middle-distance run. I was still building up my fitness, and he was bursting full of energy. It was a nice way to spend time together and during that holiday we went out for a run most days. It felt like life was returning to normal once again and it was reassuring.

We went on long walks in nature, and I shared what I could about the wildlife. I taught them how to identify various trees by the shape of their leaves, we watched birds and walked through different terrains. This was how I liked to spend time with them most, connecting to nature, chatting through life's challenges with the sun on our faces. Dorset has some beautiful places to walk, either coastal paths or country trails, it really is an idyllic place to spend time when the weather is good.

We'd all had a really good Easter break; it was family time and I'd needed it so much. I drove the kids back to Oxfordshire and then went on to my next house sit. It was a small flat in Farnborough where I'd spend a week looking after two house cats. Adele was coming to spend the week with me before she headed off to South Africa for a month. She'd changed her mind about me joining her in South Africa, but instead of going for the initially planned three months, she was cutting her trip down to one month as she said she didn't think I'd wait three months for her. She seemed to be making all the decisions in our infant relationship without consulting me. I'd raised my concerns about that approach; I liked to work with someone, to build a shared vision for the future, not to always be told what was going to happen. I'd been looking forward to going to South Africa and was disappointed.

As I let myself into the flat in Farnborough I noticed a huge metallic map on the wall, it was the exact same piece of art that I'd seen on the wall in the house in The Forest of Dean. Was it a sign for me about the war in the Ukraine and potential for escalation? I couldn't say, but it was such an unusual piece of art, and like the bear with the bow and arrow, it seemed to be following me around.

Adele arrived the day after me. I picked her up from the station where she was waiting for me with a big smile and her yellow bumblebee suitcase. I'd been looking forward to seeing her and spending a romantic week together. There was a nature reserve near the house, and we walked hand in hand along what was a former golf course, which had been handed back to the community. There was a little ditch full of water, and I shared a story with her about how I used to jump a ditch like that as a child with my friends to test our bravery. She laughed and dared me to do it again, so without giving myself time to think it through I took a run up, and jumped from one side to the other, landing safely on the other side. She laughed and was thrilled by it, it felt like we were adolescents playing in the park; it was such fun acting childishly again. She couldn't believe I'd managed to make the jump, which on reflection was bigger than I'd first thought.

That evening Adele made a salad niçoise and we played a game about music; she used her music collection, and I used mine. We would play the intro to a song, and the other person would have to guess the artist's name. We listened to great music, we nibbled on chocolate, and we reconnected with each other. We were still very much in the initial honeymoon phase of getting to know each other, and it felt like things were going well.

On one of the days, we drove to nearby Windsor and walked old busy the streets with my camera, stopping occasionally for me to photograph the sights. We crossed the bridge to Eton and saw the college and sat in the sun with a coffee and cake outside a little café and enjoyed a fine day out together. On the way back to the car, she bought me an ice cream and we kissed each other beside Windsor Castle's great walls. It was a day that I would hold dear to my heart and remember fondly.

That week was full of delicious food, walks in nature and love making. It went by way too quickly and it would end up being the last time I'd see Adele. On our last day we tidied up the flat and I drove her to Heathrow. We said our goodbyes and I had absolutely no idea that we'd soon be breaking up. Sometimes it's best not to know what the future holds, otherwise it would ruin the present moment. As Arthur had left Caroline to go and be with his parents in the present day, Adele was leaving me to go back to her parents in South Africa. Despite my efforts in the rewrite to keep Caroline in my life, it was unavoidable. I would have to find love in my second novel with someone new, as Adele was just playing her role in the book that I had written all those years ago. I didn't want to keep searching endlessly for my life partner, I knew she was out there somewhere, and I wouldn't give up until I found her. Adele had helped me enormously as I had helped her; we were just stepping stones for each other in the grand picture painted in the stars.

As April 2022 came to a close, I travelled to Hungerford for a short stay looking after two cats in a beautiful house that was being renovated. There was scaffolding outside and workmen on the roof. They'd made me feel very welcome by leaving some lovely food in the fridge to eat whilst I was there. They'd left a wild boar sausage, some tasty artisan cheese, and a loaf of sourdough. The house was very stylish, and it had everything I needed.

The days were getting longer, and the weather was getting warmer. There were no curtains on the window in the bedroom, so I woke up to the sun shining on my face at six o'clock in the morning, and as the sun woke me up so bright and early, I decided to photograph the small town before all the traffic started driving through the main street. I worked with the light to capture some lovely images. I wasn't great at getting up early in the morning for travel photography, but due to my close proximity to the centre of town and the light waking me up, on this day I'd managed it.

The following day, whilst enjoying a leisurely breakfast at the house in Hungerford, I received a message from a photography client, Miranda, asking if we were still meeting that morning to do the photoshoot? Shit! I had completely missed it; it wasn't in my diary, and it was a Bank Holiday Monday so I completely forgot. I had just enough time to get there, so I rushed down my breakfast, loaded the car and headed to Thame for the shoot. It was an hour's drive and thankfully I arrived on the minute, and I thanked my guides for giving her the nudge to remind me. We chatted about what they wanted over coffee, her, and her husband Danny, explained they wanted natural photographs of the two young children outside and some family photographs too. We went to a nearby farmer's field, and I captured beautiful portraits of the family together, there were some really special shots. I'd taken almost two hundred images, and we then sat down and went through my price list. We arranged a time for me to show them the photos and I said goodbye.

In the evening I went for a long walk along the canal in Hungerford, I took my camera and cleared my mind. It was a new way of life for me and I enjoyed the peaceful walk by myself, passing the narrowboats, dog walkers and teenagers hanging out on their bikes. It was my last night there and when I got back to the house, I had a message from Adele telling me that her parents did not approve of our relationship; they hadn't accepted her divorce due to religious reasons and were refusing to talk to her about me. And she wasn't challenging it. I couldn't understand, her parents were in their eighties, and it was her life to lead, not theirs. Like the busker who'd let her boyfriend go in Rotherham, the same thing was about to happen to me. I knew I had lost her to an old-fashioned religious point of view. I knew I had lost her, and it hurt very much. I was angry, not with her, and not with her parents either. I was angry that I'd written that plot line into my book. How could I be mad at anyone for just playing their part in the prophecy that I'd found myself in? I realised that Arthur's father had banned Arthur from going back to see Caroline, by telling him he couldn't use the time portal again, and Caroline's parents had banned her from seeing Arthur too. A real Romeo and Juliet moment and I was living it in my reality. However, for a time, Adele had given me what I so desperately needed, and now I'd have to face the hard reality that I was going to be alone yet again.

I arrived in Hambledon in Buckinghamshire in early May. The village was set aside idyllic rolling hills and lush countryside, and it was spectacular. I knew the area but had never heard of the little village where I was staying before; it was a well-hidden secret in the heart of middle England. I'd been booked to pet sit, but after a mix up with dates, Frank and Philippa, the homeowners were not going away anymore, so they let me stay in their house for free for a week. I had a self-contained room with a kitchen, that reminded me of what you might find in a holiday villa. It was basic but would get me through the week and I was extremely grateful for it. I was close to my friends and family, without any responsibilities of looking after any animals and having to be back by a certain time. I could get my head down and canvass in the local towns of Henley, Thame, and Marlow, which were three affluent towns nearby. I was also close enough to help with the children; Leo needed a brace, and I would be able to drive him to Oxford to get it fitted.

The walks through Hambledon were magical; I would take my camera and photograph the horses in the pristine meadows, and that week it seemed that the sun always worked with me, letting me capture some stunning images. It seemed like I had the whole valley to myself. The trees were now full of leaves and the countryside was brimming with every hue of green, vibrant and full of life. It was a time to reflect on my relationship with Adele and how I would have to let go of my hopes for a future with her. I'd had so many disappointments over the previous couple of years and sadly I seemed to be becoming an expert in letting go of things that were no longer meant for me.

The following house sit was nearby in a village called Haddenham. The house was a typical terraced house on a housing estate. The family were renovating, so it had a few issues, including a shower that only dribbled cold water. The night before I arrived, I received a message saying that one of the two cats, Mitsy, had gone missing. I was to keep the other cat locked in and when Mitsy arrived back home, I was to lock him in as well. These were two cats that were not used to being housebound, but now they would have to be. On my first afternoon there I got a message from Grace, the homeowner, telling me that Mitsy had turned up safe and sound at their old house, and that a helpful neighbour had skilfully captured him. Grace asked me to go and collect the cat, which was easy enough as it was a short drive on the other side of the village. Mitsy had been bribed with treats and was hiding in a wardrobe when I arrived. We managed to get him into his carry case, and once he was back home, he looked mightily relived that his adventure was over, I could relate! Mitsy and Bramble were pleased to be back together, and a drama had been averted. I was as relieved as the cats were, and as they snuggled up together, I could feel the tension leave my body. I set myself up in the little office and got to work.

I needed to keep all the windows closed as the cats were apparently great escape artists, but the temperatures were soaring and there was no fan. It was uncomfortable and sticky, and canvassing in the mornings was a struggle because of the heat. Despite the weather, and the fact it was hard to work, things started to pick up during June. I completed my first few sales and the money that had been eluding me up until then, finally started to flow. It felt significant, my hard work was finally paying off, and I allowed myself to feel a tinge of pride. I had planted the seeds, and now the shoots had broken through the earth and were growing towards the sun. Yet I knew my new little business was still vulnerable.

On the bookshelf I found an interesting book about the Enneagram. The Enneagram is a personality typing system that uses nine specific personality types to describe patterns in how people interpret the world and manage their emotions, and it would lead me to another area of growth and understanding of who I am. Over the next few weeks, I was about to be given many answers to the questions about the journey I'd been on, and this would eventually lead me back on my spiritual path, with a deeper understanding about my life. That book was the first of a long line of books that would open my eyes even wider and help me to understand more about myself and why things were happening the way they were. Apparently, the Enneagram was first discovered in ancient Mesopotamia four thousand years ago. I worked my way through the book, determined to finish it before the week was up.

I was amazed to read that the nine personality types matched the Greek mythology of Odysseus' hero's journey, and I marvelled at the way the universe was able to share its wisdom throughout the ages using a variety of perspectives and voices in different ways, yet sharing the same vital information. According to the book, I identified mostly with the character type number eight, and the reason I was an eight was because of my childhood and the experiences I'd been through back then.

There are moments in our lives when events shape us; they teach us lessons and help us to grow. Sometimes these moments can be quite traumatic and have a long-lasting impact upon us, and one moment in my life had done just that. I was eight years old, and on the school playing field messing about with a group of my classmates; good friends and some others I didn't get on so well with. With rackets in our hands, we were trying to keep the ball up in the air, much like you would do at the beach. But something happened, to this day I'm not sure exactly what I'd done, but I can only assume I must have done something wrong because I ended up getting pushed to the ground. The group of children then circled around me, there must have been at least a dozen boys and girls. Surprisingly, and totally out of character, they all began to kick me. I lay there huddled up in a ball, being kicked from all angles. As I lay there receiving blows to my back, legs and arms, the world I knew instantly changed forever; the world was no longer a safe place as I was introduced to its darker side for the first time, fate was changing my future. The strangest thing of all about that day, was that my best friends were there too kicking the hell out of me. I closed my eyes until they were done.

I kept what happened to myself; not telling my teachers or parents or even my brother. And that would be a habit I kept throughout my childhood; when I was hurt, I kept it to myself.

After many years I'd started to assume this memory had been nothing but a strange dream; it would occasionally pop up in my mind, but I'd dismiss it as something that hadn't really happened. Then one day on social media I connected with one of my old school friends, Simon. He was living overseas and had done so for many years. After we had connected, he sent me this message:

Hello   Ben,
How are you? I have been living in Brazil now for many years. I married a Brazilian woman and moved here to be near her family. I'm an architect and have built a good life for myself here. There is something I have been carrying with me for all of these years. That day on the school field when

you were beaten, kicked on the ground by all of us. I'm really sorry about that and wanted to ask for your forgiveness. I was your friend, and it should never have happened.

It was a significant moment for me because it meant it had happened; the ordeal was real. I became very emotional as the acknowledgement came flooding in. I forgave him, and he immediately disappeared again from my life.

According to the Enneagram book, because of this event and others like it which had put me in extreme situations during my early years, I'd created an anti-establishment and anti-religion side to my personality. I defended the downtrodden and stood up against bullies, believing I'm far more capable of achieving things in life than I actually am. Apparently, my superpowers were my strength and resilience, but my shadow aspect was in dealing with my vulnerability, hiding my pain and loss and not processing it. All of this was revealed in the book, and I was finally understanding how events in my life had played such a major part in shaping it. It also reflected in how I was tackling my life during my current situation.

Understanding this concept would help me rise above my ego and make decisions from a different perspective. There are parts of my character that are really helpful, and I wouldn't change, which have done me well throughout my life. But understanding the aspects that were still holding me back was a tremendous advantage. When I first started working with my spirit guides, they had led me to work on my vulnerability, and that was a year before me being here uncovering the knowledge in the enneagram book. It was reiterating what my guides had been previously teaching me, that perhaps back then, I hadn't been ready to learn or understand.

The cats weren't happy, and neither was I, we were all feeling hot and bothered. At night I'd been instructed to lock them in the kitchen where their litter tray was; but Mitsy had decided that this new, authoritarian keeper was not to his liking and so he started to protest. He would wait until I was asleep, and then go into my food bags that I'd left on the kitchen counter and pee all over them. Unfortunately, it took me a little while to figure out where the smell was coming from, and I had to throw all of my food out. The following night I left the kitchen door open to make it a little better for them, but Mitsy decided it wasn't good enough, found a bag containing my books and peed all over that one instead. I did my best not to get annoyed, but again the contents of my bag had to be thrown out. The following day, I decided this could go no further as the house was starting to smell of cat urine despite my best efforts, and the heat was making it a whole lot worse. In the kitchen I left a small window slightly ajar, it was high up with no surface underneath it, allowing some air into the kitchen without the cats escaping. However, I came down in the morning to discover that the two cats were in fact as good at escaping as their pet parents had warned. I wouldn't have believed it possible, but to my horror there were not cats in the house. This was the first time I'd lost pets on a pet sitting job and I was extremely stressed about it!

I left the back door open in the hope that the cats might return of their own free will whilst I got dressed to trawl the neighbourhood in search of them. It felt good to momentarily let some air into the house, but the cats didn't return. I closed the door and locked the cat flap so they could come in but not leave again, and put some food out to tempt them back. I tried to keep calm, these were regular moggies, they were used to the great outdoors and they'd probably return when they were hungry. I decided not to tell the homeowners quite yet, it would just stress them out, and they'd already been so upset to leave without knowing where Mitsy was. By ten o'clock in the morning Bramble had found her way home, and I was so grateful to her.

I didn't go canvassing that morning, I was too worried about Mitsy, although I suspected if he didn't return, he would just go back to his old home, like he did before. By lunchtime he appeared, to my huge relief. From that moment on, all my bags were kept in my room and the windows were kept closed. And needless-to-say I was glad to say goodbye to Haddenham by the end of my time there. At least it had been a successful week with my business, and I'd also learnt a lot and been able to see my kids, but Mitsy had got the better of me and I was looking forward to an easier experience at the next house. I was heading back to Wales and Agatha's house on the border with England; she'd invited me to return and it was the perfect place to be for the summer, with a secluded garden, two well behaved cats and a house full of books.

I was excited to be back in Wales. Agatha had a private courtyard with sun loungers, and it was so beautifully sunny that I decided I'd let my body soak up some rays. It felt good to expose all my skin to the power of the sun.

I called my friend Jennifer, and we chatted for some time over coffee. During the conversation she suggested I read a book on shamanism and mental health, so I read the bio and decided she was right it would be a useful book for me. I'd recently been trying to reach out to a few shamans online that offered coaching and counselling, as I'd wanted to speak to someone who could help me unpick my ordeal, and understand what had happened through the rewriting of my book. I'd messaged a few people and I'd received the same response from all of them, nothing; I'd been completely ignored. So, I'd asked my spirit guides for help, 'Send me my mentors' I'd asked, and here was their answer, they'd sent me what I needed in the form of this book. That evening my friend Quinn sent me a photo, and it was the cover of the very same book, he was suggesting I give it a read too. To have these two people send me the same recommendation on the same day for the same book, after asking my guides for some assistance, was quite incredible. I downloaded the book and decided to read it straight away.

I spent many hours that week reading. The book took me on a journey of deep understanding about the path I was on. In the book was an explanation of the 'shamanic sickness', apparently those selected by the spirit world to become a shaman would have to go through a great ordeal; they'd first lose their health, at which point they'd have to find a way to heal themselves. I'd done this when I'd learnt about energy and how to generate energy through my body to heal myself. It had taken me almost a year to get through my physical sickness, but the book spoke of many shamans that would die through that initial ordeal or take many more years to heal themselves. I'd been lucky I guess, to get through it as quickly as I had. The author then went on to describe how after recovering their physical health, the shaman would lose their mental health and have to find their way back and heal themselves again. I could relate; I'd been taken to the edge of my sanity and survived the ordeal, with the opportunity for a period of huge inner growth and reflection. The reason the shaman was pushed to the extremes was to gain great knowledge and become a healer. I was totally gripped as I turned each page, I had experienced almost everything I was reading. I knew I was supposed to be reading that book in that very moment; my guides had given me this information at the perfect time. I was a shaman; I couldn't ignore what I'd been through. I needed to get back to what I was really here to do, my shamanic work. The book said that a shaman doesn't have a choice; once selected for the work by the spirit world, he would have to surrender to his path. I understood that now, as when I'd gone against the wishes of the spirit world, very bad things had happened, like crashing into the tree in the snowstorm.

The next book I picked up was on NLP, neuro-linguistic programming, which is a pseudoscientific approach to communication, personal development, and psychotherapy. I had read books on NLP in the past so the concept wasn't new to me. I skim-read through the book in one day, it was more of a recap for me more than anything else. However, there was one section that would lead me to an incredible discovery and throw me right back into my own novels, literally. I found myself doing an exercise; I had to retrace my timeline and revisit my past. I chose Agatha's hallway downstairs to do this. The floor was covered with black and white square tiles and there was a wooden staircase up to the first floor. I stood still on the chequered floor and visualised my life, gradually taking small steps backwards, to represent stopping at various stages of my life. Through a visualisation I pictured my past three years; I pictured making love with Adele for the first time, crashing into the tree in Pembroke, experiencing heightened awareness in The Forest of Dean, speaking to Neptune in Edinburgh, meeting Jo in a café in Nottingham, standing on the Glastonbury Tor and bumping into Eleanor, leaving Gabriella, being baptised as a druid... I was travelling back along my timeline.

Suddenly I understood. This house was representing the time portal in my book; Agatha's office was stacked wall to wall with historical books from each period of history, in meticulous order. I Had just travelled back in time, on my past timeline. In the house there was a reading room with a little table, just as I had written about in my book. Every detail matched, my characters travelled back in time by picking out a historical book and the pages came to life. I'd picked out a book on NLP which took me back on my own timeline. It was the perfect metaphor. I couldn't avoid it, I was back in my story, I was back in the 'Tree of Time' – this house seemingly represented the inside on the tree in my novel. It was time to allow the spiritual adventure back into my life. It was time to complete the second edit of my novel and look for literary agents once again. It was time to try and find a healthy balance; a spiritual path and success in the non-spiritual world. I had to find a way of being in the flow, riding the wave without falling off.

Later that day on a walk around the little village I was staying in, I received texts from my mother who was visiting her elderly aunt. My mother sent me two photos; a photo of my novel, Arthur Archer and The Time Traveller's Chronicles, and a photo of a hand-carved wooden owl. My mother said her aunt was rereading my novel, twelve years after reading it for the first time, and she wanted me to see the owl, because every time she saw it she thought of me and my book. It was a message through my great aunt from the spirit world, I knew it, I was being drawn back into my story. I had unfinished business with my novel, and I'd been ignoring it.

The next two stops on my British housesitting tour were in Scotland. I had a few days in Selkirk, in the Borderlands, followed by a week looking after Mikey again, in Portobello in Edinburgh. I had a plan, I'd finish the 2nd edit of my book by the time I'd left Scotland, if I worked hard, it would just be about be doable. The drive to Selkirk was long and I arrived around six o'clock in the evening. I was welcomed by a widower, Helen, who was a tall, friendly woman with red curly hair and big glasses. She was heading to the U.S for a few days and needed someone to look after her two Labradors and a rather cute, black cat called Leonard. She'd prepared a delicious vegan meal with beans and veg.

The old house was set on three floors, it had plenty of character and an office I could use to do my editing. We spoke of politics and the environment over our meal, which she served generously with ice cold beer. We shared similar views of the world, so it was an easy and relaxed conversation. We complained about the government and the mess U.K. politics had found itself in, and after we had eaten, we headed out to walk the dogs before bed. We walked on the land of what was a former stately home with stunning grounds that had been given to the local community, after the death of the previous owner. The walk was beautiful, and the two dogs were well trained and a lot of fun to be walking with.

Helen left early the next morning, and after I'd walked the dogs, I set about working on my book. I became engrossed in the story as I chopped and changed it; some aspects I'd recently added I removed and other passages I developed more. I found my rhythm; a long walk around the stately home with the dogs first thing, followed by editing for a while and in the afternoon, I'd do the same with a lunch somewhere in between. The dogs were proving to be great company, the walks were entertaining and the people I bumped into on the walk knew the dogs and greeted them with treats. Helen was clearly well liked and respected. Leonard the cat, on the over hand, did cause me some stress, disappearing for two of the five days that I was there. But thankfully he decided to turn up the night before I was due to leave, like a rebellious teenager.

Intuitively I decided to switch my dating app back on. I was a long way from my children, so meeting someone in Edinburgh was far from ideal. However, I had a strong urge to do it and so I did. By the end of the day, I'd received lots of matches, and I'd started the long process of chatting to people and finding out who was suitable. My heart wasn't in it though, did I really want to put myself through more rejection and endless text messages? I felt that the universe was using my desire to be in a loving relationship to fulfil scenes from my novels.

I photographed the little town of Selkirk and whilst I was walking the streets, I popped into a barber and had a trim. I soaked up the atmosphere in the barber shop, enjoying listening to the people having their conversations, and soon enough I was fully emersed in the local chatter, they advised me of what I should be taking photographs of locally.

I'd enjoyed my short stay in Selkirk, I was flying through the editing of my book and felt good within myself I was ready to move from the disappointment of losing Adele. I thought about the stately home nearby, one of the ideas I'd had in my document matched what happened there; handing back the land to the local community through inheritance. The stately home was almost half the size of the little town, it felt absurd that half of the land was owned by one person, and only common sense that the land should be opened up for everyone to appreciate and get value from. We accept so much that is unfair and wrong, simply because it seems to be the way things have always been.

I went on to my second stay at the beach house in Portobello, which was just a short drive from the centre of Edinburgh. I arrived to find the family loading up their car for a week in the Highlands. They offered me a warm welcome, updated me on the changes in the house and were soon off on their vacation. The weather promised to be amazing, and they'd left the hammock up in the garden for me to use. I was starting to get a regular and unfamiliar pull to the sun, I felt my body needed it and was demanding I simply do as it requested.

I met a Scottish woman on the dating app, her name was Leah; we'd been chatting for a few days and she'd endeared herself to me. She was quirky, confident, and attractive, and she had a few days coming up without her son, so I asked her out on a date. I warned her that I wasn't staying in Scotland long, but she didn't seem to mind. I was pleased, it would be nice to meet someone up there, and give me something to look forward to. I didn't have a desk to write on, so I sat on the sofa with a small low table placed in front of me; I was determined to finish my book in the week I was there. After a day of writing, it was time to meet up with Leah in a suburb of Edinburgh called Leith.

Instead of driving I walked from Portobello along the coastal road, so I could have a few beers and relax into the evening. My stomach was starting to turn, I was actually getting excited, I had a really good feeling about Leah. I enjoyed the view, and the walk gave me time to prepare myself and switch gears from my writing mind to being sociable, which wasn't an easy thing to do. We'd arranged to meet in the street, but when I got there Leah messaged that she was stuck on a bus, and it wasn't moving. The whole of Edinburgh seemed to be full of road works at the time, so I told her I'd meet her in a bar and found one on the waterside that offered a wide range of beers. I like real ale, I like trying different ones from each area I travel to, but sadly in Scotland I had yet to find one I liked. I asked to try a handful of ales and, as I took a sip from each glass, I became increasingly disappointed, I settled on the one that was the least offensive to my taste buds. I guess I'd been spoilt in England, foreign people often make fun of warm English beer, especially the Australians, but for me I really appreciated the difference and what we had to offer. English beer was the king of beers as far as I was concerned.

Leah turned up an hour late, she'd told me she'd almost given up and gone home as the road works had hampered her journey so much. I was glad she hadn't. I ordered her a cocktail and we sat outside overlooking the water. She had a huge smile on her face, which delighted me, it was contagious. She had shoulder length red hair, worn up in a way that reminded me of a Celtic warrior. She had blue eyes and silver eyeliner which added a touch of sparkle. Her clothes were really unusual, stylish and they stood out. She wore a thin, figure hugging, royal blue long flowing dress with gold patterns and her shoulders were bare. She was almost ten years younger than me and had a youthfulness about her which was so appealing to me. The chemistry between us was there almost immediately, and I was excited to be in her company.

We connected over music; she told me there was no grey area for her with music, she either loved it or hated it. Her favourite artist of all time was David Bowie, closely followed by Fleetwood Mac. With that information we played a game where we picked an artist and I guessed if she liked them or not, and I had an uncanny knack of getting every one right. She loved Blur but she didn't like the Beatles, and it went on like that, she was surprised that I already seemed to know her tastes so well. Leah was an Anglophile, she loved Britain and the English in particular. She was originally from the Highlands but had lived in Edinburgh for many years, and was deeply frustrated with the Scottish independent movement and shared with me how people in Scotland either fell in one camp or the other. I enjoyed talking about Scotland, the people and culture. I'd travelled the world but now I was learning about Britain.

After our drink we headed to another bar she knew, there was a chill in the air, so it was good to get inside. The barmaid said it would be last orders shortly, so I ordered a bourbon, and Leah had another Expresso Martini. As we chatted in a quiet corner of the pub I asked her a personal question,

'What do you miss most about being in a relationship?'

She thought for a moment, and then smiled when she had the answer.

'I miss being cuddled. I haven't been held by a man for so long,' she said.

That was my cue, I looked deep in her eyes, smiled, stood up, walked around the table, sat next to her and held her in my arms. I felt all the tension in her body melt away. Her sweet scent filled my nostrils.

'That was lush.' She said with her rather sexy Scottish accent. I loved her voice, it was so rich and full of character.

I kissed her, and we snuggled up until they asked us to leave because they were closing the place.

As we left, I told her I didn't want the night to end. We had very little time to see each other before I headed back to England, as the following afternoon she would pick up her son from his dad's and she would have him for the rest of the week that I was there.

'I know it's a bit cheeky, but would you like to come back to the house I'm staying at? I can take you home in the morning.' I asked with a seductive look upon my face.

She didn't have to think about it.

'I'd like that, yes.' She said, and we kissed again.

We walked the long walk from Leith to Portobello hand in hand, and as we passed the beach, I suggested we walk down the steps and look out at the sea.

'I'd love to but I'm desperate for a pee.' She said rather unromantically.

I laughed, the romantic walk along the beach would have to wait.

'Come on, let's get you back,' I said.

We increased our speed until we got back to the house and she immediately ran to the loo.

The house was full of pictures of musicians, album covers and posters. Leah was quirky, and so was this house, so she was in her element. I put on some of my music, and we opened a bottle of wine. We kissed a little and then she told me she was really hot and took off her dress to reveal matching black laced underwear, on a slender and athletic body. We kissed a little more before I led her to my room, and we lay together on the bed as I explored her body gently with my fingertips. She told me she liked how I was touching her and to be gentle and take my time. We were soon naked and connecting with each other at a deeper level. Our bodies entwined in different positions, rhythmically moving in time together in the half-light of the bedroom. It was beautiful, gentle yet still very passionate. She was opening herself up to me and I was accepting her gratefully. The pleasure I was feeling intensified and as she let out a sigh from deep inside of her, my muscled tightened and then relaxed to the ultimate sensation. She turned to look at my face and the let out an almost apologetic little laugh.

I will never forget that night, it was so tender and almost perfect. We'd met as strangers and we'd wake up as lovers.

The following morning as we woke, we made love again and then I brewed a coffee which we shared in bed. It became apparent that I needed to take her home sooner than planned, she'd forgotten her allergy medicine and was starting to become uncomfortable and was scratching her head. A little like Cinderella racing home after the ball, I drove her home as quickly as I could. She lived in a district near the centre of the capital, and she invited me in. Her flat was small and stylish, and contained all that she needed. She quickly took her medicine and told me to hang around until it kicked in. She put on some music, and we had another coffee. I was a little uneasy as she clearly was suffering from her allergies, but as we chatted about our lives, our children, and our work, she began to find her body coming back in harmony with itself once again.

After she'd recovered and felt back to normal, she led me to her bedroom, and we made love once more. She lay there stroking my face and looking into my eyes.

'This better not be the last time I see you, Mr Molyneux,' she said challengingly, pointing her finger at me playfully.

'I wasn't looking for a one-night stand,' I said reassuringly. 'I think you're rather special. I really want to get to know you and find out what's in that head of yours, what makes you tick. I love your quirkiness, I'm a little quirky and you'll get to know that about me soon enough.'

'That's good then.' She said as she snuggled up into my hairy chest, and I stroked her thick mass of red hair. We'd connected deeply in the short time we'd spent together it had been so special and I had a spring in my step when I finally left her.

I got back to the beach house, and decided I'd spend the day editing and in between I'd catch some rays in the garden. As I lay there in the hammock, I re-lived the magical evening and morning in my head. Leah was unlike any woman I'd ever known; it felt like she was a breath of fresh air in my life, and my intuition had guided me to her. I pictured her white delicate skin, and I retraced the contours of her body in my mind. The disappointment of losing Adele had created the space for something new and exciting.

The following day Leah told me she had a couple of hours free after work, she was a graphic designer for a small local business. She asked if I wanted to pick her up and see her for a little while to say goodbye, as it would be our last chance whilst I was in Scotland. I jumped at the chance. We walked hand in hand along the beach and chatted about how things could work between us. I told her I'd taken myself off the dating app, she smiled and looked pleased. We looked at dates in our calendars and there was a gap in my diary when I didn't have a house sit, which matched when her son was visiting her parents in August. It was less than a month away. She invited me to stay with her and what's more, it was during the Edinburgh Fringe Festival, what a fantastic opportunity. I had something really special to look forward to, I would be returning to Scotland within a month.

On my last evening, armed only with an uplifting playlist of nineties British music, I managed an eleven-hour editing bonanza and completed my goal. My second edit was finished, and I felt ready to find an agent and a publisher. 'Arthur Archer and the Tree of Time,' was ready at long last. That night I spoke to the universe, 'Here you go, I know you wanted me to finish this book, it's now over to you. It's cost me so much; you've pushed me to the edge and often well beyond it. Send me the opportunity to put it out there, so it can reach a massive audience. Send me a publisher, a good one, and make it easy. I'm done with struggling. Let it flow to me, make it glorious and worthy of this whole incredible chapter in my life. Thank you.' I had set the intention, and within two days my first big opportunity would arrive, quite magnificently and unexpectedly.

I cleaned up the house, said goodbye to Mikey the cat and headed back down south. We were in the middle of a heatwave; and I'd escaped the worse of it by being up in Edinburgh. Temperatures in Southern England were in the forties and my car's air conditioning was broken. That day I spent twelve and a half hours sitting in heavy traffic, as there were road works and closed roads due to accidents. It was a tough long day and an horrendous drive. I spent time thinking about my book and wondering if my intention had been heard. I arrived at my parents' house for a quick two days of restocking clothes and catching up; they were fitting a new kitchen and the house was upside down. The following day I made the short drive to Wareham, to pick up a few things I needed for my travelling kitchen supplies. After I bought what I needed I decided to grab a coffee, there would be no opportunity to brew a proper cup at home that day as the kitchen was out of bounds.

I found a little café by the river and a waiter took my order whilst I sat looking out at the children on their paddleboards. A woman was sat alone in the sun reading a book at a nearby table. She had a stylish white hat and a serene look about her, she sat peacefully, and I was curious as to what she was reading. She seemed to be a similar age to me and looked like she might be on holiday, I saw she was reading a book I knew well. She noticed me looking at the book, and she said hi and introduced herself, her name was Aggie. I told her I'd read the book and it was one of my favourites. We got into a conversation and as the waiter appeared she asked if I cared to join her with my coffee. I was surprised, but pleased so said yes and changed my seat. As we chatted, I discovered that she too was a fellow house sitter; she was currently looking after two dogs and some ducks, and was trying hard to stop the dogs from eating the ducks. That was a scene from my book, so my attention was immediately alerted, this wasn't a chance meeting. There were some serious coincidences happening again.

She had arrived the day before and was based in the small quaint town of Woodstock in Oxfordshire. She asked me what I did and I talked about the novel I'd just finished, and she told me she was a director for television and cinema. Now my interest was truly peeked, and my heart began to beat faster. Had I manifested this opportunity straight away? I asked her about her work, she directed for the children and teen market, mainly films but she had done a few mini series' as well. Two days ago, I'd told the universe I was ready, and I had asked them to send the right person to me, and by chance here I was sat by the river enjoying a coffee with a successful director. Play it cool Ben, play it cool! We shared stories about our housesitting adventures and she told me an hilarious story about being locked out of one of her houses without her phone in just her knickers and bra. I told her about Mitsy and Bramble and their great escape. Aggie was good company and by the end of our coffee she'd asked if she could read the manuscript of my novel. No way! It was unbelievable, I was in the flow; nothing was guaranteed but the universe was creating the most incredible opportunity for me almost immediately. This was the stuff science couldn't explain and to many it would be just another coincidence; being in the right place at the right time yet again.

I drove back to my parents full to the brim with excitement. I'd had a great time in Scotland, I'd finished my book and it was being read by a successful television director. Life was one big, beautiful adventure, and I was most certainly living it.

I went back to Newbury to the cottage I'd stayed at for a few days the previous year. It was always nice to be invited back and I was starting to feel like I had many homes; the houses and animals were becoming familiar, and I was getting used to the areas where I was staying. It was still extremely hot, as the heat wave continued; climate change was clearly showing its colours and I was finding it too hot to work. I was staying in a little village just outside Newbury, I'd been keen to explore the countryside, but besides a path through a farmer's field it seemed like all of the countryside was out of bounds. I was bitterly disappointed; there I was in the middle of the countryside, and I couldn't even explore it. I thought about our right to roam and the book I'd read the previous year; In Scotland people have the right to roam the countryside as they do in many parts of Europe, yet in England we have only got access to a tiny percentage of the land, and with each new generation we lose more of our rights and the landowners gain more. I was tempted to break the rules and trespass through the ancient forest that was closed off to the public, so I started walking down the path but then realised I wasn't in a particularly rebellious mood after all, and besides, it was already getting too hot so I headed back to the house to start work on some of my photographs.

On my walk back I saw a slow worm crossing the path, I stopped and took a closer look. I'd never seen one before, and when I got back, I researched its spiritual meaning. A slow worm represented transformation and new beginnings, which felt apt and symbolic as I was after all at the beginning of a new relationship. I posted the picture on social media and one of my friends Quinn liked the image and made a comment; we chatted, and I invited him out for a drink that evening. Quinn had been the bard who'd told the stories the day I'd been baptised by Jay as a Druid. We worked out our halfway point and it turned out to be on the ridgeway, which was a site of major historical and spiritual significance, and it was actually the exact place he'd planned to take me the day we'd met last when my guides had suggested a different location. It all felt very significant. If the slow worm hadn't been on my path that afternoon, I wouldn't be heading out with him that evening. We both grabbed a couple of cold drinks and an icepack and drove to the carpark on the ridgeway. It was great to see him, he was always such an interesting character. It was a barmy summer evening, and the sun was beginning its slow decent as we walked along the ancient trail. Quinn shared stories of ancient Britain and how our civilisation was much more advanced and older than common knowledge believes.

We found a great spot on a ridge overlooking the spectacular scenery, there were wild deer and a couple of hares bobbing up and down. The sunset was magnificent and as we watched it descend behind the horizon, I shared with Quinn all of the events that had shaped my life since I'd seen him last. I asked him why they'd baptised me that day at the start of my journey.

He shrugged. 'Don't ask me, that was all Jay's idea,' he said.

'Well, at least it makes for a good story,' I replied.

Chapter 13

Manifest

The hot weather continued as it reached the end of July, I was back at my parents' house and happily had my children with me for part of their summer holidays. It was our usual quality family time together, with the exception that Sara had decided not to join us. She was a seventeen-year old after all, and understandably preferred to stay near her friends.

Leo and I took a long walk to Cole Woods in Wool, and as we re-emerged back out of the woods a herd of cows had decided to congregate at our exit, blocking our way out as they were crowded around the gate. We had two choices; we could either walk through the closely packed cattle or take a much longer route back. We had once as a family been chased by an angry herd of cows and only just escaped, and since that day I was very cautious around cows. As I had my son with me, I decided to take the longer route back. We were tired and eager to get home for lunch, so we were both a little frustrated, the cows were watching us curiously. We headed the long way back, along a quiet country road. As I looked ahead in my path, I saw a snake. I knew straight away that it was the adder I had always wanted to see in the wild. It was injured and was trying to roll off the road. I didn't feel in any danger and knew I needed to get the poor creature off the road. A car approached and I protected the snake by guiding the car around us, I then found a long stick and gently nudged the adder to the side of the road and into the long grass and we left it there hoping for the best.

The following day, with Beatrice along with us, we went back to Cole Wood. As we entered the woods I noticed another animal in trouble, it was a little robin whose claw had got caught in some barbed wire. I got the children involved in rescuing the little bird; Leo held the robing gently whilst Beatrice untangled her and the robin flew off unharmed. We walked around the woods and as we came out through the wooden gate, we discovered the cows had repeated their efforts from the previous day. It was as if they'd deliberately moved from one side of the field to the other whilst we'd been walking, and they were standing their ground by the gate once again, looking at us mischievously. To Beatrice's dismay it meant we needed to go the long way back again. As we retraced our steps, I decided to look for the snake to see if it had survived, but sadly I found it where I'd left it. It had died soon after I'd taken it from the road. Beatrice and Leo held it up and examined it; it was so beautiful. I'd always imagined adders to be black, but it was full of intricate colouring and was more orange than anything else.

Leo wanted to see if he could preserve the snake, so we took it back with us and I put it in one of my wooden boxes. A couple of days went by, before I noticed a peculiar smell started emerging in my room. I'd forgotten about the snake, but by the third day I realised where the smell was coming from; the dead snake had created the most horrendous odour that was permeating around my room. I took the snake out of the house and left it to decompose in nature. I couldn't understand how it had got so smelly so quickly, or why I'd allowed Leo to put a dead snake in a box in my room in the first place. I had to throw my wooden box away too. Later that week, the actions of the snake, the cows and myself I would all become clear.

Whilst there I decided it was time to read through my second novel, 'Arthur Archer and the Warrior Queen,' I was apprehensive as I hadn't wanted a repeat of the previous experience; but I wanted to see if it also needed to be rewritten and if there were any meanings in the book that I'd missed. Like the first book, I read through it all in one day. Halfway through, I was reading a scene where Emily and Boudica had gone for a walk in the countryside. Boudica had brought food with her, only to pull out of her bag a snake to eat. Emily was horrified and declared that the snake smelt so bad she wouldn't touch it. Clearly the second book was also full of moments in my life that I was experiencing. I had deliberately tried to close my attention to all the coincidences, or at least I hadn't gone looking for them, but they were still happening regardless. I identified that I'd already experienced through synchronicities, like that of the smelly snake, around half of the scenes from my second novel, and yet I was still here and in one piece. The book was a powerful piece of writing that was manifesting events into my life, but it was no longer derailing me; that put my mind at ease.

I reflected on the cows and the snake; I believe it is easier for the spirit world, or universe, to work through an animal or the weather, rather than a human being that is conditioned by their thoughts and society's norms. Animals are more likely to act on instinct, the cats and dogs I'd been looking after had played out many scenes from my books as unknowing but willing actors. I thought about shamans throughout history reading omens, signs, and messages in nature; like a flight of birds, or discovering a dead animal, and allowing themselves to be guided by them. And that night I had a powerful dream, I was one of a dozen people spaced out along a huge sandy beach facing the ocean. We didn't know each other, and we didn't speak; we were all alone in our thoughts looking out at the sea. The waves were higher than a three-storey building, and all of us had to face them on our own. I was terrified but knew I would do it, others were already in the water, ahead on their journey.

I decided to do a shamanic journey to speak with my guides for more insight into the dream and the animals I'd come into contact with. As I reached the familiar place deep within my subconscious mind I was immediately greeted by Tomahawk. We sat together in the sunshine at the top of a cliff looking out over a luscious landscape.

'Last night I dreamt I was facing huge waves, and I knew I had to face them alone but there were others there too. What can you tell me about the dream?' I asked him.

'The dream represents your spiritual journey. You are travelling alone and facing huge challenges. It is much easier for you to come off the path, turn away and walk along the beach or back into the forest. Yet you know that your journey is to face the ocean, and that the ocean is wild and powerful and so much stronger than you are. The other people you saw were others on a similar path, and although you will meet others along the way, no one else can do your journey for you. It must be you that faces the waves and you alone. You already know that you can do it, otherwise it would not be on your path.'

Intuitively I knew what he said before he told me, and hearing his words did not give me any comfort.

'Why must we face such huge challenges alone?' I asked.

'You are never truly alone; the universe will always give you everything you need if you allow it to come to you,' he said with the hint of a knowing smile.

'Ancient shamans would draw in the soil or perhaps the sand, they would take a stick and draw a circle and inside they would draw everything the community needed for its survival. That might have been rain, sunshine, oxen, pigs, or horses. They would tell their gods exactly what they wanted. Cave dwellers would do the same thing on the walls of their caves. Shaman's have a powerful energy and can manifest their wishes through writing and drawing,' he continued.

'So, it works like a vision board.' I said understanding exactly what he meant.

'Yes, and your books work in the same way. You wrote about a rotten snake, and you received a rotten snake!' A much wider smile spread across his face.

It was all making so much sense, I was manifesting my two novels and also the changes I'd made to them. I had been training in the art of manifestation through energy, written words, and feelings. I thanked Tomahawk for his wisdom and came back to my waking state to reflect on his wise counsel. My attempts to change my books had only created new scenes into my life, you can't change your destiny, but you can certainly add to it. I reflected on how I wrote about Caroline's parents disapproving of Arthur and banning her from seeing him, and how I'd written that scene fairly recently not understanding that I was bringing it into my reality.

I started thinking of the positive impact I could bring with all of the knowledge I was assimilating. I understood the law of attraction, I knew all too well that we are a magnet with our thoughts; if we visualised our desired results, and added emotions and feelings to them we could manifest those desires into our life. I'd read about visualising the desired result as if you had already achieved it; writing affirmations in the present tense, as if whatever you longed for had already happened. I reflected on how I could have a positive impact in the world through my manifestations. I wanted to know how this knowledge could be harnessed on a larger scale to impact the world, to help humanity with the issues it faced. To help the planet and the multitude of species residing on it. I considered our current society, our media told the *bad* news, there was rarely a positive story to be found and they spread sensationalism, drama and fear. I had to ask the tough question, were we responsible for our plight with the narrative we were spreading?

Authors, film makers and journalists wrote things that played to our lower emotions - fear, lust, shame, greed, gossip, and chaos. It was hard to find an uplifting inspirational story, but what would happen if the mass narrative changed? Could we as a species start manifesting a more positive future for ourselves? I had proved to myself beyond any shadow of a doubt that I could manifest my writing into my life, so could we as a people manifest a vision for the future? Could we learn to move away from our need to spread fear and fatalism, and replace it with hope and optimism? I had read that week that the Chinese Government had changed the ending of Western movies and given them a positive ending when crime wasn't rewarded with success. Were they aware of the power of the written word in manifesting a future? I was just theorising, but I suspected there was some powerful truth in all of this. My big question remained, how could my manifesting be magnified to impact more people positively, and potentially the environment we lived in too? Could a massive group of people writing a positive future together, change the trajectory we were currently heading towards?

I took the kids back to their mother's, and headed straight back up to Scotland, consumed with thoughts about how good it would be to be spending time with Leah once again. I was really excited to see her; we'd been chatting over the phone all the time whilst we were apart, and we were getting to know each other slowly but surely. The drive was long, but I filled the trip with audio books. I arrived just after nine o'clock that night, and Leah answered her door with the biggest smile I'd ever seen in my life, which my words cannot do justice to; she couldn't believe I'd driven all that way to see her again. We kissed, we held each other and chatted excitedly about the few days ahead.

After we'd emptied my car, she suggested we go to her local pub for a drink as there was live music as part of the Fringe Festival. We walked hand in hand to the pub which wasn't far away. They had a folk band playing covers, we ordered a couple of drinks and sat down, I had a beer and she had her usual cocktail. The band was great, the beer not so good and the company delightful. I was talking about the power of manifestation and gave the example of music; I shared with Leah how often I'd heard music matching what I was thinking, feeling, or experiencing. I told her to experiment with it; to think of a song, the first one that popped into her head. She said she was thinking of Fleetwood Mac and their song 'Dreams'. I then told her to tell the universe that she wanted to hear that song next, so she did, within five minutes the band were singing it! Her face lit up with astonishment as the first cords were played.

'That's how it works,' I said, 'That's the power our thoughts contain. The more you believe in it, the more powerful it becomes. You've just got to believe it's possible.'

She grabbed my hand and led me to the dance floor, 'Let's dance,' she said. We stood in front of the band, and we danced along to the song she'd wished for. I watched her slender frame move in time to the beat, she looked so beautiful and so happy. I allowed the rhythm of the music to enter my body, despite the long day, I was ready to let myself go and have some fun! The band had been somewhat ignored by the clientele in the pub, but now we were engaging with them, they perked up and looked appreciative. The energy was passing from the band to us and back again; she'd somehow brought the whole place to life and other people got up danced too. When the band finished Leah chatted to them for a little and I proudly watched her. She had a way about her that people warmed to immediately. She was captivating.

We left the pub and headed back to the flat, and as soon as we got in, she put on some more Fleetwood Mac so she could continue dancing, she mimed along with the songs, and I was mesmerised by the way her body moved in time to the music. She was sexy, she was stimulating all of my senses, and despite the long day all I could think about was making love to her. She kept dancing and singing and I kept my desires under wraps. She changed her clothes to fully get into character; she put on an outfit that matched that of her idol, Stevie Nicks. She was totally engrossed in her dancing and utterly lost in the moment. It reminded me of people at a rave or shamanic ceremony, when people truly connect their body, mind, and soul to the music.

I watched Leah solo dancing for a while, and when she was finished, she fell into my arms on the sofa, laughing, ecstatic. I held her tightly to me and could feel her heart pumping fast after all the dancing. We made our way to her bedroom, where we took pleasure in slowly undressing each other. We kissed, we explored each other all over again, and we made love. It was magical, we'd instantly reconnected; like our bodies needed to be in union again. We fell asleep, shattered, and I held her tightly in my arms, as if I was worried. I'd wake up and find her gone. If I'd had to leave Edinburgh that very next morning it would still have been worth the drive; she was so different from anyone else I'd ever met. I wanted to get to know her, to understand her and learn from her simplicity and unabashed quirkiness.

I woke before Leah and lay there looking around the room. Time travel seems to have always been an integral part of my life; as a young child growing up, I loved Mr Benn, a cartoon where my namesake would enter a room full of clothes and come out dressed in a new outfit from the time period he was about to explore. Leah's bedroom was like Mr Benn's wardrobe; she had many wardrobes all open, each packed full of colourful clothes. Leah stirred and I gently moved my naked body against hers and wrapped my arms around her. She rolled over and looked at me in the eyes and smiled, then she kissed me. She climbed on top of me and slowly slid down underneath the bed covers. I felt her nibble my chest and then my stomach. My body came alive to her touch; her soft lips brought life to everything they kissed. I let out a moan, it felt like she was using her powerful magic to bring life to parts of me that had been in a deep dark sleep; even though we had made love just a few hours before. I was completely in the moment, feeling every sensation. I tried to relax all of my muscles and just allow myself to reach the full potential of the moment, and when the moment arrived, and I came, I let out a moan of sheer unadulterated pleasure. It had felt sensational, all the tension in my entire body left in that moment. And then she returned to my side and hugged me tight.

'Your turn,' she said with an expectant look upon her face.

I allowed myself a few minutes to recover and then headed under the sheets to return the favour.

I left Leah in the shower whilst I wandered down the street in search of some fresh bread for breakfast. I found a little bakery and the smell of the fresh bread wafted under my nose and made me realise how our morning antics had left me with quite the appetite. I picked a brown and white sourdough loaf and headed back to the flat where I found Leah wrapped in a towel, doing her makeup in the mirror. I got started on breakfast; I put on some music and searched through the kitchen cupboards for a pan, so I could poach some eggs, and whilst the water was heating, I looked around the little kitchen to see what signs spoke to me. On the table was a model of a hand; the type artists would use that could be repositioned, and it was pointing up to the sky. My name, Benjamin, meant right hand of God. On the wall were two pictures and as soon as I noticed them the hairs on my neck went up on end and I got shivers down my spine. They were the clearest signs so far and confirmed I was exactly where I was supposed to be.

There was one piece of art of a woman's face made with bits of cloth, it was a portrait of Leah that an ex-boyfriend had commissioned for her as a gift. The face had long red hair blowing in the wind, she was wearing an aqua coloured dress with a gold trim, and had bright red lipstick; the picture was almost identical to the woman representing Boudica on the cover of my second novel. I remembered the day I sat down with the designer who created the cover, he'd chosen Boudica for the front, and the initial two designs I'd sent back because I didn't think she was attractive enough. Now I knew why I insisted she was to be even more beautiful. I was mesmerised by the image, it was a perfect replica of the character on my book cover, meaning I was in the right place with the right woman at the right time. The picture above was of a bear wearing a jumper, my jumper, the exact jumper I'd worn during my journey. Here in a tiny space were three powerful images representing my journey. I was with the love interest in my book, and I was allowing spirit to flow through me. And then Leah walked into the kitchen wearing the exact same outfit from the picture, including the identical belt that matched my book cover. I remembered when I first met her, she'd reminded me of a Celtic warrior, and here she was playing Boudica, who in my novel marries Arthur, and he becomes King Arthur!

I grabbed a copy of my book that I'd left with her as a gift when we'd first met and showed her the comparison, she was shocked and didn't quite know what to make of it all. Who could blame her? She told me when she'd shown my book to her son that he'd immediately asked,

'Is that you mum?'

How perceptive children can be.

In her front room was another picture of a bear carrying bags, as if arriving from a long journey!

We walked into the city, with Leah wearing her stylish flowing head turning outfit. Women stopped her to comment on what she was wearing; and I could see it was an exchange of energy that Leah was accustomed too. Whilst we had a coffee she shared her long-time dream with me, that she wanted to be fashion designer; she said it was a pipe dream but I hoped one day she would find a way to make it come true. As we chatted, I noticed something about her energy; it was so uncluttered. She had organised her life to be a simple one. A single mum with her ex around the corner offering support for their son, she had a part-time job and a couple of dreams; to be a designer and to find a man and live in a country cottage with him. I was attracted to the simplicity of it all, how straight forward and uncomplicated she was, or at least she seemed. I was so drawn to her clean settled energy. By comparison, I gradually revealed to her my somewhat complicated life; the synchronicities and my search for meaning, my understanding of my life purpose and at times how lost I was. We shared a piece of cake with our coffee and the little café starting filling with people and noise, before long we were back on the street heading along the royal mile.

Leah took me into a retro second-hand clothes store. It was a full of interesting clothing from bygone eras. She looked me up and down and went off in search of some new clothing for me. Before long she returned with a couple of shirts, wearing either would push me outside of my comfort zone. However, Leah was inspiring something in deep within me, dare to be different, dare to stand out. It was Leah and her confidence to be different that would give me the courage to write this book and share my journey with the world. I tried on the shirts with the long collars that belonged in the seventies and purchased one and returned the other to the rail. She was pleased with me, perhaps I'd passed her little test.

Now it's fair to say Leah liked a cocktail, I was quite surprised at the rate she started to knock them down; but she told me she only drank like that when she was on holiday. I wasn't one for drinking during the day, it just made me sleepy and lacklustre, a state I didn't really enjoy. Where I wanted to explore the city, enjoy an occasional coffee, and spend a lazy afternoon making love, Leah wanted to go to the pubs and drink cocktails.

When her son was with his father and she was off work, she liked to let her hair down in that way.

That evening we ate out; Leah got changed for our evening and looked gorgeous, I felt so proud to be seen walking down the street with her. The restaurant had seating outside and as it was covid times, restauranteurs had devised clever ways to keep people away from each other. This restaurant had cable cars from a ski resort positioned around the garden. We were shown into our cable car which had a table for four inside. It was so quirky, like Leah, and then it dawned on me, in my second novel Boudica and Arthur had ridden in a chariot together, this must be that scene playing out. I shared my thoughts about it with Leah and she laughed, in that little cabin it certainly felt like we were riding in a chariot.

It was of the time of the Fringe Festival and we had tickets to two shows. The first of which was an Australian David Bowie tribute band. We arrived just in time, as Leah was keen on getting a fresh cocktail to take inside the marque. The band didn't just do the David Bowie back catalogue justice, they performed acrobat stunts and little comedy routines whilst the lead singer was singing. I was very impressed. I soaked up the atmosphere and wondered what it would have been like to see David Bowie in his prime, the creative genius, live on stage. I hadn't seen live music for such a long time, it was such a treat. As the show came to a close, we walked back through the city, stopping at a few pubs along the way, ending the evening at a cosy little Spanish Tapas bar. I finally made an important discovery of how to survive pub crawling in Scotland, I switched from beer to wine, why I hadn't thought of that before was beyond me. Sadly, I never did find a drinkable beer in Scotland. Perhaps one day a Scottish brewer will take up the challenge and prove me wrong! I did later discover though, that I had written in my novels that Arthur didn't like the beer on his journey back in time, it was such a shame I'd written that bit in!

Love making with Leah was unbelievable; it was tender, passionate, and it felt like we became one soul together. I loved her body, although her insistence of keeping her socks on during sex, quirky as it was, didn't quite work for me, but occasionally I'd manage to get the little buggers off. We spent a lot of time in bed making love over those few days as we got to know each other intimately, we connected physically and emotionally. I started to imagine a life with her in that flat, how my children could come and stay and explore Edinburgh. I allowed myself to dream of a life with her, I allowed her in to my heart and let all of my barriers down.

We went to see a comedy act with a Boris Johnson impersonator in a local theatre. There was a boisterous crowd and as the comedian walked out on the stage, it really felt like I was looking at our former Prime Minister. He gave a hilarious performance and told so many truths about the way we were governed and how our leaders acted. A Scottish man asked him what good Brexit had done, and the impersonator proudly mentioned the terrific new blue passports, everyone laughed. In part it was funny, but it was also sad. Although I had belly laughed at many of his jokes, I had been reminded about the state the country was in and how desperate the world was for wise leadership, truth and integrity at the top.

On my last morning with Leah, I made us a breakfast of scrambled eggs and sourdough, and whilst I was packing, she made me a sandwich for the journey back; it was the thickest doorstep sandwich I'd ever seen in my life. It was a subdued morning together, not knowing when we'd see each other again. I left Edinburgh loved up, happy and sad to be leaving, not just Leah but Scotland, which, beer aside, will now always have a special place in my heart.

My next stop was in a village just outside of Witney in Oxfordshire; my friend Jennifer lived there in a small one-bedroom annex connected to a beautiful large old house with a little orchard. At last, I was staying in a house within walking distance of my children. I was going home, the place I'd lived for the past 20 years.

When I pulled up the weather was extremely hot, and I still hadn't fixed the air conditioning in the car, which I regretted after the long drive. Jennifer welcomed me in, she wasn't going away until the next day, so we had a night together before she headed off for a long weekend with her friend. She would be going to New Zealand soon for six weeks, and I would be looking after her house and her cat Jet, whilst she was away. We were good friends. She was increasingly becoming the only person I could speak openly to about the workings of the universe and my shaman's journey. She'd been on a similar journey of letting go, becoming a nomad and going through a long period of meditation and reflection. Jennifer had a deep understanding of the workings of the world that the vast majority of the people on the planet couldn't relate to or understand. Together we were like two scientists debating a complicated theory of mathematics that no one else could grasp, only for us it was on subjects like energy, manifesting, different dimensions, time travel and timeline shifts.

We spent a fascinating evening together and I got to know Jet, a black rescue cat who was very shy. Jet spent his days hiding underneath Jennifer's sofa and would only come out when he needed to, but by the end of that summer Jet wouldn't leave me alone, it just took some time to win him over.

In those days in that little annexe, I had a major realisation; you could say the penny dropped once more. I had written other novels that had not been finished, let alone published, was it possible that these too had played out in my life? My heart sank, and I could feel my stomach turning. I searched for them through old hard drives and eventually found them, and as I saw the titles my heart sank even more; they were dark and desperate novels. I got nervous and spent the day reading through them, one after another. There was one common denominator in all of the stories, the dad had left, been killed, or simply disappeared. They had all been written years ago, but an idea formed in my head, had I inadvertently written my father out of my life? I'd only seen my father once in seven years; events and circumstances out of my control had kept him from being an active part of our lives.

It saddened me to think that it was possible, that I may have played a role in my father's absence through my writing. I took myself out for a walk in the forest, my mind racing with the impact of what I may have just discovered. I had reached the point where much of my two novels had manifested already, so I decided to reopen the books I'd never finished and use them as working tools for my life. I would keep them unfinished, and write the future I wanted to live. They would work as pieces of magic, telling the universe exactly what I wanted. Each book would transform into a different aspect of myself, one would represent my family life, one my personal growth, my health and fitness, my relationship with my partner, and another for my career. Where I didn't have a book, I would start one with a new character that emulated everything I wanted to be. I knew I had the power through my writing to manifest, and now I could start a clean slate. I'd played out most of the drama in my life that I'd caused through my earlier writing, surely now it would work even better if I was doing it purposely. I felt better, I felt inspired; I had control, I could sculpt my future using the very same tool that had sent me on my shamanic adventure and journey of self-discovery. The impact of this realisation was truly profound, I could write a new path to my life.

That night my good friend Tony invited me for a walk around Oxford, followed by a pizza in a little Italian restaurant he knew. I was hot, it was sweltering but I needed to keep the windows shut so Jet couldn't escape. When I got in the car to meet Tony, and put the key in the ignition the temperature gauge in the car read fifty six degrees Celsius! It was an insane temperature; the impact of global warmer was ramping itself up and the future world with extreme temperatures had well and truly arrived.

Tony and I walked through grounds of Christ Church College and along the little river, and I shared with him my revelation about my writing. We had a fascinating chat and as we ordered pizza it dawned on me, our evening was a re-enactment of another part of my book; we'd followed the exact same route my characters had walked when they had left Oxford with the King, only they hadn't eaten the delicious pizza that we'd had.

It was whilst I was staying at Jennifer's house that I received another one of those damn messages that I dreaded; Leah had decided to end our relationship before it really got started. She said bringing a man into her life just complicated the simple existence that she'd created. She wanted to invest all her time into her son, who she was deeply committed to. She felt the geographical distance between our two lives was too great. I was completely blind-sided; I hadn't seen it coming. Again, I was gutted. It came a day after I'd written about my future life partner; who I'd described as someone who was nothing like Leah; she could never have been that person. Had I manifested this immediately? I couldn't know, but I suspected at some level I had told the universe what I wanted, and as Leah didn't match with it I got the dreaded text. Could I have just written her straight out of my life? Oh my, that was a tough thought to digest. The high feeling of having control of my life was immediately undone by my own doing once again.

I was conflicted, I wanted to see Leah again; I wanted us to fall in love with each other. But I knew deep down we were not a perfect match if there is such a thing. We had different interests, and she lived so far from my children. I was hurt but wondered if it wasn't for the best? I was trying hard to find my life partner and again had chosen someone that had offered me something else; something I wasn't looking for but was worthwhile and would help me grow and learn. I thought about my reply and decided to be as kind as possible; I told her how hard it must have been for her to write that and how conflicted she must have felt, I said thank you for what she'd brought into my life and that I hoped we could remain friends. Later that day I called her and we had one final chat and we wished each other good luck for the future. It was sad, but at least I had the chance to say goodbye this time. And that was that, Leah, like Adele disappeared from my life. I allowed myself to work through the loss, again. I was sad and disappointed and moped around Jennifer's place for a couple of days, then I let it pass. I was learning how to let go of people and pain. Leah had showed me how to stand out and how people looked up to her because of her courage to be different.

Sara had come down to Dorset to stay at my parents with her friend Daisy, and it was such a treat for me, as I joined them after leaving Jennifer's. I'd missed her earlier in the summer holidays. I spent quality time with her and her friend, and when they took day trips on the train to nearby seaside resorts I' started to develop a new idea in my head; I would create an online course to help people to manifest things they wanted into their life. The course would guide people in writing a series of stories as if they had already lived the life that they wanted. It was a natural progression for me after what I'd been through; if I could write my life as I wanted it, then surely, I could teach people how to do the same. I could teach them how to change their energy field so they could manifest things into their lives with ease, and write each section of their life as a story. I thought about all of the aspects of a person's life; their family, their relationship with their partner, their career, their personal development and their health and fitness. I was excited and had something new to get my teeth into; it was time to bring my coaching back into my life. To use this incredible experience in order to help others.

For my next housesit, I was going back to the house near Thame I'd been to earlier in the year with Adele. It would feel empty there on my own in such a big space. I arrived and unpacked, and even if I was on my own, it was still great to be back, as this was one of my favourite houses. It was a beautifully sunny, and I'd have the chance to relax a little in the garden whilst I was there. Leo got in touch and suggested we play Minecraft together from our computers in our separate houses; he would create a world, and we could be online building things together. Like playing chess with my dad, I could play Minecraft with my son and keep a daily connection through the computer game. I agreed, and that first night we played all evening together; we rode horses through the countryside looking for food and we fished in a stream. I realised it matched a scene in my book, when Tom and Arthur did the same; the magic in the book was still fulfilling the prophecy and ticking off everything I'd written, scene by scene like a shopping list. The universe was simply waiting for an opportunity to match my writing.

I wanted to explore the local countryside. Something was calling me, and I couldn't ignore it. I felt like I had to go somewhere, but I didn't know where or why. I'd seen some pretty cottages by a stream nearby, so I thought I'd start there, take some photographs and tie it in with a nice long walk. I put some shorts on and headed off with a bottle of water, we'd had very little rain, and everything had turned the colour of straw. It wasn't far to the cottages, I enjoyed taking a closer look and working out the angles to get some great photos. Once I was finished, I was drawn to continue exploring the area; I didn't know where I was going, I just knew to keep walking and allow the universe to guide me.

I passed fields, a disused office block, long winding country roads and farms until I emerged in a picturesque village that I didn't recognise. I sat on a bench and drank some water, and after a brief respite, I felt encouraged to continue onwards so I strolled leisurely through the village until I suddenly recognised it; I'd had a portrait photography client who once lived there. I found their house and it came back to me in a flash; the boy I'd used as a model for Arthur in my books had lived there. There was a little bench outside the house on the opposite side of the road, I sat down sure I'd been led there, but why? I felt like there was something important I needed to see, so I sat for a moment looking at the old country house. Then I saw it, the house had once been a pub. I remembered them telling me how they had converted it from a public house, and now I saw there was a plaque on the front of the house which had the old pub's name, The King's Head. I had used the face of the boy that once lived there to become the face on my cover, who later became King Arthur in the book. And I'd been led back here across fields to be shown the significance. Incredible, just incredible I thought.

Finding Arthur's house wasn't the only strange thing that happened that week; the following day I had a photography assignment, to photograph a woman's art collection in Witney. She wanted to make prints of all of her paintings, so I needed to photograph them all so she could turn them into digital images. It was a fairly easy job if there was sufficient diffused light available. I was met be a lovely lady in her late fifties. She'd prepared all the paintings to be photographed and we had a cloudy sky, which was perfect, I could photograph the paintings in the garden and get what I needed. She made us tea and I set about taking the photos. As we chatted and she talked me through each of the paintings it dawned on me, I was back in my book again, when King Charles the First showed Emily his art collection. And afterwards, in the book, with Prince Rupert, the three of them had feasted on swan; and this woman had just brought out her three most prized art pieces, a swan taken in three separate poses in three paintings. I smiled spotting the synchronicity, her three portraits of a swan, and a swan served up for three. I chose not to share it with her, it would make no sense to her after all.

That day, whilst I was working on the art photographs, I received a message from an old friend of mine, Dawn; she'd decided to hire a shop for a week to sell her paintings and she wanted to know if I wanted to share the cost with her and sell my paintings, drawings, or landscape photographs with her too. I'd been talking with my client the previous day about how to sell her art, and as I was doing so had wistfully thought I'd love to have a gallery one day, and within twenty-four hours I had manifested the opportunity. I grabbed it with both hands and immediately agreed. I had almost ten months to prepare, which was plenty of time and I was excited. Things were unfolding quickly, but now I was able to remain grounded as the world around me danced to my tune.

I turned up in Thame with my photograph and clip board and started canvassing again. As I wandered around, I realised something; it just no longer felt right. People were not interested in me or what I was selling, and why would they? I was a shaman and a storyteller. I was trying to create safety and security but I wasn't being true to myself; I'd left this path once before and was trying to force it back into my life. I stopped canvassing and went for a coffee, reflecting on what I was feeling. Everything felt wrong. I remembered finding Arthur's house, I didn't know what I was looking for that day, but I'd still I found it, and I'd need to do the same with my work; I needed to trust my path or write the career I wanted into my life. I had already written about being an author, was I supposed to focus all my attention there? I packed up and decided I'd never canvass for clients on the street again; which felt good, like a weight off my shoulders. When I got back to the house, I found a clear sign that I'd made the right decision and with it another synchronicity with my novel; my picture frame was smashed in the boot of my car, and in my novel the family portrait had fallen from a wall and smashed, burning in a house fire.

There was still a lot of things missing from my life, I had however gained a vast amount of new wisdom that I could take forward with me. Never one to give up easily I went back on the dating app and started chatting to people again; I was forever hopeful that someone out there would want to share their life with me. But something had profoundly changed for the first time in my adult life; I felt that I no longer needed a woman to complete me, now I just wanted one. I was in a much healthier position.

Chapter 14

Dreaming Big

My next stop was in a little village called Tackley; I was staying in a lovely old cottage near a train station close to Oxford. I'd been chatting to Lorna, a woman I'd met online dating. She was an unpublished author and had shared her manuscript with me, which I was very impressed with. She was a natural wordsmith; much better at writing than I was. One afternoon we had a video call over coffee and chatted about our lives; I'd had a few disappointing first dates recently so I decided to get to know someone a little via phone or video calls before setting up a date. After over an hour-long conversation, Lorna asked if I wanted to navigate a second date, and we discussed how we could meet up, given the distance between us. But I didn't want to rush a decision, I needed time to think it over and I was honest and told her that. I wanted to check in with myself as I really wasn't sure if the connection was there. It felt positive; she was smart and seemed to have a high level of emotional intelligence which I'd been looking for. She was also a good listener and of course we had writing to chat about. But I'd been hurt by Hannah, Adele and Leah and I wanted to make sure that I dated people who were looking for the same thing as me, someone who was ready for a relationship.

Lorna didn't think much of my answer, she wasn't used to rejection and later that day whilst I was out on a walk, she texted me to say that I was making a big mistake; that she really was awesome and I'd be missing out on something rather special if I didn't get to know her. Lorna's reply made me smile; I thought it was quite gutsy and confident, and I was drawn to it. Sometimes when I'm about to make a mistake the universe makes it very clear what I'm supposed to do; so I replied saying that I agreed, she did seem rather awesome, and I hadn't said I wasn't interested only that I wanted time to think about it.

We spoke on the phone again and discovered we were more similar than I'd originally thought; the more I found out about her the more I realised our personalities matched, she reminded me of a female version of myself but how I was before I'd fully embraced my spiritual path. Slowly, we were beginning to get to know each other, which would eventually lead to her coming to stay with me a few weeks later.

One morning Lorna called to tell me that the queen had died. It was a strange time as our nation went into deep mourning, and the news channels covered the events in real time, as the royal family's every move was followed in close scrutiny. Charles became king, and in doing so would create another coincidence with my novel; As Arthur and Emily had brought King Charles back through the time portal into 20th century life, Britain would have a new King Charles on the throne for the first time since the 17th Century. The days that followed were sad; I felt the mood of the nation and I mourned with them. The former queen had been an ever present in all of our lives; times were changing and the world was becoming more and more unsettled.

I was progressing through the creation of my online course, 'How to manifest the life of your dreams through writing'. I was writing examples of 1,000 words or more on each topic, knowing the power of the written word, I was setting out to help others whilst sculpting parts of my future life too. I spent time every day working my way through eight stories. It was a fantastic opportunity to experience in the written word what I would hopefully bring into my life in the future. I started with my future family life; I wrote fifteen years forward, with my children having their own children and my parents still being with us. I wrote about a day we spent together with the four generations. I covered all the feelings and emotions and different relationships, including my children's partners.

I was also keen to keep exercising, especially since I'd just written the section in my course about health and fitness. I'd written a bright new future where I was fitter than I'd ever been before; I'd be running long distances, swimming, and eating healthily. By the cottage where I was staying, there was a farmer's field that was rectangular and had a muddy track around the outside. I ran around that track every day, feeling like I had my own private athletic running track, slap bang in the heart of nature. I knew my writing had helped push me, and started to manifest a new healthier and fitter version of me into reality.

I was still searching for a greater understanding of my path and my role as a shaman within my community. How should I spend my time? What were my goals? It was time to visit Tomahawk again. I journeyed and found myself walking beside him through a deep dense forest. I had many questions that I hoped to find the answers to.

'I remember so clearly the dream I had when the spirit world told me to follow the shaman's path. But did I ever have a choice in the matter?' I asked him.

'Once a shaman has been chosen, they have little choice in whether they accept the role or not,' he started. 'If your path is that of the shaman you will have powerful spirits working with you, controlling events to keep you on your path. If you choose to stray from the path or not accept the role, you may find yourself sick and unable to live a normal life; everything else you try and pursue will simply not be available to you.' He said this almost sympathetically.

I thought about his words, they rang true despite the unfairness contained within them. We walked past a little stream, and I noticed two large swans paying us close attention.

'It seems unfair. Why was I chosen?'

'It is a great privilege to be chosen. Some are chosen through their ancestry, whilst others are picked by their interest and aptitude. You have always been interested in aspects of shamanism. As you know, your role as a community builder and as a storyteller, are aspects of shamanism. You have been on the path a long time already without even knowing it.'

'Why couldn't I have a human mentor to help and guide me? Everyone I have reached out to so far has ignored me.'

'Some shamans are taught by other shamans, whilst others are taught by the spirit world. When you are taught by the spirit world you are not influenced by other human's egos, you are learning only what you need to learn, exactly when you need to learn it,' he said.

It was a lonely path, but I saw the value in the perfect timing of each lesson they were teaching me.

'Okay, then can you please tell me what I need to work on next?'

Tomahawk chuckled out loud.

'It's good to have an eager student. I think you should continue to reach out to certain deities.' He advised, as we crossed a little bridge over the stream and started to head back in the direction we had come from.

'I wasn't expecting that. Which deities?'

'I think you should connect with Ra, the Sun God next,' he replied.

'But how?'

'You can make an offering to him. Be creative, show him you are worthy of his attention. I have an idea for you, why don't you dedicate your exercise to him. Push yourself even further and tell him, it's for him.' He said, nodding enthusiastically at his own idea.

I had a lot to reflect upon, so I thanked him for his wisdom and returned to my waking state.

The next day I returned to the field wearing my sports kit and started running around the field, or rather my own private athletic track. The sky was full of thick heavy clouds, and as I reached the halfway point I looked up to where I imagined the sun would be and said out loud.

'Ra, Sun God, I dedicate this exercise to you.'

A few seconds later the sun shone through a gap in the clouds, and a buzzard flew immediately into the gap in the sky and just hovered there like a statue in the sun rays. Did that really just happen? I wish I could have captured the moment with my camera. I finished the run, and as I reached the imaginary finish line, I found a scarab beetle lying upside on the ground. It was alive with its wings out and was trying to turn on to its underside. I bent down and flipped it over, it climbed my finger, before flying off. I made a note of it as it felt significant, I'd need to search for the meaning of a scarab beetle. That evening it was Leo's birthday and we were eating out at a restaurant with my parents and Maria, and as I climbed the stairs to the restaurant, I noticed a framed picture of the same type of beetle I'd seen earlier in the field. It was reinforcing the significance, now I definitely needed to check the meaning.

Later that evening when I'd got back from the meal I put on the television, as my mother had suggested I watch a particular television show. As I was watching I did an internet search for the scarab beetle's spiritual meaning, and to my amazement, it meant Ra, the Sun God! I was impressed, Ra was good at this. I looked up at the television screen just as some elves were sailing towards what looked like a Sun God, and a few minutes later there was a ball of flames shot from the sun which landed on the earth. There was a man lying on the scorched earth; a wizard, he was naked curled up in a sequence of rings. Unbelievably, the sequence of rings matched the new logo my web designer had just designed for me for my new website! And she'd only just sent me the new logo design earlier that day. My head was spinning with an overload of signs and the impact of it all. I also remembered that morning I'd posted a photo on social media of the sun shining through a patch of clouds and written, 'Notice all the little signs nature sends to you; it speaks to you when you pay attention.' And it certainly did for me that day; Ra had heard me and sent me an incredible sequence of coincidences I'll always remember.

From that moment on I felt close to the Sun God, and I remembered how I felt I needed to sunbath naked that summer, like I was allowing Ra to penetrate my skin and enter my energy field. It's a special moment when you truly connect with a deity, a feeling that is hard to explain; it changes your perspective of the world, the planets, and the universe.

It had been six weeks since I had sent my manuscript to Aggie, the director lady I'd met in the café in Wareham. I had been trying to keep cool, but my curiosity got the better of me, so I sent her an email inviting her for a coffee in her home town. Luckily, I was just a short drive away.

'Dear Aggie, How are you?

'I'm staying near you in a lovely country cottage for a couple of weeks and I was wondering if you'd like to go for a nice walk around the grounds of Blenheim Palace, and stop in Woodstock afterwards for a coffee?

'Kind regards,

'Ben.'

I didn't mention the book, I knew she'd let me know if she was interested or had any feedback. She replied within a day.

'Hey Ben,

'Lovely to hear from you and what a great idea. I was just thinking about getting in touch with you, I've finished your manuscript – I loved it. From the perspective of a novel, it works really well, you may need another edit though as I've seen some grammatical errors, but it's a great story. Let's chat about it on a walk. How about next Sunday?'

It was such an encouraging reply! We arranged a time and I decided to start re-enforcing my message to the universe, and I decided I would use a little magic to help the flow. It was time to explore creating new magical pathways for the book. This was powerful magic I did within my mind; I had created a mystical world in my imagination where I could plant the seed of an idea that I wanted to bring into reality. I'd had plenty of success with the technique and believed that it was the power behind visualisations; how high-level sportspeople were able to harness this human ability. In my mind I created an iron age settlement where I was the benevolent ruler of my tribe; here I could create a story that I wanted to manifest, much like how I had brought my books to life through writing. It worked in the same way, but without words, just visual images deep within my mind. I used an ancient setting as it took me back to a time closer to our natural heritage, before technology had transformed our lives to a new way of living, that had taken us out of harmony with our environment. In this setting there was no interference from modern technology, it was unstripped, an unplugged human existence. I meditated and fully relaxed my body and then allowed the images to form in my mind's eye.

I saw the dun, which was an iron age roundhouse with a straw roof. It was set in the centre of the small settlement which was surrounded by a high wooden fence. There was a well, and other small houses and livestock in small fenced off areas. I checked on my horse, a beautiful chestnut stallion, I gave him a carrot and stroked him lovingly. There were buildings scattered around the settlement including an armoury, a treasury and a small sacred building which I used for performing rituals and magic. Today I was here to use that space; I entered to find Oliver, a young man who had been preparing what I needed for the spell. I'd once read that magic created within the astral plain was more powerful than magic performed in our waking reality, it was also a lot easier to do there as well. Oliver left me in private, the room felt real, like I was really there; it was a sacred space and contained all I needed. A wooded altar was set in the centre of the room, and there was a brilliant bright light entering from an open window. I placed a copy of my new novel on the table and created a magic circle of bright blue light with my silver sword. I was within a sphere full of shimmering blue light. I placed an emerald in the centre of the table and surrounded it with gold nuggets, and a fire sprang to life in an open pit within the sphere. I called forth my spirit animals to help me with my magic; an eagle stood behind me, a leopard was at my left and a bear to my right, and a crow flew onto the table and looked closely at my book.

I called loudly to the elements.

'Earth, Fire, Water and Air, lend me your power.'

And then I asked Ra the ancient Egyptian God of the sun to aid me with my spell. Ra appeared inside the room, he had the body of a man dressed in Egyptian clothing and the head of a Falcon. There was a cobra on his head with a glowing disk that looked like a small sun that he was coiled around. Ra had an imposing presence; he walked towards the altar and placed his large golden ankh on top of my book, he then nodded at me in respect and stepped backwards. I then called upon Neptune to join us and add his power; he initially appeared as a shimmering ethereal figure and then his image became stronger. Neptune now stood opposite Ra, as he lifted his trident and pointed it at the book. A spark of light left the spikes of the trident and hit the book and whilst the energetic connection was made, I called out.

'I call on those here to ask for their help, for my story to reach all corners of the globe, for my tale to be heard for generations to come, for people to open their minds and their hearts to the words held within.'

I felt an immense power rise up within the space. The spell was complete. I thanked the deities and my guides; I closed the circle and then opened my eyes and came back to my seated position. It had felt powerful,

I knew my intention had been heard loud and clear.

My three weeks in Tackley flew by; I'd finished writing my online course and I was ready to move on to something else, but I didn't yet know what that would be. My nomadic journey had begun when I'd first been told about the pet sitting website by David who had shared with me Rebecca's love for house sitting; it was that chance phone call that led me to all the houses with all the signs, and led me to meet Jo in Nottingham, Adele in Buckinghamshire, and Leah in Scotland. One phone call had changed my whole life path, and now it was time to go back to where it all started and look after David and Rebecca's house. They lived in a sweet cottage in Charlbury, West Oxfordshire. When I arrived, David had already left so Rebecca showed me around and gave me the instructions; the cat, Rita, was an old cat that needed very little attention, just some food twice a day.

I shared some of the adventures on my journey with Rebecca, she'd been pet sitting for years so we had lots to chat about. I explained how the pictures in people's houses reflected what was going on in my life at the time, and how each book led to the next one on people's bookshelves. As I chatted to her one of her books jumped out at me, she was happy to let me read it, it was a book about the magic of storytelling. I'd just been writing the stories of my future life, and here was a book that talked about writing the stories of your past. I learnt through that book, and later in practice, that by writing a new narrative of the past helps you to gain a greater understanding of your situation and is also an aid to healing; letting go of trapped emotions by changing the energy around your attachment to the memory and to the people in the story. I would later discover that as a shaman rewriting the past added extra significance, and there were schools of thought that believed that powerful shamans or sorcerers could actually transform the past. The book encouraged me to be bold and share my story, and not worry about conforming to people's views of how the world is and what a book should look like.

Rebecca asked me to scrub her door with whitewash while they were away, but that there was no need to clean the rest of the house, I should rather just relax and enjoy the place. I was sure there was some hidden message in there for me; maybe the door, like in my novel, represented the past and by rewriting my past I got to clean the energy from my history so I could move forward with less baggage. The door was shining by the time I left their cottage, and I'd begun writing stories from my childhood; the book I'd read had led me to start rewriting my past, to change the aspects that no longer served me.

I had managed to pick up a photography shoot in Oxford, I would be working with another photographer taking photos of students who had just graduated. There were three photographers and two hundred students in the splendid surroundings of New College, part of the University of Oxford. Despite all my experience I was a little nervous, I hadn't worked at speed with my flash gun for many years and it was the first time I'd ever taken photos on behalf of another photographer. Karl was a little older than me and was a kind a patient man; he took time showing me exactly how each student needed to stand, with the certificate held in a particular way, their feet needed to point in a certain way, and the mortar board needed to point forward with the tassel hanging on the left side. It was all so exact and every time I missed a tiny detail he would patiently step in and make the correction for me; I was seriously impressed with his leadership skills.

As I worked on the photographs that evening something dawned on me; in my novel Emily worked at Oxford University too and was a maid to the queen. It was her job to help dress the queen and make sure her clothes were on right, and Emily had a boss who was patient and kind to her. It was a part written into the new version of the book and it was all still coming true.

I made time each day to continue writing parts of my future that I wanted to bring into my life; I did this in the way of writing a fictional diary, explaining what I'd done that day like it had already happened, making sure to add all of the things I could think of in plenty of detail. One evening in Charlbury I wrote that I had added to my coaching cards filling them with incredible wisdom that would help people. Surprise, surprise, the next morning I received a message from Rebecca, she wrote: 'Ben, whilst you are there if you want to make any cards, I have a set of card-making materials on the bookshelf.' It would have been such a random thing to have written, had I not been writing about making my cards the previous night.

I'd been chatting now to Lorna almost every day on video calls, we hadn't met in person yet, but I was excited when she agreed to come and stay with me for four nights at my next house sit in Oxford. She was a remarkably clever woman and we chatted at length about our children and our mutual love for storytelling. She was attractive, smart, and thoughtful, and most importantly she seemed to accept my spiritual path and how I was evolving into a new version of myself. Our daily video coffee chats were like mutual coaching sessions; I would give her readings to help her move through emotional problems and relationship issues with her friends and ex-husband, whilst she would read my stories about my past and encourage me to speak my truth in the business arena. Like the books always seemed to do, the universe had sent me what I needed in a woman for this next phase in my life.

I decided it was time to revisit a painful memory in my life; when I had long covid I had taken a run around the estate I'd been living in which had triggered my relapse and added months of illness to my life. I decided I wanted to go back and run the route again; I wanted to prove how much I'd healed, I wanted to feel good about how far I'd come. I turned up with my sports kit and parked my car at the house I'd lived in with Gabriella, and set off on the route I took, my mind flooded with past memories of that day, and all the struggles I'd been through. It felt like I was closing a chapter and rewriting the memory; the new me running with renewed strength and energy. That day I ran further than I'd ever ran in my life, and when I found myself back at my car, I knew I could have even run further. The achievement was significant, and I was proud of myself.

I met Aggie outside the town hall in Woodstock, funnily enough it was inside that building that I had found the person who would lead me to find my publisher, Janus. Now I was here again over a decade later, meeting a director who I hoped would see enough in my book to help me reach a global audience. After a five-minute wait I received a text message, 'I'm just parking, I will be there soon.' I realised I was nervous, I had clammy palms; I told myself that I had nothing to lose, she'd either like the book or not, I couldn't convince her either way. I saw her approaching, wearing a hat, like last time. This time the hat was just as stylish, with an even wider brim and in an off-white colour which framed her face perfectly. She greeted me with a smile, a gentle hug, and an air kiss either side of my cheeks. Her hair was shorter than before, she looked different, the new look suited her.

We walked towards Blenheim Palace which was only a short distance away; we continued through the large iron gates and into the magnificent palace grounds. We talked about the queen who had recently passed away; Aggie told me a story about when she had met her and what she had said. I imagined many people were sharing similar stories across Britain during those days. She asked me where I'd been and what I'd been up to,and she told me she was in between projects.

'So, your book... I loved it! I think it has huge potential.' She said encouragingly.

I let out a huge sigh of relief. If nothing else, I would gain so much confidence from her words. She said she felt strangely drawn to it and once she had picked it up she had been unable to put it down. She had read through the whole book in just three days.

I asked her if she felt any of the chapters needed work. She told me that she thought I would benefit from getting an expert to edit and proofread the whole thing. I realised I would have to bite the bullet and invest in that before publishing but I had hoped an agent would see enough in it and the publishers would take care of that side of things. I am dyslexic so editing is hard for me. We ended up in a beautiful old pub and ordered a couple of coffees. Whilst we waited she told me she had ordered the sequel to my book. That was another amazing compliment. Where was this leading to? I thought. I wanted to remain cool but I also wanted to ask her if she thought the book could be good for television. However, now she was going to read the second book, I thought it would be best to sit tight and wait and speak to her again afterwards. I was networking, it was about building relationships with people who had the contacts I needed. I knew enough about the market to know that the movie industry didn't like taking risks; they would see if a book was successful before bringing it to the big screen. I would bite my tongue and wait and see, at least for now. We finished our coffees and said our goodbyes. It had been promising. I'd have to see where it would lead.

My next house sit took me to Wytham, Oxford, where I had grown up as a young child. Instantly, I felt nostalgic; I pictured myself knocking on doors and asking whether my friends could come out to play. It was special being back there for me. My cousin and her husband still lived in the village, so we arranged to meet. I had a couple of days to fill before Lorna arrived and then I would take some time off, to be with her. Before then though, another part of my book was about to manifest itself into my life.

I had received an invitation quite out of the blue; a networking colleague I had known almost a decade before, had got in touch, inviting me to an event in Oxford. The timing was ideal as I was staying close to the city. The event wasn't business but philosophy. He had formed a group of like-minded individuals who were interested in discussing how humanity could transition to a new way of being, an evolved society. I knew this was no coincidence. I had written a document outlining how I believed it was possible. I reviewed my document; I hadn't thought about it for some time and I still felt good about what I had written. But was I ready to share it with the world. Had its time finally come?

I agreed to go to the meeting, it was in a picturesque old pub in the centre of Oxford. I was the first to arrive and grabbed myself a drink from the bar. I found the room that the meeting was taking place in and met up with my old friend, Andrew. He hadn't changed much in the decade since I'd last seen him; his hair had thinned a little and perhaps he had gained a few extra pounds but he was looking much the same. He had a calm presence about him and a lovely nature. He told me about the group and that he didn't really know why he'd started it or where it was heading but it felt important to him, and he enjoyed running it. Others gradually arrived and we sat around a few tables. They were a friendly, intelligent bunch of international people and I guessed many of them were attached to the university in some way. As the meeting went on, Andrew spoke about the challenges we face as a species and then deliberated on how best we could tackle the impending problems facing us. I was itching to speak, I believed I had at least some of the answers to the problems written in my document.

Eventually, as the meeting was opened up for us all to share, I took my chance and asked if I could read some of my document. I strongly felt that was the reason I was there. I stood up and all eyes were fixed on me as I cleared my throat and read the document. I was nervous, this wasn't just any group, I was in Oxford; the seat of knowledge and learning and I was talking with a group of academics, former politicians and students. I was testing my ideas in public and opening them up to scrutiny for the first time. I was being tested, putting myself forward, just like Arthur was in my novel. Except that for him it was to a room of kings and warriors in ancient Britain, giving his ideas on how to defeat the Romans and unite the tribes in a common cause. And here was I, delivering my ideas of how we could transition to a moneyless society and unite the world with shared resources and knowledge; it was an antidote to Capitalism as Arthur was offering up a way of defeating the Romans. The universe had ticked off another scene from my book in fine form, and I was relieved when I had finished speaking and sat back down. The room was buzzing with questions. There were immediate challenges about the logic, the implementation, and the ideology. It matched Arthur's scene splendidly.

'How could we pay for energy without money?' Said one.

'Why would people work if they didn't get paid?' Asked another.

'How could we defend ourselves from dictators?' Piped in a third.

We didn't have the time to address all the questions there and then as it would have taken over the whole meeting, but in smaller groups, I gave my answers and I felt I'd addressed their points as well as I could. I could see that people loved money too much, and in that group the idea of moving away from it was a big leap that they could never imagine possible. The evening had been invigorating. I had embarked on a new path and had no idea where it would take me. I would just let the universe lead the way but I suspected it had something more up its sleeve.

Aggie messaged me that she had just finished reading my second book, the sequel. She congratulated me, saying she had really enjoyed it and asked if I would be writing a third. It wasn't the first time over the years I had been asked that question and I had, actually, started a third book, set in Stone Age Britain. Perhaps one day I would finish the book but how different it would be now! If I did continue writing it I would write with an eye to manifesting what I wanted in my life and my characters would have a fine time, full of pleasure, fun, love, achievements and personal growth. I'm not sure the world was ready for such a book!

What now in regards to Aggie? I asked myself. I decided to wait and see, just hold tight, the magic was working, my novels had found someone influential.

The time had finally come for me to meet with Lorna. We had got to know each other really well over the previous couple of months so I was excited to be able to see her in the flesh. I had moved my car off the drive and on to the road so she could park in the drive as she had a bigger car than mine. She pulled up and I went out to greet her. Her journey from Wales had been smooth and she was as eager to meet as I had been. We gave each other a big hug, holding back on a kiss as this was the first time we had actually met each other in person.

We chatted in the kitchen over coffee and it felt a bit strange to at last be in her presence. It was real now and I could feel we were both full of optimism. After our coffee I drove us to Woodstock. We walked hand in hand around the striking grounds of Blenheim Palace. She had never been there and enjoyed the picturesque scenery, the old trees and impressive architecture. She was full of chatter but all I could think about was kissing her. I loved her energy and passion for everything. I saw a big old knotted oak and led her to the tree, gently positioning her back against it. I put my fingers to her lips and she stopped talking. She knew what was coming next, we both did. I kissed her on her lips, gently and delicately. I smelt her perfume. It matched her skin perfectly; it was sweet and musky all at once. I could feel my heart's pulse quicken. It was the perfect first kiss. There had been a build up to this kiss over many weeks. The anticipation had been electric and the all-important chemistry was definitely there, in abundance.

We stopped at a little pub on the way back through Woodstock. It was called the Black Prince and she told me of the time she had once had tickets to come and see Prince perform at a concert at Blenheim Palace, but he had cancelled because of sickness. I looked down at the menu and it said: The Black Prince apologises... It was another little coincidence that made us both chuckle.

As the barmaid took our order for drinks, she looked at Lorna as if trying to remember something.

'I'm sorry but are you Lorna Nicolson?' She said sheepishly.

I was a little baffled, Lorna was a long way from home and her book was unpublished.

'Yes, that's me.' She said with a lovely, knowing smile across her face.

'Wow! It's really you! I thought it was when you first came in. I love your movies!' They both grinned.

I was seriously taken aback. What was going on? I thought with a little unexpected tinge of excitement building inside me.

'Thank you, that's kind,' Lorna replied.

The barmaid then asked if she could sign an autograph and have a photo taken with her. Lorna obliged politely and I was handed the camera. I took a handful of photos whilst giving Lorna a questioning look. When the waitress finally left us in peace, I looked at her with an expression that said: You've got some explaining to do young lady!

'Do you remember I told you I had done a little acting?' She said in her gorgeous Welsh accent.

'Yes, you told me you had be in the theatre and done a couple of plays.' I said, and she nodded, pleased I had remembered.

'Well, I did more than that. I have made quite a few movies as well, and I was quite successful at one stage of my career.' she added, paying close attention to my reaction.

I stared at her face. She certainly was familiar. I felt embarrassed but intrigued as well. I got shivers all over my body, telling me this was an important moment.

'I'm sorry I didn't recognise you. Exactly how famous are you?' I asked.

'Don't be daft! You've got nothing to be sorry about. I was glad you didn't know who I was. I haven't acted for fifteen years, not since I had my girls,' she laughed. 'I don't expect anyone to remember me or know who I am. I knew you didn't, otherwise you'd have mentioned it. I used to get recognised all over the world at one stage.'

I could tell she was glad her secret was out in the open.

I asked her about her movies, why she had stopped acting and why she hadn't told me. She had been the lead female actress in a handful of movies that had been successful. She apparently had fans all over the world and would often get approached and asked for her autograph. She had stopped acting once she had her daughters as it was too demanding. Also, her husband had left her so she had to navigate being a single mum.

I was finding it hard to digest all this information. I was dating a world-famous movie star. How did that make me feel? Good was the answer, in fact my ego was soaring through the roof! Had I manifested this into my life, had I done a piece of magic somehow in my book or through my writing about my future life? I'm sure I had, as this kind of thing didn't exactly happen every day. But then there was no longer any normal life for me; now I was in flow with the universe anything was possible. Knowing how to manifest things easily was leading to a new and very exciting time.

It suddenly dawned on me, Arthur had fallen for Boudica, and they had married. And Boudica was the most famous woman of her time, just like Adele, an actress was playing the leading role in my book and in my life.

Now we were on the subject of movies and fame she started chatting about Hollywood and the A-list celebrities she called friends. She talked of two people even I had heard of who were now her daughters' god parents. What a strange upturn in events. I started dreaming about a possible future, walking down the red carpet of a movie with this world-famous actress. I asked her if she wanted to go back to acting, and she said she planned to one day when her girls were a little older. I was seeing her anew and tried hard to remember her movies.

By the time we got back from the pub we were both feeling very connected, and once in the house we knew exactly what was coming next. We held each other tightly, nervously. We kissed and both became increasingly excited as our sexual energy began to build, my heart pounded fast.

'Let's go to the bedroom. I think we both need this don't we?' I said.

'I thought you'd never ask!' She said playfully.

As we reached the bed we started to kiss. I could feel the desire in her energy. I kissed the delicate skin on her neck as she lifted her sweater over her neck to reveal beautiful French lingerie. I undid her bra and as it fell on the floor I could feel how self-conscious she was; she hadn't made love for over two years. She wanted me but was worried how I would receive her. I wanted her to feel wanted and desired, in the same way she had made me feel. I studied her breasts longingly before putting one of her nipples in my mouth and sucking gently. As I did she kissed my neck whilst delicately unbuttoning my shirt.

'You are so beautiful, and I feel so privileged to be here with you.' She said with so much tenderness, those words filled me to the brim with love.

She pulled me to her, and we melted into each other. It felt as if our bodies had always known each other, everything felt so natural, so effortless and electric. We'd left nothing to the imagination as we had both allowed ourselves to fully let go during sex. As I lay there afterwards looking at her naked body, I knew that this wonderful experience was just the beginning, for both of us.

It had been a beautiful day, with us connecting in every way together at the highest level; we both knew we had found something special in each other and it became quickly apparent to me that I needed her in my life. The next day we sat drinking tea in the lounge, cuddled up together under a blanket. I asked her about her name, I wanted to know the meaning of it. She told me it was a fictional character from a book called Lorna Doone, invented by the author R.D. Blackmore. So it didn't have a meaning, I thought, unless of course there was a connection with the book. I suspected there was, as everything seemed to have a hidden meaning of some sort, especially names. A few minutes later I was getting something from the bedroom when I noticed six books that were in the room. Five of them were crime novels but the sixth one was so old that I couldn't even read the spine. I lifted it from the shelf and, to my absolute astonishment, it was an antique copy of Lorna Doone! I laughed out loud and called Lorna upstairs. When she saw it, she also burst into laughter. We both knew we were exactly where we were meant to be; the timing was immaculate. We were in perfect flow together.

Then I received an email from Aggie.

'Hello Ben,

'I trust all is well with you. I had a conversation with a fellow director. You may have heard of him, James Walsh. He's new on the scene, young and really creative. He directed 'My Town Wednesday' last year which is a lovely arthouse film. Anyway, he's looking for a new project and I mentioned your books to him. I hope you don't mind. He's had a look through and would like to chat with you, shall I send you both an introduction?'

Incredible! On reading the email, I smiled from ear to ear. I immediately told Lorna the news.

'I've heard of him,' she told me. 'He's got a growing reputation. It sounds amazing Ben, you should definitely find out what he's got to say for himself. I'm so proud of you.' She said supportively.

I was beside myself with excitement. Had the universe effortlessly delivered my chance at success like it had all those years ago with my first publishers? Time would tell. I replied to Aggie's email immediately.

Lorna left Oxford and I shortly followed. We had had a wonderful, romantic few days together and created memories I would never forget. I received a phone call from the owner of the house in Wytham saying I had left my trainers in the downstairs cupboard. It was annoying, I always seemed to leave something behind me. I arranged a time to go back and collect them.

After an agonising few days of waiting, I finally received a call from James Walsh, the director. In the intervening time I had researched him, watched his new movie twice, read all the reviews I could find and generally stalked the poor guy. I was becoming a fan.

'Hey Ben, it's James Walsh, Aggie's friend. I've been reading your books. Well done, I really like them.'

'Hi James, great to hear from you. Aggie said you'd call. I'm really flattered you liked the books.' I said, trying to play it cool.

Just don't mess this up Ben; don't say anything you'll regret, I thought to myself. James had a crisp, well-polished English accent; it was southern, and he was clearly confident.

'Aggie says you're a nomad and you've been travelling around writing this story whilst looking after pets. It sounds like a fascinating story. Listen, I'd love to meet you and buy you lunch. Do you fancy coming to meet me in London?' He said. I wanted to jump up and down and cheer!

'I'd love to, thank you.' It was as articulate as I could muster in the moment.

We arranged a meeting two weeks later. London had been calling and I would soon be on my way. As he lived in Hackney he invited me to a little seafood restaurant nearby. Now I could allow myself to get excited. Things were really happening; the book was pulling people in who were drawn to the magic contained inside it. The same magic that had caused havoc in my life was also drawing in the people I needed to make my dreams come true.

In the house in Wytham, Margaret let me in. I slipped off my boots and we sat together in the lounge. Her daughter was with her, I hoped I hadn't disturbed them. I had been thinking about the old Lorna Doone book and had a sense that there was more to the story than I had first thought. Margaret made us both a pot of tea and I shared a story of how I had captured her cat after it wouldn't come in and she told me about her trip to Greece. I decided to ask about the old book on the shelf.

'When I was staying here, I asked Lorna about the meaning of her name. She told me that it was first used in the book Lorna Doone. Five minutes later I found the book on your bookshelf. I was wondering, is there a story behind your old book?' I asked.

'It's funny you should say that,' she said. 'My sister bought the book a long time ago now from an antique shop, it's a first edition. The house where the story Lorna Doone is set was owned by my great, great, great, grandfather,' she said proudly. I smiled, I knew there was a connection and a story behind the book.

And so, Margaret's current house would be the setting for my very own story, containing a new world-famous Lorna, with her repeating the cycle of her ancestor.

It was finally time to head to London to meet James. I set the intention of a successful outcome over a tea in bed that morning; I had visualised a contract being offered to me to sign and the feelings of accomplishment and excitement that came with it. I was nervous and wanted to make a good first impression; I made a real effort with my clothing, picking out something that made me look successful and understated, creative and stylish all at once. It was a challenge, considering most of my clothes were either a few years old or recent purchases from local charity shops. However, I just about pulled it off. After arriving in London, I changed on to the underground and made my way across the capital. I arrived ten minutes early and, after scouting around the restaurant, I saw that James wasn't there. I ordered a bottle of water. I was so nervous that I couldn't drink anything else, as I sat at a small table and waited for him with anticipation. Ten minutes passed, then another ten. I had been sitting there for almost thirty minutes when my phone rang. It was James.

'Hi Ben. I'm really sorry, I've been caught up. Grab yourself something from the menu to keep you going until I get there. I won't be long, I'm really sorry.'

I did as he said and ordered some battered prawns with a garlic dip and I people watched from the back of the restaurant. James arrived carrying a rucksack over his shoulder. He was tall, with sandy long hair and a thick brown beard. He was good looking, with striking features. I stood and shook his hand. He had a firm grip. We sat down and he looked at my plate of prawns.

'How are they?'

'Lovely, really tasty,' I said.

'I'm so sorry I'm late.' He apologised.

'Don't worry, I've been quite comfortable.' I said, as he got the attention of the waiter and then James asked me if he should order for both of us.

'If you like,' I said.

It was his local restaurant, he was paying, and I wanted to make a good first impression, even if that meant eating clams and mussels with a smile on my face!

He ordered the food quickly and the waiter brought a bottle of water for the table and some bread. I told him I had watched his movie. He was genuinely pleased. He told me he was interested in new stories that were unknown; he was a risk taker and wanted to find the little gems hidden in unusual places and bring new undiscovered stories into the public domain. He wanted to know about my journey, so I shared my story about my sickness, leaving Gabriella, my businesses and setting out on my spiritual journey as a nomad. I watched him, he was engrossed as he rubbed his beard and asked more and more questions. I had had no intention of sharing any of this, yet before I knew it, I was talking about being baptised as a Druid and how I was seemingly manifesting my book into my reality. He was fascinated but I wanted to reign it in, to get back to the characters of Emily and Arthur Archer. Yet me and my characters were seemingly intertwined. I was both Arthur and Emily, their stories were also mine. I had lived in their house, I had shared their adventure; I had foraged for food when they had foraged for food, I had found the same friends, made the same mistakes and I had felt the raw emotions that they had experienced. With James I shared my dating stories, the car crashes, my experience with magic and how it had changed my view of reality and how it could be manipulated. I was over sharing. Was I blowing my chances? James was a good listener; he considered his words wisely before responding to my serious overshare.

'Ben, it sounds like you've been on one hell of an adventure. I think there's a story here about your journey and what you've learned and experienced when you're ready to share it with the world.'

'Yes, I think you're right. And I've already started writing it.' I said, feeling like I had been heard and taken seriously.

'Listen Ben, I'm interested in your books, the time travel novels. I have an idea if you'll entertain it. I would like to take out an option on them to make them into movies. Give me a year, just a year and I'll see if I can find a producer interested in investing in them. I love them, I think they can be really successful. I can't talk about money at this stage, there's a long way to go, but what do you think?'

I couldn't contain my excitement, although I tried. I offered up a big smile and thanked him. It felt right but if nothing happened with him, I would have lost a year waiting.

We chatted more about the novels, his latest project, and his contacts in the industry. Things were moving fast and I allowed myself to get excited as we ordered a couple of glasses of wine to go with the food. Thankfully he'd stayed clear of the mussels and clams. He ordered salmon and some monkfish, all of which was delicious. James was an impressive man and I felt like I was moving in new and exciting circles. I told James that I would give him a year to find a producer and when he had news we'd take it from there, one step at a time.

The news came through only three weeks later. James had his first meeting with a producer! To talk about, Arthur Archer and the Tree of Time. It was all happening so fast. At last, my long-held dream was looking like it could become a reality! My novel could soon be reaching a global audience and with that, new opportunities and a whole new adventure could unfold before my eyes. I was beyond excited, I was ecstatic. What a rollercoaster ride the last couple of years of my life had been!

And now as I bring my magical story to a close, and finish writing this final chapter, I am still very much allowing the universe and my spirit guides to lead me on my whirlwind adventure through life. In this novel I have only shared some of the incredible synchronicities that I have experienced over the past couple of years. Many more remain untold. As my shamanic life unfolds, I continue to make notes each day of what I see, learn and understand. If you would like to know what happened next on my journey, the first chapter of my untitled, follow-up novel can be found on my website: www.benmolyneux.com and details of my coaching, online course and other novels can be found there too.

My desire for this book is to encourage you to open up your connection to the spirit world, to watch out for the signs from the universe as they reveal themselves to you and to pay attention to the words you use and the energy behind them. You too, have the power to manifest your future into reality.

The End

If you have enjoyed

THE JOURNEY TO THE EDGE OF REALITY

please post a review on Amazon.

You can also 'follow the author' on Amazon
to get notified of new titles as they are published.

Find out more about Ben's coaching and online courses
and read the first chapter of his follow-up novel at
benmolyneux.com.